"Shake my hand and I'll show you the ropes"

A BIOGRAPHY OF GEORGE W PIPE

"Shake my hand
and I'll show you the ropes"

A biography of George W Pipe

by

John Loveless

First published in 2020 by The Ringing World Ltd, Andover SP10 1LJ

ringingworld.co.uk

Copyright 2020 John Loveless

Designed and typeset by The Ringing World Ltd

Printed and bound by Ridgeway Press Ltd, Pewsey SN9 5LU

ISBN 978-1-8381590-0-9

Illustrations

Front

Left: George outside St Mary-le-Tower, Ipswich,
with a new bell about to be installed for the Millennium.

Right: George in his study at Lansdowne Road, Ipswich, preparing for an
exhibition of bellringing memorabilia at Felixstowe in 2015.
A print of Great St Mary's, Cambridge is on the door behind him.

Background: 'Early autumn at St Mary-le-Tower' by George. Commissioned by
the PCC in 2001 as a Christmas card; later used for calendars, coffee mugs and
as a frontispiece for service sheets and reports.

Back

A set of seven Suffolk towers sketched by George for the fiftieth anniversary
of the Suffolk Guild of Ringers in 1973. The image was used on the front
cover of *The Ringing World*'s celebratory jubilee issue (6 April 1973),
which began with a history of the Guild written by George.

Contents

Illustrations

The opening of Washington Cathedral bells in 1964

Outside the belfry

The loss of Bristol Maximus, the Beresford family and 'Wilfred'

The remarkable story of St Mary-le-Tower, Ipswich

The roaring '80s

The 1990s – a decade of decades

The Pye brothers and their legacy

Momentum maintained in the late 1990s

Foreword

George Pipe wrote in early 2020:

I am both touched by John's writing this biography, with great support from Linda, and by his very generous words. I am conscious too of having one of the Exercise's finest ringers ever undertaking the research, collecting the photographs and creating what I hope is an interesting book, emphatically not just about the art of ringing, but instead painting a much broader canvas whose chapter headings speak for themselves. Linda's compilation of the photographs is a happy extra dimension.

After George's death, Diana Pipe completed this foreword on behalf of them both:

These were George's words written just before he was admitted to hospital. Sadly he never made sufficient recovery to continue and his sudden death (although we knew he was very ill) still came as a shock. I had not discussed with him what or how much he wished to say. I know we would both say a huge thank you to John and Linda for their vision even before George said 'yes' and for the mammoth amount of time, research and work since then. Also to Will Bosworth for his help and time and to the readers, Christine Knight from Clare, Richard Smith from Cambridge, and to all of you who have helped in any way.

I have tried to follow on showing how George had to quickly grow up from being a boy to taking great responsibility in his working life – in managing people often much older than himself, he had to be adaptable, strong and willing to do manual work, to travel in order to communicate with the dealerships (his customers) and Ransomes' directors in England, to demonstrate the machinery using his salesman's skills, and above all to be fair, honest and compassionate. I have also tried to demonstrate a bit of his true self, the driving force behind his achievements, his empathy and, yes, patience. He was hugely sensitive.

George's first visit to us on the farm at Bedfield in Suffolk was naturally a memorable one. We were sixteen and had met several times at ringing dos and I had been a few times to practices at Grundisburgh. I had learnt to ring at Rushmere, a six-bell tower on the outskirts of Ipswich. My family knew nothing about ringing but George was fitted in and became a much-loved regular visitor. I was then invited to Grundisburgh, often to Sunday lunch, and would stay and ring for evensong.

When George was old enough to have a licence he bought a Norton Dominator motorbike which took us many miles round the towers and Suffolk countryside, one evening ending up in the ditch somewhere in West Suffolk just as it was beginning to rain. What fun! George played rugby for Ipswich so we used to go to club dances, friends' parties, family celebrations, etc., and of course we did lots and lots of ringing!

It was on one of George's father's tours to Cornwall that we decided we wanted to spend our lives together, though sometime in the future, as George was an apprentice earning a pittance and I wanted to do a nurse's training course. Keeping all this strictly to ourselves, little did we know that before long George would be offered the manager's job in Australia, we would be married, he would sail to Melbourne and I would follow ten months later. Frantic activity ensued with a mixture of nearly every emotion to cope with for so many of us – but most of all for George.

As my great liner, the *Southern Cross*, sailed into the Melbourne Dock there was George on the quay with a large bunch of flowers, an even bigger smile, and a small Ford car too. It was a reunion of a lifetime. Then followed a whirlwind of being introduced to so many things and people amid the excitement. George was already in charge of the ringing at St Paul's Cathedral, Melbourne, a ring of twelve bells, so usually on Sundays it was ringing for morning service and coffee with the ringers afterwards, and then back again later to ring for evensong. He had also made lots of friends through work, becoming involved in the city and surroundings, and they were a great support and help to us in those early days.

For six months we shared a bungalow with an elderly lady, paying rent of course, having only one room to ourselves – it was not ideal, but it worked, and she was a great friend by the time we moved on to renting a flat, still close to the factory but nearer the city and St Paul's.

Naturally we missed our family, friends and beautiful Suffolk but Australia was a complete change and we had six years there, the first period of our married life together – George had already spent nearly a year on his own. We travelled as much as time and money would allow, visited so many places and people and saw some breathtaking scenery. Sunshine and beaches to die for, making sure we kept clear of the box jellyfish! It was the people, though, who made us so welcome, and although a lot of them have died I'm still in contact with many and have received lovely cards and letters from them.

Saying farewell on our return to England was tough; there were tears and more than a few bottles consumed to try and drown our sorrows. We had to sell our house (Ransomes finally helped us to purchase), pack everything that we were able to bring home, and of course we had our own precious little family, Sarah (nearly five) and baby Stephen (eight months). They had been baptised in St Paul's Cathedral on separate occasions, each accompanied by special celebrations, with godparents in Australia and England.

A great welcome awaited us on returning home and very soon we were back into the swing – George's work at Ransomes, Sarah started school, and after looking at forty properties we purchased 8 Lansdowne Road, Ipswich, which we were able to afford as it was in rather a run-down state. In 1967 Alison was born. She was a beautiful baby but it was soon apparent she was different from our other children at that early age. She was finally diagnosed autistic at the age of five or six but we really knew much sooner. Family life was difficult for many years but she has always been dearly loved and now at 53 years she is very well cared for and happy in her rented flat in Ipswich.

Moving on, I find myself surrounded by so many letters and cards of sympathy giving me and the family comfort and support following George's death on the 3 March 2020. I shall always be grateful for this.

Looking back over nearly 68 years together I realised what a remarkable person George was, but at times quite a complex one. Always enthusiastic, larger than life and always willing to get involved, he loved being with people, often having a considerable influence on their lives. As someone recently said to me, he was 'completely unique in so many ways'. He had loads of talents which he used to advantage and was blessed with an amazing memory. Occasionally, though, he had bouts of depression and needed lots of tender loving care to get him back on track. He was a bundle of nerves before a peal, regardless of whether it was Bob Doubles locally or Orion Maximus in Birmingham. Being late, or even thinking about it, was one of his worst nightmares. The family would say 'Dad always has to have something to worry about.'

As well as being a loving husband and father he was always concerned for the wider family, interested in their progress and welfare, remembering birthdays and writing encouraging notes. He so enjoyed nursing our latest (and third) great granddaughter, Summer, eight months old, when she and her mother Fleur visited not long before George died. Amber, six years old and Amelia, three years old, were also a great joy to him.

Another of his special gifts was being able to speak completely off the cuff or deliver a eulogy he had prepared, doing notes and bringing in a bit of humour at just the right time. I have often felt proud and thankful for his use of such a wonderful talent.

Underlying all these ups and downs, and giving him strength during periods of ill health over many years, was his Christian faith. He loved all aspects of his church and latterly made a supreme effort to listen to the ringing, have coffee with the ringers and attend the 10:30am service at St Mary-le-Tower. The power of prayer, his own or from others, was a great comfort and he thanked our God daily for all the good things he received and treasured throughout his life.

After three weeks in Ipswich Hospital he returned home to enjoy being with the family, seeing the garden and sitting in the lounge, optimistically making plans for the summer.

On Tuesday evening, 3rd March 2020, he passed swiftly and peacefully away, leaving his home for the last time – a lasting wish fulfilled.

Keith Jones, Dean Emeritus of York, Vicar of St Mary-le-Tower, Ipswich, 1982–95:

The subject of this biography may be mostly celebrated as a most distinguished campanologist. But the good influence of his life and character extend further than that, and George Pipe is revealed here as among those people of whom we may be glad to have been contemporaries. And we may be still more glad to have been among the many people who can count George and Diana as friends.

When I arrived as Vicar of St Mary-le-Tower in Ipswich in 1982, George and Diana Pipe were among the first people I met. An early sign of their significance lay in their defiance of the habit of some bellringers to regard the belfry and the church as separate places. For to understand George and Diana it is necessary to see them in terms of their Christian faith. The Sunday morning prayers in the tower, during the ringing for the main service, were clearly an act of rejoicing in the blessings of God.

The same joyful confidence rang, further, in George's active Christian discipleship. It may have been in his words of encouragement and advice in getting people to donate generously and systematically to the work of the Diocese of St Edmundsbury and Ipswich (he became adviser for Christian Stewardship); it may have been in his undertaking the considerable labour of being a churchwarden of a parish which now encompassed the whole of Ipswich's old town centre; it may have been in his exquisite designs for notice boards, or magazine covers, or programmes for concerts; it may have been in embarking on the next project for the care of the building, or supporting the social life of the parish: in any of these activities George could be relied on to take on the task and do it with gusto and thoroughness. If progress in a job ever got him down, his resilience triumphed. And his and Diana's diverse abilities ensured good results.

George was known throughout Suffolk. The network of ringers ensured that, but his character and his gift for friendship turned acquaintance into something like renown. George became the lay chaplain to one of the bishops of the diocese: and there was little wonder in that, given his knowledge of the whole of a county in which localities and local loyalties have always been more important than their relationship with the official centres.

That these gifts have been exercised from a family deeply embedded in Ipswich and its surroundings has always been an advantage. So often the initiators and visionaries in a place are found among those who have recently arrived, so that their energy has been known to grate on those who are indigenous to a place. George's contacts and friendships, of course, extended round the world. But George's knowledge of Ipswich, its history, its buildings, its characters, and the long memories of such an ancient place, were part of a deep love and commitment to this part of the world. His enthusiasm fanned my own growing delight in the town, and for that I shall always be grateful.

But this book makes clear why many people are just as grateful for George and Diana Pipe.

Introduction – A word about biographies

Recording our bellringing achievements

Much of our ringing history stays in the tower, often as historic performances on beautifully painted and written wooden peal boards. These are seldom seen by people apart from bellringers – mostly we don't tell them! Ringers love seeing their peals and quarter peals in print and communicate them via *The Ringing World* and social media. Others take the statistical side further, to keeping a tally of number of peals, quarter peals, number of towers visited and many more statistics. These days, publication on BellBoard and PealBase is free. Thousands of obituaries of ringers have been written – typically one or two pages and a photo in *The Ringing World* – but little more about ringers than that, and very few biographies.

The eighteenth and nineteenth centuries saw books about bells in churches in each county and on bellfounders. No *Dove's Guide* before 1950, of course. People such as Trollope and Snowdon wrote books on the theoretical side of ringing, methods and compositions. In the early twentieth century, a particularly weighty tome appeared, *Among the Bells*, by Revd F E Robinson, the first person to ring 1,000 peals. This autobiography ran to 638 pages and was effectively the story of Robinson's ringing career. *A Great Adventure*, by J S Goldsmith/W H Fussell (131 pages), is a fascinating account of the first ever group of ringers from England to visit Australia and New Zealand in 1934–5.

More recently, John C Eisel's two *Giants of the Exercise* books have given excellent accounts of notable ringers of the nineteenth and twentieth centuries. Bill Butler has made many valued contributions in the areas of training, handbells, Central Council biographies and more recently, his *On this Day*, a huge collection of notable ringing events sorted by date, with up to a dozen for each day of the year, is innovative and different. Robert B Smith's autobiography *My Life among the Bells* (1999, 203 pages) focuses on the author's ringing career and his years running a bellhanging firm. In 2007, Mike Davies, who learnt to ring with ringing composer Albert Pitman at Port Talbot, wrote *An Unassuming Genius – The Life and Times of A J Pitman* (169 pages). Richard Pullin's recent excellent work on Pitman and several other composers, a set of articles printed in *The Ringing World*, brings to the fore the lives and work of these talented men from over 100 years ago. Apart from these, biographies or autobiographies of ringers are rare.

So why a biography of a bellringer?

There are plenty of specialist biographers in fields such as the arts, literature and sport, but none for bellringers. Respect from a wide range of people for a would-be subject is often top of the list. In George's case that is beyond doubt. For the biographer, getting the opportunity and taking it is another critical aspect. In reality, it's about a range of intangibles really. The 'wow' factor, the charisma of the individual, certainly helps. Many people asked me what it was like to be writing his biography. This initiative has attracted interest from many people, from 'Hasn't there been one already?', or 'That must be quite a job' to, 'I'm really looking forward to reading it, when will it be finished?'

One drawback: I felt I needed to retire in order to do the project justice. Then when I retired I was just too busy! Finally, in April 2018, we agreed to go ahead on what I was sure would be a huge exercise. The agreement was that I would have complete access to everything, peal books, papers, etc. and George would supply much other information relating to the many areas of his life about which I knew very little. I wasn't too sure about the meaning of 'huge exercise' in this context – but I certainly wasn't reckoning on 80,000 words! I should have done, if only because as a lover of the written word he wrote upwards of 10,000 letters in his lifetime. Living in Australia for six and a half years gave them a good start.

Much later, in the last three or four years, it was an Australian ringer, Simon McMillan from Armidale, who helped keep this biography simmering as a concept. My thanks to Simon in this regard. We had the odd 'wobble' when George wasn't feeling great and at other times George had occasional attacks of profound modesty about the project which I managed to overcome!

So why a biography of George Pipe?

If you're going to write a biography, then choose the best to work with. We had several conversations over a couple of years and I knew I should do this. After all, having known him for fifty years, I knew that he was the most famous ringer of his generation, a charismatic, universally popular individual who should be added to the very select list of biographies of ringers. George came from the closest thing to a ringing dynasty we have seen, certainly in modern times. His father Jim (Cecil W Pipe, born in 1906) and his brother Rod (Roderick W Pipe, born in 1940) were both excellent ringers.

Jim was a dashing character who came from very poor background in Grundisburgh, went on to become a guardsman in London, later became part of the St Mary-le-Tower, Ipswich, band before and after the 1939–1945 war, and managed the restoration and augmentation at Grundisburgh. Rod made his ringing career in Birmingham and was one of the finest ringers, conductors and technicians we have ever seen. Jim, George, Rod and David (Rod's son, George's nephew) are all thousand pealers. And now new generations are coming through, David's sons Henry and Alfred, the team wonderfully managed by Cecilia. Time for the biography of George. What an opportunity!

George was instrumental in founding a new national ringing association in Australia (and as a 'pom' to boot) and led the development of great improvements to ringing in Melbourne during his six years there. This was testament to his natural gift for establishing friendships, working with others and his ability to get things done. He was an important member of the band that opened Washington Cathedral bells in 1964, a connection of great value to him that he always valued highly and took care to nurture. And then there's everything else.

An excellent subject

A biographer should value his subject and write about them as they really are, warts and all. Without question, George was my first ringing hero, from when I was about twelve. Until I left home, I lived about twenty miles from Ipswich so I didn't ring with him every week, but I soon realised he was a true gentleman who gave me encouragement and good counsel. His friendship to me was unfailing for over fifty years. Above all else, I respected him as a person, as a sensitive, kind, considerate man who respected and encouraged others and was a role model. All my peers looked up to him. He was a multifaceted person, first and foremost a family man, a dedicated churchman, and a top-class bellringer.

Breadth

He had many other interests and was well connected. Like many sales people, George was extremely good at securing references – be it at Ransomes, Sims and Jefferies, in Ipswich, where it all started, or Ransomes in Australia, whose MD noted George 'acclimatised himself to this country, quickly making a large circle of friends through his ability to mix well at all levels'. The MD had no hesitation in recommending George's services to anyone interested in a keen and alert personality, who had ambition and ability. Back in the UK, Vicon's MD talked of George being pleasant and unflappable despite considerable pressure at times and that he would be pleased indeed to recommend George to a prospective employer. George was always valued highly.

Commitment to the church

The church, whether it be serving St Mary-le-Tower for a couple of spells as churchwarden, ringing all over the country or in paid church employment, was a great part of his life. He worked with senior clergy in the Diocese as Christian Stewardship Advisor and later as Lay Chaplain/PA to the Bishop. One Suffolk clergyman, having arrived during George's time working for the church, thanked him for his help, understanding, encouragement and friendship from when he arrived – 'I seem to remember you were one of the first, if not the first, to welcome me here.' Similar sentiments from another clergyman thanked him for his welcome, helping him become a ringer and develop friends within the wider church community. Giving, welcoming, committing – typical George! He was a born giver, giving much of his time to stimulating and supporting bell initiatives in Suffolk, including at his church, St Mary-le-Tower, Ipswich, where creating a new, modern 35cwt twelve started in 1976 and was finished in 1999. He was a charismatic and empathetic person, a talented artist, great communicator and public speaker. His powers of recall were phenomenal, and they never left him.

The opportunity

It was my privilege to be asked by George to write this book. I knew the breadth of the story of George and Diana would be immense, and it was, as I expected. It's important to remember that as a youngster George knew men born back in the mid-nineteeth century and he also knew the St Mary-le-Tower band who broke new ground between the wars. If these links were not nurtured then in time they would erode. George's ringing career went right through to ringing with the brilliant youngsters of today, born in the 21st century (some in his family of course), many of whom he knew and even more of whom know who he was!

I'm not given to writing 80,000 words for fun, but I wanted this biography to be comprehensive and I thought the subject and content would be fascinating. When George died, the reaction from across the world of bellringing bore that out strongly, feelings of profound and genuine loss which crossed international boundaries. Behind that sense of loss was an appreciation of everything he'd done, what he'd achieved and the vast number of people he touched along the way. If you were to meet him again ten years after a previous meeting, the odds were that he would remember who you were and where you came from – and one's quality as a ringer wouldn't have come into it. Few can do that. Well done George!

Bellringing Jargon

I expect many people reading this book will be bellringers. For those who aren't, some clarification of the terms we use may help.

ANZAB, the Australian and New Zealand Association of Bellringers, founded in 1962.

ASCY, Ancient Society of College Youths, founded in 1637. An ancient London-based ringing society which does not admit to membership those who are members of the Society of Royal Cumberland Youths.

SRCY, Society of Royal Cumberland Youths, founded 1747. An ancient London-based ringing society which does not admit to membership those who are members of the Ancient Society of College Youths.

We start and finish a piece by ringing **rounds** and at the end we '**stand**' (stop) the bells. Once we've done this we can change the ringers and ring a different piece or **method**.

The order in which the bells sound can be altered to give different sequences without the ringers changing their physical position. These are called "rows" or more commonly "**changes**". So we can move from change 123456 (rounds) to 135246 by gradually swapping a small number of adjacent pairs of bells in the sequence, for example 123456 to 132456 to 132546 to 135246.

A full **peal** is comprised of a minimum 5,000 different changes, usually taking between two and a half and three and a half hours to ring, depending on the weight of the bells.

A **quarter peal** is 1,250+ different changes.

A '**touch**' is any piece of ringing up to 1,250 changes.

Typically our change ringing is on an **even number of bells** between six and twelve. It's possible to ring on any number from one to sixteen bells. Six or eight bells is most common.

The names of bellringing **methods** usually have three components: a **name** (often a place name), then a **class** (maybe Surprise, Delight or Alliance) and then a **stage**, the number of bells being rung (Minor is rung on six, Major on eight, Royal on ten, Maximus on twelve). So for example *Cambridge Surprise Minor* is a very commonly rung method on six bells, but it can also be extended to eight (becoming Cambridge Surprise Major), ten, twelve, fourteen and sixteen bells using the relevant definition.

Stedman and *Grandsire* are methods that have been rung for centuries and involve the tenor (biggest) bell being rung 'behind' (i.e. in the same position, at the end of the change). So Stedman **Triples** has seven 'working' bells and the tenor bell rings behind. For **Caters** it is nine bells and tenor behind, and for **Cinques** it is eleven bells and tenor behind.

Probably the simplest method rung is *Plain Bob*; as with Cambridge it runs from six to sixteen bells.

Change ringing is also practised on handbells. The bells are typically rung two bells per ringer, one in each hand, hence half the number of ringers is required. Most ringers believe handbells are easier to ring physically (less weight), but more demanding mentally.

Chapter 1

'The Pipes from Suffolk' – A Dynasty

Bellringers going back two hundred years

The name Pipe is common in Suffolk, particularly East Suffolk, where it goes back several centuries to the 1600s. There are many branches of the family, and historic 'sub' surnames or second names also exist, such as 'Miller' and 'Wilgress'. With just four exceptions, all the Pipes, male and female, carry the name Wilgress, which originated in Great Yarmouth. (See the family tree in George's hand on the first central colour page.) These may be used by family members who are otherwise unrelated. In a rural county such as Suffolk, certain activities are associated with individuals or families. So sitting in a pub somewhere in East Suffolk and mentioning that you are a bellringer might conceivably generate a response, 'Have you heard of the Pipes, bellringers?' or a mention of the Pipe family might be followed by an observation 'Yes, bellringers, Grundisburgh, St Mary-le-Tower, Ipswich'. East Anglia, with its rural farming heritage, is home to a number of such families, small dynasties if you like. The East Anglian Pipe family – still thriving – has included ringers over many generations: one, James Wilgress, is known to have rung a peal at St Mary-le-Tower in 1817.

The Pipe ringing dynasty of modern times started with Cecil W (Jim) Pipe, born 1906, and runs through the generations via his sons George James Wilgress Pipe (1935–2020) and Roderick Wilgress Pipe (1940–2011), Rod's son David James Pipe (1968) and David's two sons, Henry and Alfred, born 2003 and 2005 respectively. 22 Pipes have been bellringers. Therefore in modern times the Pipes from Suffolk have been a ringing dynasty for a century or more, from George's father, Jim, learning to ring in 1918, to now – and (at least by family standards) Henry and Alfie are just starting out as bellringers! An interesting point about the 22 Pipe bellringers is that although eleven of them have rung peals of Surprise Maximus, there has never been a Pipe family tower-bell peal. Until the younger generation came along – David, Cecilia (née Lansberry), Henry and Alfred, who have rung a number of handbell peals together – the only family member to have rung a handbell peal was actually George. Rod had intended to ring a handbell peal with David and Henry, but sadly this was not to be, as he died unexpectedly in 2011.

Research going back to the 1920s and subsequent correspondence between George Pipe and Geoff Pye (William Pye was Geoff's great uncle – much more on him later) in 2003 suggests at least a distant family link between the Pipes and the Pyes via the Carters of Great Yarmouth.

Cecil W (Jim) Pipe

Much of George's early life, certainly until he left home in 1956, was shaped by his relationship with his father. Jim, born in 1906 and died in 1980, was an interesting man who had come from very humble beginnings. Their relationship certainly wasn't always harmonious, but he was a very significant figure in George's story, and from a ringing perspective he provided many of George and brother Rod's early opportunities.

Jim was to many ringers a great 'character'. In his later years, he was usually the man who welcomed them to ring at Grundisburgh on the excellent light

George's father, Cecil (Jim) Pipe, taught himself to ring at Grundisburgh in 1917 at the age of twelve after watching his Uncle John.

ring of ten bells he had worked very hard to create, who would later invite them back to the house 'Easta' to see Arthur (the famous donkey, named after Arthur Barker) and the cats. Many a young man tried riding Arthur, nearly all failed. Jim was born in 1906 in the Turk's Head pub, Hasketon, near Woodbridge, the youngest of a family of fifteen. Soon after his birth he was adopted by an aunt who lived in Grundisburgh, where he went to school and first became interested in ringing at the age of twelve when he taught himself to ring, at Grundisburgh.

The Pearson effect

Cecil W Pipe in Henley Vicarage garden in 1920, aged fourteen

Soon after leaving school, at thirteen, Jim Pipe secured employment working as houseboy for the Revd W C Pearson at Henley, near Ipswich. Pearson had been at Clare College, Cambridge, was the principal founding member of the Cambridge University Guild of Change Ringers (CUG) in 1879 and rang in many early CUG peals on both tower and handbells. His contemporaries were people such as A H F Boughey, B Tyrwhitt-Drake, H S T Richardson, H Law James and C W O Jenkyn, all of whom became accomplished ringers and clerics. E H Lewis and E M Atkins followed a few years later. These were well-connected men who rang at a good standard and were regular visitors to Henley, where Pearson was vicar for 48 years.

Revd W C Pearson, founder member of the Cambridge University Guild, pictured in 1899. Vicar of Henley for 48 years, he was an early influence on Jim Pipe.

Pearson clearly made things happen – by 1902, the old mixed ring of four bells was augmented to eight. 125 peals had been rung on the eight by the time of Jim's arrival in 1919, a significant number anywhere at that time, but particularly for a small village in Suffolk. The first and second peals on the augmented eight, Double Norwich and Kent Major, were rung within two days of each other on 17th and 19th August 1902 – to a bellringer that would definitely indicate Pearson as a 'ringable vicar'!

In 1919, Pearson was in his late 50s and there's no doubt that he was clearly a very positive influence on Jim. Things could have been very different, of course – without that contact with Pearson, Jim's progress might have been slower and he may never have progressed to ring at a higher level, or indeed he may not have continued learning to ring at all.

Jim's first peal was Plain Bob Major on the treble at Henley on 31st July 1920, conducted by George E Symonds, an important figure. Pearson rang beside him on the second. The footnote stated that 'the ringer of the treble is but thirteen years of age, and he only commenced to learn change-ringing this year', added to which this was his first attempt for a peal and he had only rung eight bells on two previous occasions. Thus was established Jim's relationship with George Symonds and the culture of rapid learning that was to run through generations of the family.

George Symonds, a professional miller from North Suffolk and later a revered member of the St Mary-le-Tower band, was an accomplished ringer – he had gone to London in 1895–96 and worked at Seth Hayward's flour mill on London Bridge. Symonds had connections with both of the two elite London-based ringing societies: the 'Cumberlands' at St Martin-in-the-Fields and later with the 'College Youths' at St Paul's Cathedral, where he sometimes deputised as a ringer for Ezra Carter, an original member at St Paul's band from the casting of the bells in 1878. Carter worked shifts as a tugboat pilot on the Thames.

Both Carter (originally from Eye) and Hayward (from Marlesford) had Suffolk connections. George Symonds was still in London when the first peal of Cambridge Maximus was rung at Ipswich in 1908, but later returned and was a key member of the band that rang so many new methods between the wars. He rang his last peal at the age of 97 in 1973.

*Jim Pipe on Life Guard duty.
His horse was called Jim too!*

To London to seek his fortune

Eventually, like so many in the 1920s, Jim Pipe left Suffolk, joining the Life Guards in 1923 and moving to London, where he rang with the College Youths and at St Paul's Cathedral, the latter as a supernumerary to Thomas H Taffender. At St Paul's they had just thirteen ringers for Sunday ringing – two were needed to ring the tenor of the twelve bells in those days, so no one could sit out. Jim was also tower captain at St Andrew's Holborn for a while. A particularly noteworthy peal for Jim would have been Stedman Cinques on the heavy ring of twelve at Southwark Cathedral on 17th August 1929, to which he rang the 49cwt tenor bell. The peal took 3hrs 48mins. To draw a comparison, Grundisburgh tenor bell at the time weighed 8cwt. In those days much of London ringing was tradition-driven, and to get such opportunities, Jim, a young man from Suffolk in his early 20s, would have had to have been very competent. Jim would ring Southwark Cathedral tenor twice to Maximus again in 1957 and 1961. George did similar in 1976 and so well understood this and others of his father's achievements. Set against their many differences, George was rather proud of some of Jim's achievements – he was an excellent ringer – and had plenty of respect for his ringing ability. Jim and George rang 234 peals together so George was Jim's leading ringer for peals.

From the Life Guards, Jim Pipe joined the Stock Exchange, and then he moved into insurance with the Prudential in the 1930s. He became very well-connected in London ringing, particularly in College Youths circles. He then moved back to Ipswich with the Prudential in 1938 and soon after married Sylvia R E Bowyer. Together with Rod, their son, who would become one of the most talented ringers of the second half of the twentieth century, they moved back to Grundisburgh to live in their own house, 'Easta', Meeting Lane, which was built in 1951. In later years, Jim travelled extensively all over the world. From a ringing perspective, he was active in Suffolk, took part in early 'East Meets West' tours (an annual peal tour that continues to this day) and was a member of the 'Great Adventure 2' party, a group of ringers who toured Australia and New Zealand in 1965.

Jim Pipe was a big man physically, strong-willed and with a considerable temper when put to it, but kind and respectful to older people. He was also an excellent organiser, as those who went on his 'Pipe's Pilgrims' tours, which he organised for over thirty years, will know. He was influential in Suffolk ringing. As Secretary of the Suffolk Guild just after the war, it was he who in annual reports pointed out with passion the dire state of many of the 'prime' bell installations in the county and the need for fundraising and restoration, a vision yet to be acknowledged by many at that time, but embraced ever since, and with great success.

He practised what he preached, too, with the restoration at Grundisburgh and augmentation to a very light ring of ten bells in 1949 (later to twelve, in the 1990s), a project

George (right) with his brother Robert in 1941. Robert never learnt to ring.

that has given huge value to generations of ringers ever since, as there were no easy rings of ten anywhere in the area and this was one of the first installations of its type anywhere. Jim was a fine ringer who rang 1,018 peals. He died in October 1980.

George W Pipe and the very early years

Into this proud regional bellringing dynasty, George James Wilgress Pipe was born. Surprisingly perhaps, given what would be a lifelong devotion to the county, George was not a native of Suffolk. He was born to Dorothy (née Mitchell) and Jim at Egham, Surrey, on 9th April 1935. They had moved to Staines in 1933 and in 1937 they had another son, Robert. The years 1937–40 were difficult years for Dorothy, who suffered a breakdown, and she and Jim divorced in 1939, somewhat acrimoniously it seems, just after the war started, when George was four. There were custody and court issues. Dorothy and the boys lived in Virginia Water until 1943, when George moved back to Suffolk to live with Jim and Sylvia. He was not to see his mother for fifteen years.

Some family issues

In the summer of 2018, George talked to me about his early years, through home, school and early career. What came across loud and clear was that these years were hard for him and his parents' failed marriage was the cause of much unhappiness and instability in his childhood, together with moving from Surrey, where he was born, back and forth to Suffolk. He also felt he was undervalued and treated unfairly, often as second best to Rod, by Jim and Sylvia over many years and quoted numerous examples to illustrate the point. However, on the positive side, Sylvia encouraged George's drawing interests, which were very important to him. Since she seldom made mistakes when ringing, she advised him on ways of reducing his mistake tally, and George's records include some notes and tallies regarding mistakes made. One suspects this was an interest she also passed over to Rod.

Help from ringers

Fortunately, George and Rod, although very different, were very close, got on extremely well and had a great relationship. George was five years older than Rod, an age difference that is not always easy to bridge, but this meant that outside the family he could be his own man. On the face of it, the differences were marked. Physically, Rod was very much Sylvia's son:

George aged one with parents Dorothy and Jim in 1936. They divorced in 1939.

St Mary-le-Tower outing, 1924, leaving the Inkerman pub, which is still there today.
Note the "hood" on the charabanc in case of inclement weather.
(left to right) William F Tillett, William P Garrett, Charles W Parker, George E
Symonds (standing), Robert H Brundle, Frederick J Smith, Henry C Gillingham,
Frederick J Tillett, Alfred Bowell, William Wood, Percy May, Harry R Roper,
Hobart E Smith, Charles A Catchpole, Herbert Shemming, George A Fleming,
Charles Woodcock, Albert A Fleming, Charles J Sedgley and Mr Mayhew (Driver)

tall, thin, lightly built, a mathematician, bright, talented, driven. For over fifty years, Rod was a brilliant technical innovator and practitioner in ringing. George was Jim's son: tall, broader in build, East Anglian, a lover of the arts, softer, sociable, collector, public speaker, highly capable ringer. Perhaps the differences were complementary.

Some of the prominent East Anglian ringers of the day were very supportive – George used to go to Norwich to ring peals with Nolan Golden and stay with Nolan and his wife Iris during holidays. Bill Barrett was another Norfolk ringer who knew the Pipe family well and he and his wife Eve offered support. Leslie Mills, from Bures, Suffolk (who taught the author to ring) was a perhaps rather unlikely supporter. Leslie's wife Emily (who George regarded very highly) had learnt to ring in her 40s and their son Donald was a rising star at the time. From conversation it was obvious to me that Leslie disliked Jim intensely!

Early ringing recollections and St Mary-le-Tower

On his return to Suffolk, Jim Pipe rejoined the St Mary-le-Tower, Ipswich band, so from the age of three George had contact with many ringers. He remembered being taken by Jim to watch the ringing at St Mary-le-Tower on Sunday mornings in early 1938. This was the start of George's lifelong love for a great church and tower. He had a comprehensive knowledge of the rich history of ringing at St Mary-le-Tower, where he knew men who had started ringing as far back as the 1870s, and the outstanding exploits of these men in ringing the first peals in many Maximus methods that have formed the fabric of twelve-bell ringing ever since.

Frederick J Tillett with his pigeons, taken outside his home, 12 Bank Road, Ipswich in 1948

George recounted these experiences in his first peal book. They represent a part of our ringing social history that is becoming endangered – the knowledge of them and the characters involved remained with George only – so it is important I record some of them here. They make a fascinating read:

"The belfry is vivid in my mind, so indeed are most of the ringers in their dark suits, watch chains, moustaches and shiny black boots. Charles Sedgley was the only one I can recall who wore shoes. The kindly Robert H Brundle, then nearly 90, Bill Garrett, George Symonds with his waxed moustache, always on the 11th, the sally of which used to fascinate me as it was only fractionally thicker than the rope itself! In all George Symonds rang the bell to 104 peals. The Fleming brothers, Albert and George, would be there, Albert later becoming a recluse who played accordion on the streets for money, Harry Roper, Hobart (Bert) Smith who always rang the fourth, he had a withered arm. The immaculate William JG Brown who, like Percy May worked on the railway, Fred Smith and Ernie Fitch who rang the tenor behind, Charlie Catchpole, the drayman who also swept chimneys and little Billy (William) Tillett.

"My hero was the great Frederick J Tillett, a man of immense strength and presence, nearly always on the tenor, a kindly gentle giant of a man. He worked for Ransomes, Sims and Jefferies for 64 years and was known to do the work of three men and drink about the same! Although a keen ringer he also raced whippets with his son John F (Ben) Tillett who was a pigeon fancier. After the Sunday morning ringing Fred, having been a bare-fisted fighter in his younger days, would sit astride the tenor box and beckon me over to him to punch his nose as hard as I could, much to the amusement of the other ringers! I seem to remember that old band, characters all, so very clearly. Sunday mornings were indeed a great thrill."

Fred Tillett's ancestry in fact went back to John Naunton, an Ipswich bell hanger in the first half of the nineteenth century. As well as being the main tenor ringer at St Mary-le-Tower, Fred rang long peals of more than 10,000 changes on the tenors at Coddenham, Woodbridge and Leiston. In 1892, he rang Debenham tenor to 16,608 Oxford Treble Bob Major when only 24. Never a man to overlook those important elements of detail,

The family basket works in Grundisburgh, around 1900

George could tell you what they did for a living and even where they drank, for example Charles Sedgley went to the Albion Mills, George Symonds the Inkerman, Fred Tillett to the Boilermakers Arms, the Duke of York, the Little White Horse and the Water Lily.

Wartime change

Sylvia R E Bowyer, who later married Jim, together with Phyllis Tillett (Frederick J Tillett's granddaughter) were outstanding lady ringers of their generation, much admired and respected by the St Mary-le-Tower Society which at the time was still male-dominated. That Sylvia and Phyllis rang Surprise Maximus, something achieved by only a handful of women at the time, was to their great credit and also to the St Mary-le-Tower band's credit in that the band provided the leadership and opportunity for it to happen. This was evidence, not for the first time at St Mary-le-Tower in the first half of the twentieth century, of clear-thinking leadership that welcomed innovation, with an eye to the future.

In 1943, the Pipe family moved back to Suffolk, to the original Pipe family home at Royal Cottage, Grundisburgh, where George's Aunt Alice lived, and they remained there until 1951. For children in Grundisburgh in the 1940s, most of the village's activity was centred around the green, the school and the church (Sunday school and choir). Two pubs, the Sun and the Barley Mow, had shut twenty years before, but the Half Moon and The Dog remained. In the past, the Half Moon had been owned by George's great great aunt and great uncle, Samuel Wilgress Pipe. The Dog is the pub by the green, familiar to visitors to the village.

The Pipe family ran a basket-making business in Grundisburgh. The works had been in George's family for around 250 years, perhaps longer, and he spent many hours of his childhood there.

Chapter 2

1944 – George's ringing career starts

Wartime ban lifted and learning to handle a bell

The ban on ringing was in force then and was finally lifted for VE Day, 8th May 1945. However, some churches in the area, including Grundisburgh, rang occasionally some months before that. George, taught to handle by Jim at the age of nine, rang open rounds on the old back six (the restoration and augmentation to ten was not until 1949) at the end of 1944. George, uniquely he believed, actually learnt to handle on a walnut tree at the bottom of the garden at Royal Cottage. The Wartime ban wasn't lifted until 1944, but Jim ingeniously rigged up three pulley blocks, counterweights and guides and spent hours perfecting ringing style.

For a youngster, ringing with someone who is much, much older can be a defining experience. George's first 720 fell into that category, as in the band was a man in his 80s, William Dye. He had conducted peals back in the 1880s, including Holt's Original, and provided a living link back to the mid-nineteenth century. George as a youngster already very much liked the historical aspects of ringing, so Dye, having been born in 1859, was certainly an interesting character to the ten-year-old. Dye's contemporaries provided considerable further interest. John N Oxborrow, who came from nearby Helmingham, was one of the many who left rural Suffolk to achieve success elsewhere. He went to London in the late nineteenth century, joined the College Youths, became Head of Westminster Abbey School, was the first Secretary and Master of the Westminster Abbey Company of Ringers and rang two peals at St Paul's Cathedral in 1904 and 1906. Another very interesting character of that time was Arthur P Moore. He came from Redenhall (a favourite tower of George Pipe's) and he was a regular peal ringer in the Waveney Valley in the 1870s and 1880s. Perhaps a little dashingly, he appeared in peals as 'Captain Moore'. Clearly a very resourceful chap, he with two others jointly founded the Harleston Bell Foundry in 1878. Despite being described as excellent bell founders and pioneers, with bell fitting designs considered revolutionary for the time, the business couldn't secure sufficient work to be viable and sadly it sold out to Whitechapel in 1885.

George and John Mayne learn to ring together

At the time of VE Day Cecil, Phyllis and John Mayne were living in Grundisburgh. Cecil worked at Debach Aerodrome, some five miles away, and his wife and son spent the holidays there in a house on the green. Thus, John Mayne and George Pipe virtually learned to ring together and both rang their first peal (separately) at Ufford. George remembered Cecil Mayne being an excellent striker on all numbers on both tower bells and handbells and he always felt that it was Cecil more than any other ringer who taught him the rudiments of good striking.

Three stars for the future: John Mayne, Rod Pipe and George Pipe, at Grundisburgh, Summer 1944

Another memory was VE day in 1945, which was celebrated in style on bicycles by the Pipe family, the Maynes, Fred Crapnell the village smithy and Charles Clarke the local builder. They visited the sixes at Burgh, Clopton, Otley, Hasketon, Wickham Market, Pettistree, Earl Soham and finished at Ufford, where they were met by the Revd Herbert Drake, one of the founder members of the Suffolk Guild in 1923, prior to ringing Grandsire Triples with Father Drake and the local Fisher brothers.

Early peals and first Central Council meeting at Norwich

By September 1945, George was considered to be ready for his first peal. This was to be at Ufford, since the choice of eight bell towers was fairly limited for a ten-year-old – many were too difficult and in the case of Woodbridge and Debenham a bit too heavy. Sadly the band met short for that peal and the peal was rescheduled for 1st December 1945 at Ufford.

George remembered that it was snowing after the peal and there was a seven-mile cycle ride home but, fortunately, Willoughby E Maulden, one of the band, gave George a whole bar of Cadbury's Dairy Milk chocolate, very special with rationing still in place at the time! George's first New Year as a ringer, as he recalls it in his peal book, was spent ringing out the old year and ringing in the new with 672 of Plain Bob Triples and a further 672 of Plain Bob Major. Celebrating in The Dog, the gallon pot of gin and beer was served by the landlord, Mr Watson, a large man of some 18 stone, intriguingly nicknamed 'Gutty'.

George's second peal, again at Ufford, was Cambridge Surprise Major on 2nd March 1946, when he was still ten, also his first blows in the method. This caused quite a furore in *The Ringing World* and later at the Central

SUFFOLK GUILD
UFFORD, Suffolk, at the Church of St Mary
On Saturday, December 1st, 1945
in 3 hours and eight minutes

A Peal of Bob Major 5056 changes
Tenor 13 cwt

* George W Pipe	Treble
Willoughby E Maulden	2
Mrs C W Pipe	3
Harry Hall	4
Leslie C Wightman	5
Frank L Fisher	6
Charles Clarke	7
Cecil W Pipe	Tenor

Composed by J R Pritchard
Conducted by Cecil W Pipe

* First peal.

Council meeting at Norwich in June 1946. The *Ringing World* Editor, J Armiger Trollope, point-blank refused to publish footnotes to peals unless he felt they were necessary and debate ensued. The footnote to this peal said quite simply 'First of Surprise Major, aged ten', the 'aged ten' being the stumbling block. This was the first Central Council meeting since the war and obviously George's first meeting as well, so to become embroiled, albeit unwittingly and unintentionally, in this type of issue as a consequence of ringing his first peal of Cambridge Major, must have been an interesting experience both to witness and later to reflect upon.

Introduction to the Central Council

On the positive side, attending the meeting at Norwich, close to home, was a great way of meeting some of the great and the good of the Exercise at the time, a privilege afforded to very few 11-year-olds then, and something that should not be under-estimated. In 1946, the world was a very big place with long journey times, poor roads, few bypasses and unreliable cars – for those that owned them. There was no 'nipping up the motorway' then. Indeed, for some it was primarily about riding a bike many miles to the rail or bus station if one wanted to go any distance. Opportunity

Central Council Meeting, Norwich 1946. The caption of this photo in the Eastern Evening News read: "The Youngest and the Oldest – A happy picture from Norwich taken just previous to the Council meeting. George (aged 11) is pictured with the Lord Mayor, The Lord Bishop of Norwich, The President (Mr E H Lewis) and Mr George Williams, aged 89, of North Stoneham, Hants."

was limited and, even for the great and the good of the Exercise, ringing together at the Central Council meeting was a highlight, as there was no other similar forum. George also rang changes on twelve for the first time, Grandsire Cinques at St Peter Mancroft. Jim was well connected – George recalled meeting William H Barber, Alfred H Pulling, John W Jones, Rupert Richardson, Alfred B Peck, Edwin H Lewis, Charles H Kippin, George Williams (who was 89, an 'oldest and youngest' photo) and many others. He remembered ringing with Wilfred Williams, who was to become a lifelong friend, for the first time at Norwich.

Rapid progress in peal ringing

The bands for these early peals were of very high quality and the band for his third peal (he was now eleven), Superlative at Ufford, on 12th October 1946, for VJ Day, was a good example of Jim's ability to secure the high quality ringers he needed to do the job and support his son – in addition to three Pipes there was Willoughby Maulden from Framlingham, Leslie C Wightman from Cretingham, Frank L Fisher from Ufford, George

A Fleming from Witnesham and Leslie G Brett from Framsden. Although the pre-war peal ringers of the 1920s and '30s were starting to diminish, there were still plenty of capable performers around. Denied any ringing for several years because of the ban, they must have been delighted to ring with a capable youngster and watch him progress.

George's first peal as conductor, Plain Bob Major from the second, followed on 22nd March 1947, with five more in 1947, still aged just twelve, peal total now nine. In 1947 he rang his first touch of Stedman Cinques at St Mary-le-Tower, which included Robert H Brundle (who rang the tenor to the first peal of Cambridge Maximus at Ipswich in 1908) and Frederick J Tillett, thus a youngster could cement links with ringers going back several generations. His first peal of London Surprise Major at first attempt followed, on 11th January 1948, conducted by Leslie C Wightman. He was now the youngest person to ring a peal of London Surprise Major.

Jim Pipe the publicist

Jim was also keen on publicising his son's performances, so in George's peal book are press cuttings from the *East Anglian Daily Times*, the *Diss Express* and the *Suffolk Chronicle and Mercury*. For a bellringing festival at Bury St Edmunds in 1946, Jim gained publicity in the *West Suffolk Mercury* and even the *Daily Sketch*, which reported 'Said to be the youngest bellringer in Britain, George Pipe of Grundisburgh, Suffolk, was amongst a party of ringers from the Eastern Counties who took part in a Campanologists Festival yesterday at Bury St Edmunds'. This 'festival' was actually the Suffolk Guild AGM! Do we exploit the available means of publicity these days as diligently as Jim Pipe did, I wonder?

The Bailey brothers of Leiston – the only known photo of all eleven. Left to right: Allen (boilermaker), Frederick (boilermaker), David (the eldest, farmworker), Leonard (painter), Edgar (fitter), Herbert (maintenance engineer), Charles (blacksmith), James (painter), Ernest (known as Sid, carpenter), Norman (gear cutter), Wilfred (boilermaker)

The Leiston band

There were several strong eight-bell bands in Suffolk at the time, normally from one tower or in the immediate locality of that tower. George was familiar with these men, often knowing them personally and ringing with many of them as a boy.

The Bailey brothers, eleven of them, were particularly noteworthy – all from Leiston on the East Suffolk coast. All rang except Herbert and David, although he could toll the service bell. They rang peals in all the Surprise Major methods of the day, including quite a few new ones, and the brothers rang peals of Stedman Cinques on hand bells. They rang the first peal of Edinburgh in 1923 and also Lancashire the same year, the latter a double method of classical structure much favoured in Spliced these days, nearly 100 years later. Getting jobs as the young ones grew up was no problem, most of them worked at Garrett Engineering, a very large agricultural engineering and manufacturing business in the town, now an excellent museum.

In 1911 eight of the eleven brothers rang their first peal including only family members, Plain Bob Major, at Leiston. The centenary was marked with a further peal, in 2011.

In 1921, six of the brothers rang a peal of Stedman Cinques on handbells. For each, this was their first peal on twelve bells, an astonishing achievement.

The Helmingham band

The eight-bell band that captures the imagination of most in Suffolk with an interest in ringing history, and indeed one of the most remarkable rural bands in history, is the Helmingham band, particularly active during the 1920s and 30s. This band was drawn from the neighbouring villages, Framsden and Cretingham (pronounced 'Critnam') as well as Helmingham itself, and it typically would contain several brothers per family from perhaps two or three families, with the art being passed down through the generations. Ringing was still for the most part an all-male activity then. Some of the sons would move to the North or London for work, or perhaps join the Forces. However, most worked on the land, covering a wide range of skills, from saddlery to brickmaking, typically on the Tollemache estate, home of Helmingham Hall, with their families living in tied estate cottages. (The Tollemache family was part owner of Tolly Cobbold brewery in the late twentieth century.)

These men were very competent performers by any standards in any era. At that time ringing was highly regarded within their local parishes and seen almost as a village craft activity. Also, unless something miraculous happened, the only means of transport was bicycle; no buses or tubes as in the towns and cities, which limited their opportunities. So the Helmingham band included men by the name of Whiting (three of them: Albert E, George and William G), Wightman (five of them: Alfred S, George, Leslie C, Walter, William and Edgar), T William Last, Leslie G Brett and George Pryke, and there were others. By the standards of the day, they were prolific peal ringers and many ringers today would consider much of their output to be 'advanced'.

The Helmingham band, 1935.
Left to right: George Whiting,
T William Last, George Bennett,
Leslie G Brett, William Whiting,
James Bennett (Jr), George Pryke,
Albert E Whiting, Leslie C Wightman

They had the benefit of at least four of the band – T William Last, George Whiting (who had a withered arm), Leslie C Wightman and Leslie G (Lester) Brett – being capable of conducting peals of Surprise Major; 'the four conductors', as George was to put it. Leslie Wightman was reckoned to be the best ringer – he sometimes rang in peals at St Mary-le-Tower and also went on some of Bill Pye's tours.

Helmingham St Mary, Suffolk: bells cast by Thomas Mears II for Waterloo in 1815, rehung in 1900 and again, on one level, in 2011

New methods at Helmingham

Their 'everyday' repertoire was very much the standard methods of the time: Cambridge, Superlative, London, Bristol, Double Norwich and Stedman. Between 1930 and 1939 they rang 244 peals in these methods alone, including 68 of Double Norwich. Apart from George Whiting, who rang 84 peals during these ten years, Leslie Wightman, George Pryke, Bill Last and Brett rang over 100 peals each. Bear in mind that for agricultural workers, as many of the band were, weeknight peals were limited and the summer was busy with a harvest break from ringing in July and August. Of course they were creatures of habit – George Pryke usually rang the third, even though his handling style meant that he often caught the clock case with his elbow!

The Suffolk Guild report for 1939, written in July 1940, spoke of a wish for the Helmingham men to resume their previous output of peals, 'somewhat interrupted by the dark days of war', as Charles Sedgley put it, but soon the war would have a detrimental effect on the band, and it was never the same afterwards. What they rang in the 1930s was impressive, though – Cornwall, Deben, Devon, Dunwich, Edmundsbury, Helmingham, Lavenham, Lincoln, Monewdon, Silchester and Yoxford, to name just a few, are all excellent methods and were all rung as firsts in the method by the Helmingham band between 1932 and 1938. Several of these are regularly rung today, eg Cornwall and Lincoln, often in Spliced. One wonders who was the arbiter of what was worth ringing and what wasn't. Maybe the methods were composed by one of the ringers themselves or perhaps given to them by Gabriel Lindoff, together with a true composition. Lindoff was a noted composer, originally from Leiston. Perhaps George Pipe would have known.

There were no method banks and no computer generation in those days, as is standard today, and hence there was little choice of new methods – you had to compose them yourself. Even as late as 1964, fewer than 600 Surprise Major methods had been rung. Interestingly, the band's method complexity was toned down after the Second World War, presumably because there were fewer ringers in the band (due to ageing and service in the Forces) and those remaining were less experienced. Lester Brett was one of the younger ones, a very tall, narrow, strong, sinewy chap who worked on the land, but so broad Suffolk one sometimes needed to work hard to understand him. A very nice chap and a very good ringer who rang anywhere with anyone, a former Ringing Master of the Suffolk Guild and the first native of Suffolk to ring 1,000 peals, he died in 1991.

The Tollemache family was a substantial benefactor to Helmingham from as early as the fifteenth century. They gave a ring of eight bells, tenor 19¾ cwt in E flat, all cast by Thomas Mears II at the Whitechapel Bell Foundry in 1815 to commemorate victory at the Battle of Waterloo, and the bells were originally hung in an oak frame on two levels. They were rehung by Alfred Bowell of Ipswich in 1900 and around 250 of the 300 peals on the bells up to 2001 were rung after Bowell's work, a credit to him. However the bells became very tough to ring in the late 20th century and ringing stopped in 2001 when it was discovered that there was movement in the frame and work was needed to the tower. The bells were returned to the Whitechapel Bell Foundry for retuning and are hung, now on one level, in a new cast iron frame on a galvanised UB steel grillage, which is desirable as bells on one level are easier to ring.

The project proceeded with the blessing and assistance of Lord Tollemache, whose family, nearly 200 years on from 1815, was fully involved in deciding the new configuration, raising funds and helping with the removal and restoration. The Suffolk Guild of Ringers contributed towards the project, as did English Heritage. The main sponsor was the Heritage Lottery Fund, and, appropriately, the heritage project was about French Revolutionary and Napoleonic Wars culminating in victory at the Battle of Waterloo and the involvement of Helmingham people during these years. The restoration of an excellent and historic ring of eight in a fine tower represents a significant success. The dice is so often loaded against those undertaking major projects – for example, the structural elements alone at Helmingham required an investment of £290k.

Chapter 3

Developing his ringing career and Woodbridge School

Post-war resumption of ringing gathers pace

One of the most exciting aspects of ringing after the long silence of the war years was the resumption of district meetings, a new experience for George. They were eagerly anticipated by the pre-war members, providing a means of meeting old and new friends and making available a higher standard of ringing than was possible in the individual towers. The ringers' tea continued to be a significant attraction!

He recalled memorable meetings at Lavenham on Midsummer's Day Saturday 1946, where over 200 people attended, and Beccles, another great event where the belfry was packed and Edith K Fletcher rang the tenor to Cambridge Surprise Royal. By the 1980s, a great event going back decades, the 'Lavenham Ringing Day', had dropped off the calendar through poor attendance.

In the summer of 1947, a weekend outing from Suffolk to Leicester was organised. Apart from war duty, Ipswich to Leicester was the furthest that some of the party had ever travelled! Leicester was a developing city for ringing after the war and they rang at the Cathedral, St Margaret's and other city towers, meeting Ernest Morris, the Poole family (whom George would ring with again in 1953, with great success) and others.

Expanding peal-ringing horizons

George rang 21 peals, mostly as a thirteen-year-old, in 1948. These were mainly in Suffolk and included some peals of Minor at Clopton, a tough assignment, Hasketon, Burgh, and Tuddenham and his first peal of Bristol Surprise Major, at Framsden just after his thirteenth birthday. In August 1948, the family, together with Les Wightman, spent a week in East Kent on a tour organised by A Patrick Cannon and Frank C W Knight. George rang five peals and met people like Frank L Harris, Ronald N Marlow, Ronald H Dove, Thomas Cullingworth, George R Newton and Mark S Lancefield, quite an array of noted ringers for a thirteen-year-old. Mark Lancefield was starting out at that time, but would soon become an early and great exponent of conducting peals of all-the-work Spliced Surprise Major in the 1950s.

The ringing highlight of 1948 was George's first twelve-bell peal on 19th September, Stedman Cinques at St Mary-le-Tower, aged thirteen. The band was composed mostly of members of the local band, which still remained strong at the time, including Charles J Sedgley who conducted it, and George E Symonds. George noted it was 'a long-awaited ambition to ring a peal on twelve bells. I'd listened to so many at the Tower even in that short time so it was a great thrill to ring one at last in such a historic tower'. Alas, by then Fred Tillett was too old to ring, and George never did ring a peal with him. George was at the time the youngest person to ring a twelve-bell peal, the previous youngest being Phyllis Tillett, Fred's daughter, who rang Grandsire Cinques at fourteen. The peal details are given here.

George's first peal of Stedman Cinques was for the 97th birthday of Robert H.

SUFFOLK GUILD

IPSWICH, Suffolk, at the Church of St Mary-le-Tower

Saturday September 19th, 1948

in 3 hours and 35 minutes

A Peal of 5007 Stedman Cinques

Tenor 32 cwt

William F Tillett	1
Sylvia R E Pipe	2
George W Pipe	3
Charles J Sedgley	4
Harry R Roper	5
William J G Brown	6
George A Fleming	7
Leslie C Wightman	8
George E Symonds	9
Cecil W Pipe	10
Ernest W Pye	11
Herbert G Jillings	12

Composed and conducted by Charles J Sedgley

Brundle, a man who he liked and admired and who rang the tenor to the first ever peal of Cambridge Maximus at St Mary-le-Tower on 15th August 1908. Sadly Bob Brundle died soon afterwards. He had remarkable ringing longevity – his last peal, one of Cambridge Maximus, was rung at the age of 87.

Further evidence of the post-war decline of the St Mary-le-Tower band manifested itself soon afterwards with the death of William P. Garrett of Ipswich, which occurred in the belfry of St Mary-le-Tower in August 1948. Bill Garrett was a first-rate ringer, the first person to ring 100 peals of Maximus, and he rang in most of the firsts of Maximus at Ipswich as well. The Suffolk Guild report noted 'Bill Garrett was a gentleman of the highest character and everyone who knew him loved him.' Jim Pipe, as Suffolk Guild General Secretary, continued to issue annual warnings about the state of the county's bell stock and the need to teach new ringers, the Guild wasn't 'replacing' those it was losing.

Albert J Lancefield, a ringing poet

Another tour, this time to Suffolk, took place in August/September 1954 and involved some of those on the 1948 tour. Albert J Lancefield, Mark's brother, was on both tours. Bert was an interesting chap, a bachelor, railwayman/enthusiast and a capable ringer who rang 250 or so peals. He was a little younger than another Ashford area ringer, Harry Parkes, who would undertake Whitechapel's bellhanging work at Washington Cathedral (more of Harry later). Both had undertaken five-year steam apprenticeships at Ashford Railway Works, the sort of 'work' plenty of modern-day ringers drool about.

Albert, or 'Bert', followed his father before him into the works. He was also a keen traveller and, perhaps uniquely in his time, was a well-known and highly rated poet who was also a very good ringer. He made frequent visits to Australia and New Zealand, to where he emigrated in 1948. He was ringing master at Christchurch Cathedral, where he developed change ringing on all ten bells, something which had never been achieved before in that part of the world.

One of his works was *On younger soil: a working tour of New Zealand in verse*. Most of these poems and verses were printed in 1955 under the title *By wandering tempest − a journey to New Zealand in verse*, with the rest written on a second visit during 1965/1966. Bert also travelled to Australia, writing *Footfalls : a working tour of Australia in verse*. Later he submitted some of his early offerings, *Early Poems*, to the then Poet Laureate John Betjeman, for appraisal. Betjeman had never mastered the art of the sonnet and Bert offered to give him some instruction, thereby beginning a lifelong friendship.

Still only 32, Bert returned to England in 1952, via a grand tour taking in Sydney, Hobart, Adelaide and Melbourne, reaffirming his love of Antipodean life along the way and then joined the band headed by his brother Mark that was making history in Kent at that time.

In 1961 he returned to Australia by sea, firstly to Perth, where he got a job in the railway works. Having done a lot of work trying to improve the heavy eight hung at the top of St George's Cathedral, he decided to recruit new ringers from Perth University, to whom

"Victorian Gathering" − Ringers from Melbourne, Bendigo and Ballarat at St Paul's Cathedral, Melbourne, 1963. George, Diana and daughter Sarah are in the front row. Bert Lancefield is in the back row, third from left.

WOODBRIDGE SCHOOL

REPORT for the _Lent_ Term, 1949.

Name _Pipe G.W._   Age _13.11_

Form _Remove_   Final Position _1_   No. of Boys _27_   Average Age _14.0._

SUBJECT	Diligence (key below)	Term %	Exam. %	Place in Form	Remarks on Term's Work
DIVINITY	1				Very good. GP.
ENGLISH	1	69	—	7/27	Very keen and hardworking. In essay work he must guard against losing himself in the music of words and writing nonsense.
HISTORY	2	67	—	5	His written work is usually well set out, and he is quick to grasp points & detail. A good term's work.
GEOGRAPHY	1	78		1	His work is uniformly good. GP.
LATIN	1	66	—	3/9	Excellent. A most enthusiastic and promising Latinist, whose worst enemy is occasional carelessness.
GREEK *or* GERMAN					
FRENCH	1	71	—	6	He is alert and painstaking. He should continue to improve rapidly.
MATHEMATICS	2	67		4	His work never lacks enthusiasm; the pity is that this often interferes with concentration on the point at issue. RH
PHYSICS / CHEMISTRY	1.	74		2	Has worked well throughout the term and made excellent progress. a.R. Most interested in the subject he does consistently excellent work.
ART / Music	1				He continues to do excellent work. GP.
NATURE STUDY MANUAL TRAINING					

DILIGENCE: 1=Good   2=Satisfactory   3=Moderate only   4=Poor

ATTENDANCE	Absent — sessions. Late — times.
FORM MASTER'S SUMMARY	He is keen, industrious and attentive to detail. He has done very well to come top of an intelligent form.
HOUSE MASTER'S REPORT	He is a most enthusiastic member of the House & ever willing to contribute to his utmost in all branches of school life. — RNB

Excellent.

George's Woodbridge School Report 1949, when he was thirteen. Note the comments about English!

he floated the idea of installing a ring of bells in an empty tower on the campus. Was this forward thinking, or an idea already belonging to someone else? This would be a five-year tour and Bert took care to stay a reasonable time in each location – Adelaide, Melbourne, Tasmania, Canberra and Sydney – so he could assist with developing local bands.

Bert was a popular chap wherever he went, visiting George and Diana in Melbourne in 1963, shortly before they returned to the UK. He appears in a photo of a Victorian ringers' group on the steps of Melbourne Cathedral in 1963. Despite all the travel, he finally settled back into a simple life in the Kent countryside where he started, immersed in local and family history, keeping in contact with his many friends around the world and becoming something of a cult figure. He must have been an unusual chap, a poet living as a '50s equivalent of a backpacker, dropping off for a spot of bellringing along the way.

Woodbridge School

George went to a prep school, Bacton House in Felixstowe (part of that time was funded by a family friend), and then gained a scholarship to Woodbridge School. In the view of his father, his strengths were drawing and writing and his career possibilities were either in surveying, becoming an architect or taking a trade. Attending Woodbridge School and then moving to a trade is not as odd as it might seem these days because we were a manufacturing nation. So it could have been agricultural engineering, an important industry in East Anglia, with a major employer, as it turned out to be, but going into a trade was quite a logical thing to do, even from a public school background.

The call that never came

When Bishop Richard Brook confirmed George at Woodbridge School Chapel in 1949, he remembers feeling moved to hope for the call to the Ministry. The chaplain at Woodbridge School at the time was the Revd George Darley, an Anglo Catholic from Skibbereen, County Cork, a Trinity College Dublin man and a splendid priest. He was also a great encourager, who offered to guide George if he did feel the call to the Ministry. He also gave non-timetable tuition in church architecture to George and a couple of his friends, which was a History of Art module as part of the School Certificate. George saw this as a natural adjunct to his theological hopes, but after two years he knew deep down that he hadn't got the call, which was disappointing. Of course, God has a wonderful way of working his purpose, and this was definitely the case with George. As well as a lifetime as a churchman, he spent the later part of his career deeply involved in church work.

Expanding his ringing career

George's peal books, five of them, are a wonderful record covering his 1,418 peals in a peal ringing career spanning 67 years, from the start in December 1945 through to his last peal in December 2012. These records are all handwritten, with lots of flourishes, notes and comments. As a social history, they provide untold riches and there's always a surprise waiting on the next page.

A little piece of social history from one of George's peal books. A copy of a wonderful photograph of James Heffer of Framlingham, chimney sweep, ringer and thatcher, who died in 1899. George Symonds rang with him.

George had a huge collection of postcards, notably of East Anglian churches, and was a collector all his life. Thus, most of the peals have an accompanying postcard of the venue. Any devotee of ringing-related history could profitably spend a day or two with this collection.

From the late 1940s through to the mid-1950s, George was working at Ransomes, Sims and Jefferies in Ipswich and lived in Grundisburgh. Peal Book 1 records a burgeoning ringing career, mostly in Suffolk, and his first six hundred peals. At that time opportunity was limited, most ringing was local and most people travelled by cycle and motorbike rather than car.

1949 saw forty peals, mostly in standard methods, some achievement for a fourteen-year-old. 8th January 1949 saw George's first peal of Maximus, Cambridge, rung at St Mary-le-Tower, making him the youngest person to ring a peal of Cambridge Maximus, aged thirteen.

Frederick J Tillett, George's hero and one of Ipswich's prize fighters, who had retired from ringing at St Mary-le-Tower, gave George two new half-crowns. This memento, the fruit of many hours of Fred's labour, we suspect, is still in George's peal book. This achievement was later superseded by Margaret E L Beamish (Chapman), who rang a peal of Cambridge Maximus at Birmingham Cathedral on 19th March 1949.

George's fourteenth birthday was celebrated with a 'George' peal of Bob Major at St Margaret's, Ipswich, on St George's Day! The first peal on the restored and augmented bells at Grundisburgh was rung in May, his first peal of Royal, enabling him to complete peals of Cambridge from Minor to Maximus, quite a rare achievement in those days, but usually quoted in *The Ringing World* when it happened. In early June, coinciding with the Central Council weekend, he rang a peal of Kent Maximus at Wakefield Cathedral with Harold and Olive Rogers, Ron Dove, Harold Walker and Gilbert Thurlow.

It's difficult to know when the habits of a young person develop into values in their own right. By now, having rung a couple of twelve-bell peals and spent many Sunday mornings as a youngster watching the premier band of its time in action, I'm sure George was well aware of what really mattered, and his historical interests and perspectives were already well established. Chris Pickford takes that view:

SUFFOLK GUILD

IPSWICH, Suffolk, at the Church of St Mary-le-Tower

On Saturday, January 8th, 1949

in 3 hours and 58 minutes

A Peal of 5280 Cambridge Surprise Maximus

Tenor 32 cwt

William F Tillett	1
Charles J Sedgley	2
George W Pipe	3
Hobart E Smith	4
Harry R Roper	5
Cecil W Pipe	6
Sylvia R E Pipe	7
George A Fleming	8
Leslie C Wightman	9
Leslie G Brett	10
George E Symonds	11
John F Tillett	12

Composed and Conducted by Charles J Sedgley

"When any question about Suffolk ringers and ringing arises in discussion, "George Pipe would have known all about that" is what immediately comes into the mind. That's because George, as a passionate advocate for the future of ringing, was always deeply interested in the past too. He personally knew many of the 'greats' of the old Ipswich band that broke new bounds in Surprise Maximus and he always spoke of them with enormous respect. His knowledge of ringers and ringing spanned several generations. For George, the bond between ringers – across age, social standing, gender, etc. – made ringing what it was."

Cheshire ringers tour of Suffolk and the loss of a hero

In late August 1949, George was invited to join the Cheshire ringers tour of Suffolk and Norfolk, an amazing privilege because this was probably the best peal band in the country at the time, comprised of people like C Kenneth Lewis, W Eric Critchley, John E Bibby, Walter Allman, J Edward Cawser, Wilfrid F Moreton, Ralph G Edwards and James C E Simpson: revered company indeed for a fourteen-year-old, and he was on his own, amongst a band he hardly knew. He rang four peals with this band, Liverpool Surprise Major at Stowmarket, London Surprise Major at Clare, Bristol at Lavenham on the same day (a very big day for anyone!) and Pitman's Four at Ufford.

George's peal book notes that James C E Simpson was one of his heroes. Simpson was a doctor who died in 1951 at the age of 43 due to complications occurring during a routine operation. The peal book contains Ken Lewis's *Ringing World* obituary of Simpson, 'a well-known and brilliant conductor (he specialised in conducting London

Surprise Major) and ringer'. He was the first person to call 'Pitman's five' and 'Pitman's six', difficult compositions of spliced requiring an unusually good memory, and he rang a number of long peals in the north-west, including the then record of Spliced Surprise Major. Although he was of slight build he was a noted heavy bell ringer of his time, carefully considering each tenor that he rang and the amount of energy he needed to do the job well. He rang the tenors at Beverley Minster, Wells Cathedral and St Nicholas, Liverpool. His friends were surprised at his unexpected death as many considered him to be the fittest man amongst them – his other interests were fell-walking, tennis, badminton and singing.

James C E Simpson: one of George's heroes, a noted heavy-bell ringer and conductor

100th peal at sixteen

1950 was a year of consolidation during which George rang 13 peals, including Plain Bob Caters and Plain Bob Cinques. He'd also started work. April 1951 saw George's 100th peal, at Wickham Skeith, of which he conducted 21. I expect Jim Pipe picked up the publicist's role once again! The *Suffolk Chronicle* and *Mercury* and the *Children's Newspaper* noted that George 'had attained his ambition to ring 100 peals on tower bells before the age of sixteen, thereby setting up a new national record'. It was carefully noted, however, that all his 100 peals were on tower bells, as a rival had rung some of his on handbells (this a reference to Edwin A Barnett, some of whose 100 peals had been on handbells). George's 100 peals were rung in 33 different towers, for five different guilds or associations, and with 115 different ringers. Even young Rod got a mention as 'much promise is given also by the younger son, now aged 10': such promise that Rod rang his first peal the following month, Kent Treble Bob Major at Grundisburgh at the age of eleven. By 1951, George was starting to raise his profile, ringing tenors and regularly conducting peals in the local area.

Ringers helping

I mentioned earlier that George's childhood was tough, but that some of the noted ringers in East Anglia were aware of the problem and were keen to assist, for example, providing a few days ringing for him during the holidays. So in September 1951, he spent a few days in Norfolk with Bill Barrett and Nolan Golden. They rang peals at St Giles, Norwich, Loddon, Aylsham, and St Michael at Coslany and St Peter Mancroft, Norwich. Postcards of those wonderful churches add to the peal records in George's stylish hand. Peal number 113 marked 50 peals with Ronald W Steward and William J Button, Suffolk men who were supporters of George's early ringing career. Meanwhile, another stellar ringing career was just starting. In November at Grundisburgh, still at the age of 11, Roderick W Pipe rang his first peal on ten bells, Kent Treble Bob Royal, and he composed and conducted the peal.

Peal ringing certainly wasn't all plain sailing in the late 1940s and early 1950s. George noted that peals in those days were never guaranteed and far from a certainty in many cases. This was because of a lack of capable ringers and conductors with the ability to really sort things out if there were mistakes and the bells got into a muddle. It seems unbelievable these days, but as an example, attempts for a peal of Cambridge Royal at Beccles in 1947, 1948 and 1949 were lost on all three occasions, and at the time there were no other ringers capable of coming into the band. He also commented on the help he was given by the St Mary-le-Tower ringers and also the bands at Framsden and Helmingham, people like T William Last, the Whitings, the Wightmans, Leslie Brett and others, who helped him in his early ringing and peal ringing career.

First peal of Major on the back eight at Exeter Cathedral in 1954

In 1952, a 'double-handed' peal (with two people ringing the tenor together) of Grandsire Triples was rung in 3hr 52min on the back eight of the 72cwt ring of twelve at Exeter Cathedral. In 1954 this was eclipsed by a double-handed peal of Plain Bob Major in 4hr 47min, George on the box with Jim Pipe strapping (ringing from the floor), supported by a star-studded band of the day to do the job – Frank Harris, Pat Cannon, Ron Marlow, John Mayne (conductor), Richard and Tony Price. Norman Mallett and Fred Wreford wrote to *The Ringing World* complimenting the band on their performance. There is a wonderful peal board in light oak very prominently positioned in the tower. Chris Kippin notes:

> "George once told me that he'd wanted to ring Double Norwich, but Jim persuaded him that Plain Bob would be a better/safer option. I also seem to remember that they rang the tenor with two separate ropes attached above the sally, rather than with a conventional extra tail end. I don't think the idea of the extra long sallies which are used these days had been thought of."

THE GUILD OF DEVONSHIRE RINGERS
Saturday October 30th 1954 in 4hrs & 47mins
A PEAL OF PLAIN BOB MAJOR
5056 CHANGES
Tenor 72cwt 2qr 2lbs in B flat

FRANK L. HARRIS	TREBLE
A. PATRICK CANNON	2
RONALD N. MARLOW	3
HILDA G. SNOWDEN	4
JOHN R. MAYNE	5
RICHARD E. PRICE	6
TONY PRICE	7
GEORGE W. PIPE CECIL W. PIPE	TENOR

Composed by John R. Pritchard
Conducted by John R. Mayne
The heaviest ring of bells yet rung to a peal of Major

Peal board which now hangs in the Exeter Cathedral ringing room, recording father and son ringing the 72cwt tenor to Major. "Four hours and 47 minutes of joy!"
This was the heaviest peal on eight bells, a record that stood for 54 years until a peal of Cambridge Major was rung on the back eight at Liverpool Cathedral in November 2008.

Hilda G Snowden

Hilda, a prominent North Essex ringer from the 1930s through to the 1960s and a friend of Tony Price and Jim Pipe, rang the fourth in the peal of Major. Hilda was part of an unusual breed at the time – she was a fine heavy-bell ringer at a time when relatively few women rang big bells, a classic bell handler with an effortless style who rang peals on

Hilda G Snowden, pictured in 1994. She was from North Essex, a pioneering and very fine lady ringer who rang heavy bells superbly.

many heavy bells in Essex and Suffolk (Woodbridge tenor, to name one, a challenging 25cwt bell), and she was still around and very much revered, justifiably so, at the time I learned to ring in the mid-1960s. She was 'old school' and a Christian lady who served her local church and community. Interestingly, she travelled to Exeter in November 1953 and rang the 33cwt tenth to Grandsire Caters, perhaps a warm up to the Major? Frank Harris conducted this peal and he said 'it was truly an amazing performance on her part, for not only did she ring the bell beautifully, but she seemed as fresh as a daisy at the end whilst the rest of the band were lost in admiration – what a woman!' At the earthier end of the spectrum, Sam Twitchett from Clare, an early mentor of mine, once described Hilda, inaccurately, as 'the heaviest lady bellringer I ever saw.'

Chapter 4

Apprenticeship, getting married and preparing to leave the UK

Apprenticeship at Ransomes, Sims and Jefferies

In the 1950s, apprenticeships were a little different from now. At that time, one was indentured to a business. This was rather like transferring ownership of oneself from one's father to the business and then signing up for a seven-year apprenticeship. The business George went to was Ransomes, Sims and Jefferies at Ipswich, which was a very well-established, rather conservative agricultural engineering business that was run in a patriarchal, Edwardian sort of way. After three years, there was the option to specialise – in George's case it was about going to the drawing office department of the business. Ransomes had 4,000 staff, so there was plenty of opportunity for good people to progress. Staff were very well looked after and they took on 170 apprentices per year. At that time, there were 'runners' in the business who would run from the boardroom to the managers with messages and vice versa – no sophisticated internal phone system in those days.

George was fortunate to be selected as one of those apprentices, so his move from school to career was reasonably seamless, and, of course, there was full employment in 1950. George's interest in and ability at drawing, together with his communication and people skills led to his progression to field engineer. Ultimately, he wanted to move into export sales as his longer-term objective. In the early 1950s there was plenty of management opportunity in the colonies, and Africa in particular was the place being promoted in the UK – the government wanted young professional people to go to places such as North and South Rhodesia, Uganda, Tanganyika and The Cape. Opportunities to build careers existed here and in other colonial territories. Ultimately, though, his opportunity would not be in Africa.

Outward Bound

In the summer of 1953 George was eighteen and working on the Africa desk in Ransomes export office. The Personnel Director (Lieutenant Commander the Hon Peter Carew RN Retired, (with voice and accent to match) called for George. In those days, if you were summoned by a director you tended to imagine you were guilty of some misdemeanour or other!

OUTWARD BOUND MORAY SEA SCHOOL

Name   PIPE. GEORGE J. W.

Age   20. 6

Course No. "S" 53

Watch   HAWKINS

Sponsor RANSOMES SIMS AND
         JEFFERIES LTD.

Leadership: - Will come to the front in any sphere.

Team Spirit: - Excellent.

Public Spirit: - Exceptionally well developed.

Reaction to Discipline: - To my entire satisfaction.

His Ability to continue in the face of danger, hardship, discomfort: -

        An example to us all.

Ability to concentrate: -

    Where interested   )   At all times he has shown excellent powers
    Where not interested) of concentration.

Resourcefulness: - Can be relied on to produce an intelligent answer
                    to any problem.

Manners: - Well mannered and polite.

Conscientiousness: -

    On routine, fatiques etc.   ) To my entire satisfaction.
    On special tasks entrusted to him) Whether supervised or not he is
                                        completely reliable.

Fair Mindedness: - Completely impartial in all his dealings with offenders.

General Progress & Report: - I cannot speak too highly of this boy. He
made a good Watch out of what easily could have been an indifferent one, by
his own example and powers of leadership. He has a very likeable
personality, is loyal and trustworthy. He is supremely in control of
himself at all times. He is a good Christian and a credit to his sponsor.

                    Contributing Officer's Initials

*Outward Bound assisted Ransomes in developing future management, through
outdoor education enabling young people to believe in themselves. They sponsored
George and this played a part in him realising the opportunity in Australia.
"I cannot speak too highly of this boy."*

Peter Carew told George that with a view to assessing future management potential, the company had decided to select two apprentices a year (Ransomes took 170 apprentices per year at that time) to attend one of the three Outward Bound centres in the UK – the Sea School at Aberdovey in Wales, the Mountain School at Ullswater in the Lake District or the Moray Sea School in the far North of Scotland. The Outward Bound Trust was founded in 1941 and is still operating today. It is now an educational charity partnering with schools, colleges, youth groups and employers. It aims to help young people defy their limitations through learning and adventures in the wild, the objective being that young people learn to believe in themselves. Outdoor Education, in brief.

George and his friend Michael Stower were chosen to start the scheme off. They would be going for six weeks to Burghead, near Lossiemouth and Gordonstoun and they would be very busy chaps, who would be tested by the experience. Finally, Carew said with a twinkle in his eye, 'no smoking, no drinking and no women'. They realised how fortunate they were to be selected and it was an amazing experience for them. The six-week courses were comparable really to today's Duke of Edinburgh awards courses. The regime was very strict, the food was excellent, particularly the fish from the cold waters of the Moray Firth. Those on the Outward Bound courses were assessed every hour of the day, but not in a penal way: the assessment was designed to foster improvement.

Twelve of the sixty of them at the centre took the *Prince Louis*, a 300-tonne three-masted schooner, up to the Orkneys. There was climbing in the Cairngorms and the exercise culminated with being taken by bus with the blinds down and dropped off two-by-two with just a pack of sandwiches, and a compass, to be back in Burghead in 2½ days. There was athletics, cross-country, public speaking and seamanship theory and practical: a positive experience, and Ransomes greatly benefited by participating. George gained First Class Honours following his six weeks of endeavour and he came top of the 52 Ransomes people on the course, which gave him an excellent platform from which to progress further in the future.

All this culminated in a wonderful evensong in St Giles's Cathedral, Edinburgh with a moving address by a chaplain who had sailed with Scott to the Antarctic. Finally, a day in Edinburgh enjoying the annual march past of the Black Watch and other Highland regiments down the full length of Princes Street, kilts, pipes and drums. What an experience! Then it was back to work at Ransomes with the words from Commander Michael Leslie that their reports would be sent to the directors and thence to their parents.

Headhunted at 21

Sir John Greaves CBE came to Ransomes, Sims and Jefferies as chairman in 1949, following many years as head of his long established family firm, which traded in cotton. He was a well-travelled, influential man among whose previous appointments had been Controller of Textiles for India and High Sheriff of Bombay. At Ransomes a key part of his role was growing the export business. He knew exactly what he was looking for and needed to find the right people from within the business to achieve it.

George had been away – on manufacturing duties and on Outward Bound – and hadn't seen the advertisement internally of a sales role covering Australia, New Zealand and Singapore. Such roles were not uncommon in the 1950s – the UK was still a strong manufacturing economy with a strong, although diminishing, empire. Many people wanted to work abroad and emigrated. George's original aim was to work abroad as a field engineer in Rhodesia and the Cape, or Kenya and Uganda.

So Greaves called George into his office, surprised that George hadn't seen the Australia job, and made his surprise fairly clear. There had been 70 applicants for the job and Sir John felt that George was ideally suited to it. It was subject to a three-year contract; was George interested and would he take it if offered? Greaves wanted an answer by the following Monday morning! Ransomes were providing him, at 21, with the opportunity to set up what was effectively a new business, the chance of a lifetime, setting up a manufacturing plant in Melbourne and eventually a sales network for Australia, New Zealand, Singapore and the Solomon Islands.

Clearly at 21 this was a great opportunity for George, who wanted to progress his career. The family situation at Grundisburgh

George and Diana's wedding day: 12th May 1956 at St Nicholas, Bedfield

was such was that he was very keen to leave home and make a fresh start, and he and Diana were just about to get engaged. They had met in Stradbroke belfry at the age of sixteen, with their first peal together there at eighteen, on 31st January 1954. Her family, who were farmers at Bedfield, was very supportive. George's father Jim and stepmother Sylvia were at best lukewarm.

Getting married and brilliant in-laws

The move to Australia happened very quickly following George accepting the job in Melbourne. Subject to firming up on some detail the decision was made – George (initially – June 1956) and Diana (ten months later, as it turned out) would be leaving for Australia for three years, later extended to five and then seven years. He would be getting engaged and married to Diana before he left – things were done in

St Nicholas, Bedfield, Suffolk, where George and Diana were married

the correct order in 1956! Their own great adventure! He had the weekend to ask his (hopefully) wife to be, Diana, if she would marry him. Both were aged 20. He would then need to ask her parents for permission to get engaged, married and be ready to sail to Australia by the following June.

All went well and George secured Diana's hand in marriage, with a few tears from his mother-in-law to be and a handshake and pat on the back from father-in-law to be. In George's view, Fred and Marjorie Matthew were the best in-laws one could ever have wished for. He was treated like a son from when he started going out with Diana at the age of sixteen. Diana's sister Jayne, six years older, married Michael Ashwell, from an Earl Soham milling family, so these excellent families gave George and Diana terrific support and encouragement, especially over the Australian enterprise. They got engaged on Valentine's Day 1956 with their memorable wedding on 12th May 1956 at St Nicholas Church, Bedfield, up in beautiful 'High Suffolk' with its fields of wheat, barley and sugar beet. A marquee in the garden of White House Farm, Bedfield and a honeymoon in Devon and Somerset was a wonderful precursor to George sailing from Tilbury on 24th June. Now it was really outward bound!

George commented that he was so fortunate marrying Diana. Despite the musical joke about the in-laws (or outlaws), it gave him Fred and Marjorie Matthew, the finest mother and father-in-law one could ever wish for. The Matthews were from Suffolk farming stock, from Little Stonham Hall and Pettaugh Hall where Marjorie's grandparents had farmed, a beautiful part of rural Suffolk, close to Framsden and Helmingham. George stressed 'my lot in terms of marriage and family has been a very happy one and this has led on to the wider family Diana and I have today, with children, grandchildren and great grandchildren and the happiness that runs through the generations. This is something very precious to us. God is good!'

Our parents

Sarah, George and Diana's oldest daughter, talked in 2019 about her parents:

"When I think of Mum and Dad, key words come to mind … loving, generous, caring, constant, creative, supportive, enterprising, encouraging and so much more …

"Early life was colourful for my brother Steve and I, with no TV until our teens. Exposure to all of the arts, travelling all over Suffolk and surrounding counties, being encouraged to read, make and create. Making our own entertainment fed our imaginations and shaped a love for 'all things creative', especially cooking, music, making and mending and 'all things nature'.

"Mum and Dad were always so sociable with family and loved ones, Dad often took me to visit elderly friends, sharing news and laughter – from which in turn grew a love of time spent with people of all ages!

"David as a son-in-law will always pay tribute to Mum and Dad for the generous way in which he was welcomed into our family at age sixteen. Recipient of Mum's loving hospitality and Dad's thoughtful, supportive wisdom and encouragement – constant over the years. This to us all, as children, grandchildren and great grandchildren alike.

"The arrival of our sister Alison for me aged 9 and Steve aged 5 was to change life dramatically for us all. Presenting challenges which were to increase over the

years, the diagnosis of Severe Autism – a little known condition, took monumental commitment and energy from both our parents as they struggled to understand and deal with the huge behavioural issues that Alison presented. Courageously navigating these new experiences. Something they continue to do with loving care.

"To conclude, Dad is a source of wisdom on authors, poets, people, places, scrabble word checking and always a humorous anecdote or three! His memory remains masterful despite declining health – he's sharp as a tack.

"I, we, are thankful, grateful and indeed very blessed to have such wonderful parents whose legacy is evident in our lives and those of their grandchildren – a love of people, a joy in work, a passion for life and a hope for things as yet unseen.

"In the words of Alan Bennett, 'Pass it on boys.'

"Thank you Dad – you have!! X"

Refer to the family tree (*central section*) for a visual representation! For 56 years, No 8 Lansdowne Road, Ipswich has been the family home to all of them, since George and Diana's return from Australia in 1963.

Chapter 5

An Australian adventure

Getting there: arrival in Melbourne

There were no Boeing 747 400s in those days. Most travellers, George included, went by sea with six weeks on the water. He sailed from Tilbury on the SS *Orontes*, a 20,000-ton liner on the P&O Line, used as a troop ship during the Second World War. Ports of call were Marseilles, Naples (3 days), Navarino Bay, Port Said, Aden (his ship was the last through Suez before Colonel Nasser bombed and closed it!) Colombo (three days in Ceylon, as it was called then), the Cocos Islands and eventually Australia – Fremantle, Adelaide and finally Melbourne.

George's cabin-mate for the voyage was Richard Searby, a fellow of Corpus Christi, Cambridge, who later became a distinguished High Court judge. George recalled arriving on Melbourne Quay on a wet Saturday afternoon in June 1956 with a very large suitcase, feeling cold and very homesick. But the Melbourne ringers had noticed from *The Ringing World* that a talented young English ringer was on his way to live and work in Australia and provided a welcome party. This was the start of a wonderful relationship between George and Diana and the Melbourne ringers where so much was achieved over seven years.

Even though plenty of people were emigrating at the time, it is impossible to underestimate what a massive step going to Australia actually was in the 1950s, six weeks on a boat and then landing 12,000 miles from home. For example, think of calling home, which these days is about picking up the phone and making a normal call. In the mid-1950s calling home from abroad was a tortuous process. You had to dial the operator, perhaps wait several minutes to get connected to a land-line with static, echoes and a dull voice you couldn't hear very clearly. Long distance calls were very expensive so it was sensible to speak fast for maximum value, that is if there wasn't queue at the phone box or it wasn't already full of cash! Phone contact was so difficult then that George recalled that they never rang home in the seven years they were in Australia. Like so many at that time, George communicated by letter instead.

I said earlier that Ransomes was a very patriarchal business. The convention in the UK in the 1950s was that one was not allowed to take one's wife to the 'colonies'. Ransomes' message to George was 'We'll give you six months, Pipe, to settle in and then we'll send your wife.' The travel needs of departing executives' wives soon to follow their husbands was not prioritised very highly by Ransomes and in those days organising travel was not the work of a well-organised HR department. For example, the family needed to be closely involved in not just collecting, but actually securing her ticket on the boat.

A little local difficulty

Back in the 1950s it was not customary for staff in businesses such as Ransomes to move to work abroad and then return later. It tended to be a one-way ticket – they tended to join and stay part of the expat community. The executives' waving farewell from the UK quayside was often accompanied by the likelihood they would not see them again. But this was not a view shared by George!

In addition, Ransomes had not told George about a late change of plan. The plan as far as George had been told was that Ransomes, world leaders in manufacturing grass cutting machinery, were building a new plant in Melbourne, Australia and he would be heading a sales network. However, when he arrived, he found that whilst there was a 'site', work had not started on the new plant, so a temporary and unexpected change of career ensued. This was project managing the building of the new factory, which had to be built in order for him to have grass cutting machinery to sell – all this at 21!

It was ten months before Diana joined George – because of the Suez crisis her voyage was via the West Indies, Panama, the Pacific Islands and New Zealand. Once Diana arrived, they settled in quickly. In Melbourne, they started off in one room, with their luggage for furniture, at Glen Waverley out towards the Dandenong Mountains. Following the birth of Sarah, their first child, in 1958, they lived in a flat at Bentleigh, about ten miles from Melbourne City Centre. Finally, assisted by Ransomes, Sims and Jefferies, who funded the deposit, they bought their own house at Springvale, about twenty miles from Melbourne city out towards the bush, but on the same side of the city.

George used the ten months before Diana arrived in a very profitable way from a ringing perspective, developing relationships, particularly with outlying towers. In some cases, these were towers which historically had enjoyed little or no contact from bellringers anywhere. In hindsight, this turned out to be a very useful exercise, with relationships created which would prove to be valuable in five years' time when ANZAB was founded. On the boat to Australia he set four ambitious ringing objectives:

Help bring about a general improvement in standards.

Help bring about the restoration of unringables.

To see the formation of an Australia and New Zealand Association of ringers.

To bring Great Adventure 2 to fruition within ten years.

A pivotal ringing relationship

A pivotal relationship during their seven years in Melbourne was that with the Ropers, a well-established Melbourne ringing family, Jack (John J F) and Gwen Roper. Jack had been the leading ringer in the city for many years, having learnt to ring in 1930, and he had met the Great Adventure 1 party (see later chapter on 'Great Adventures') when they came to Melbourne in 1934. A signwriter by trade, a committed churchman and a keen Freemason, Jack had rung with the first ringers at St Paul's Cathedral going back to 1889 when the ring of twelve was installed, people like John Guest and James Murray, and so had a link right through to the 1890s.

An earthy and popular Melburnian, Jack gave the city, and indeed Australian ringing, great service over sixty years, often struggling with limited resources and poor quality bell installations. He rang about forty peals in total, many of these during George's time. Remarkably, for someone who was very competent, his first peal was rung after twenty years of ringing, in June 1952: Grandsire Triples at Melbourne Cathedral. This included five first pealers and was conducted by Philip Gray. It was the first by a local band since 1925 and the first peal on the bells since the Great Adventure peal in 1934. This peal was a real triumph, but also serves as a rather stark snapshot showing the limited opportunities that existed in Melbourne, a major centre of ringing in Australia, at that time.

Jack Roper was highly respected and his contribution to Australian ringing was huge. He spent a total of eight years as Master of the St Paul's Cathedral Society of Bell-Ringers, across three spells from 1955 to 1968. Jack was a founder member of the Australia and New Zealand Association of Bellringers,

John J F (Jack) Roper – Sketch by George, 1992. Jack was George's mentor and invaluable supporter in Melbourne, 1956–1963

ANZAB, formed in 1962, served as the first President of ANZAB in 1962 and 1963 and was president again in 1968, 1969 and 1970. In 1993, he was awarded an Order of Australia Medal for his services to bellringing.

Grays replaced by Pipes

The arrival from England of Philip and Joan Gray in 1951 to live in Melbourne had helped Jack to strengthen the band, broadening its method ringing capacity to Plain Bob and Stedman and introducing handbell ringing, so it was quite a blow when they left in 1955. Very soon afterwards, however, in 1956, George and Diana Pipe arrived in Melbourne. Jack was in his 40s, no doubt hoping the new arrivals would do Australian ringing and the Melbourne Cathedral band proud.

Grandsire Cinques at St Paul's Cathedral, Melbourne. George and Jack Roper on 11 and 12 in January 1987

He would not be disappointed on either count. In Suffolk, George and Diana had been steeped in the importance of local ringing, the need to support others and of supporting one's local association. Territorial associations in the UK are sometimes decried now, but were an important component of ringing at that time since following the war there was limited opportunity and this was mainly confined to a small number of major centres of ringing. It was only a matter of time before the same rationale would be applied to the benefit of ringing in Australia, with the formation of the national association.

There were many, many happy memories, for example the arrival at Monash University of Peter Richards, a sheep physiologist from New Zealand, originally from Tunstall in Kent. George and Diana, Jack Roper, Ken Minchinton, Cecil Pearson (Deddington, Oxon), Gerald Weston (Derbyshire), Ernest Hughes (Runcorn), Howard Impey (Leigh on Sea), Harold McDonald (Belfast) and Peter Richards all went together to St Paul's Cathedral, meaning the band was stronger than it ever had been, and the foundations were laid for Melbourne ringing to make significant progress over the time George and Diana were members of the band. The newcomers strengthened the band significantly.

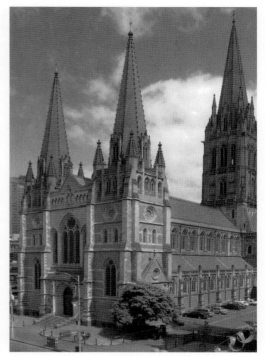

St Paul's Cathedral, Melbourne

Tower captain of St Paul's Cathedral, Melbourne

From the start, Jack and George were able to work together to improve the standard of ringing and develop the band, and they and their wives, Gwen and Diana, developed a great friendship. Jack, then tower captain at the Cathedral, quickly realised that George had the ability, energy and leadership qualities to build the band and take it forward in a way that he wouldn't have been able to and gave George a free hand to build what became the strongest ringing centre outside the UK. Jack very soon realised that given George's knowledge of ringing and conducting, he should take over as conductor, which role he undertook for seven years, and George became captain of St Paul's Cathedral Bell Tower, Melbourne, from 1959 to 1961 and from 1962 until their return to the UK on 12th April 1963.

The subtle approach

Jack Roper was George's biggest supporter throughout his time in Australia. When he arrived in 1956, Jack made sure he became properly 'integrated'. At 21, George was still pretty raw and often impatient with the standard of ringing. Not all the local ringers appreciated the new young 'Pommie' leadership style, making things happen in a way that even they, as Australians, weren't used to, with phrasing they weren't used to! References to 'cloth ears' and comments such as 'Keep it going, I think I heard a good change then' were not guaranteed to produce a 100% positive response from those used to a softer style. Helen Pettet (Henderson) recalls that he had mellowed a good deal when she and Anne Doggett (Cowling) started ringing in 1961 and that Philip and Joan Gray had built a foundation for new methods, something besides the interminable Grandsire Triples from set bells. With the addition of immigrant ringers from England, as the majority were, the band flourished, with Stedman or Grandsire Caters often rung for service.

George's first Sunday at St Paul's Cathedral, Melbourne, which he adopted as his tower, saw three touches of Grandsire Triples being rung, the tower's staple diet, followed by lunch at Ken Minchinton's house. When on his third Sunday the method was Grandsire Triples as usual, George asked Jack whether maybe they could ring Bob Major or Bob Royal. At this point one of the band stated that 'Melbourne has been a Grandsire tower since the bells were put in and it should stay that way'. Jack called for Bob Major. The Grandsire lover never came back. Jack's response was 'George, I've been trying for years to get rid of that drongo, you've done it in three minutes!'

Generating opportunity

George had rung 248 peals when he arrived in Australia in 1956, a considerable total for a 21-year-old, and by UK standards he was a well-known and very high quality ringer already; quite a number of his peals had been on ten and twelve, some with the best ringers in the country. In his seven years in Australia, things were on a different scale and he rang just 22, of which he conducted 18, these conducted more out of necessity than desire. There was less opportunity, vast distances to travel and far fewer ringers. In short, there was a lot of development to be done and he was central in that development during his time in Australia.

Thirteen of the 22 peals were rung in Melbourne and some of these were highly notable – such as one at St Paul's of Plain Bob Major in November 1956 for the Olympic Games, followed a month later by a peal of Plain Bob Triples for the Duke of Edinburgh's visit, providing early evidence of George's appreciation of public relations and then making things happen! There were three more peals in honour of Royal events during their time in Melbourne.

The Melbourne band increased in numbers and in time the method repertoire expanded to Treble Bob, Double Norwich, Cambridge Major, Kent Royal and the occasional Stedman Caters and Grandsire Cinques. This was significant progress and the ringing at St Paul's was now the most advanced outside the United Kingdom. The band rang the first peals of Double Norwich, Cambridge Minor and Major outside of the UK.

Interstate excursions

George organised and took part in visits to and reciprocal visits from other ringing towers, particularly to Victorian country towers (Ballarat, Bendigo and Geelong) and to and from Adelaide. Much could be achieved in visits to or from Adelaide on a three-day weekend by driving 460 miles each way or, on a two-day weekend, by travelling on the overnight train outward on Friday evening after work and back, hopefully in time to get to work, on Monday morning!

Then there was the wonderful Yass 'incident', gleefully recounted to me by John Fryer, comprising an 860-mile round trip to a NSW sheep town listed in 'Dove' as 'Tass' (misspelt), a 26½ cwt ring of five, to be augmented to six. Well, heavy sixes were irresistible to George, who was determined to take a band there and ring a peal on them. They arrived to find a 6½ cwt six! Peal scored but downgraded.

These interstate trips helped fuel progress, but the distances were vast. One such trip to Melbourne resulted in the first quarter peal of Maximus outside Great Britain being successfully rung. The visits to the other Victorian towers all helped either to establish bands in those centres or to raise existing standards. The visits to and from Adelaide assisted greatly in the raising of ringing standards at St Peter's Cathedral. The closest centre of change ringing was 600 miles away remember – heady stuff!

Visit to Tasmania

George recalled flying in a Dakota to Hobart, Tasmania in 1958 when their elder daughter Sarah was a babe in arms. In those days there were only six ringers on the island so he and Diana would make eight if they all came in from the bush. They did. In charge of the fine Taylor eight at St David's Cathedral and the early Whitechapel eight at Holy Trinity was Sidney Smith. Sid emigrated from Ingham, Suffolk, in 1912 and told George and Diana they were the first Suffolk people he'd met in 'Tassie' in 46 years.

Progress at St Patrick's Cathedral, Melbourne

Along with others in Melbourne, George was instrumental in re-establishing and continuing to encourage a new band of ringers at St Patrick's Roman Catholic Cathedral. That opportunity came after an approach by George and Peter Richards to the Cathedral authorities with an offer by the St Paul's ringers to ring a fully-muffled peal at the memorial service on 10th October 1958 for the death of Pope Pius XII. These bells were a Murphy of Dublin eight and tough to ring, but nevertheless a peal of Grandsire Triples was successfully rung, the first peal on the bells. He organised and managed this, including securing press coverage, at 23 years old.

The press coverage stated that 'the goodwill of the Anglican bellringers was greatly appreciated by the Catholic community'. One of the ringers taking part believed that George's ecumenical gesture was a major factor in the establishment of good relations between the authorities of the two churches. The tradition was continued when Pope John XXIII died in 1963 and a truly ecumenical team rang a quarter peal at St Patrick's, including ringers from St Patrick's, St Paul's and All Saints, Parramatta.

After the 1958 peal at St Patrick's RC Cathedral, Melbourne, a decision was made to revive the St Patrick's band. Ken Minchinton, George Pipe and Peter Richards approached the authorities with an offer of help and it was agreed that if a band could be maintained for six months, the cathedral would then supply a set of ropes. An advertisement was placed in the weekly *Melbourne Advocate* newspaper for ringers and among those coming forward were John Davis and Ivan Page. They were trained by St Paul's ringers, who also rang at St Patrick's on the first Sunday of each month, thus creating a tangible link. St Patrick's practices started in February 1959. Things went very well and the St Patrick's offer to fund ropes was unnecessary as a Melbourne rope maker donated a new set.

It is not difficult to imagine some of the pitfalls that might have existed sixty years ago when trying to set up this type of arrangement. It is also important to note that in the late 1950s the nature of news was very different in comparison to today and it is perhaps difficult to imagine how this could be big news, which it was. Radio and newspapers were still for most people the principal news medium, not everyone had telephones, and TV was in its infancy. The St Paul's ringers made two appearances on television and received good coverage in the press. (The establishment of a band at St Patrick's was highly noteworthy and demonstrates George's generosity of spirit. Claire O'Mahony refers to it a little later in her contribution.) At around this time, August 1960, at 25, George was nominated as a 'Servant of the Exercise' No 32, one of a series of articles in *The Ringing World* written by 'Jafus' (J Frank Smallwood). Jim received a similar accolade but had to wait a bit!

Handbells and media stardom

ABC television in Victoria had come in for the Olympic Games and for their very first 'chat show' whose hostess was Corrine Kirby. In January 1957, having heard the Cathedral bells being rung for the Games and for Christmas, her producer invited some handbell ringers from the city to join the show. To play safe they rang call changes on ten and the ringers were Brenda Sheppard 1-2, Ken Minchinton 3-4, Arthur Fisher 5-6, George Pipe 7-8 and Jack Roper 9-10. Graeme Heyes also appeared and rang 5-6 for the finale. This was the first televised handbell ringing ever in Australia and, probably because it was a quintessentially English art, it was very popular with the viewers.

1958 saw George in a further television appearance, on a programme aimed at linking together people with interesting jobs and interesting hobbies. Four people appeared with the well-known Australian actor Frank Thring, a well-known Olympic competitor, a velodrome cyclist and George, who took with him a model bell for demonstration purposes. Again, the programme closed with some handbell ringing, a plain course of Grandsire Triples by Barbara Beeson 1-2, Graeme Heyes 3-4, George Pipe 5-6 and Jack Roper 7-8. I'm sure to many, ringers and non-ringers, some of these very early TV appearances were seen as a novelty. Nevertheless they needed to be coordinated and made to happen once the invitation came in from the TV station, with levels of professionalism appropriate to the time. George saw the importance of this to ringing in Melbourne.

First peal of Double Norwich in Australia

There was just a little more business to conclude before George and Diana left for their holiday in the UK, namely the first peal of Double Norwich to be rung in Australia. *The Ringing World*'s Belfry Gossip column of March 31, 1961 noted:

'At the fifth attempt a peal of Double Norwich Court Bob Major has been scored in Australia, conducted by George W Pipe on the front eight of St Paul's Cathedral Melbourne. In the band were six firsts and a first 'inside' and these people are to be congratulated on the splendid performances. Special mention must be made of the efforts of the three Sydneysiders, John Fryer, Bill Watson and Ralph Clark (his first above Bob Doubles).'

Typifying the buccaneering spirit of the time, no doubt, but any conductor, band or individual who has wrestled with some of the unique difficulties and pitfalls of Double Norwich will know that much effort went into this achievement and it was a well-deserved success.

1961 – A well-earned holiday back in the UK

George and Diana's first child, Sarah, was born in Brighton, on Port Philip Bay, on May 26, 1958. This brought them huge joy. She was baptised at St Paul's and was soon attending ringing, bassinet and all! They led a very busy life whilst living in Australia, so much so that they didn't really take any leave for over four years. So in early 1961, having spoken to Ransomes, his employer, it was agreed that George and Diana would take a three month period of leave to go back to the UK, leaving Australia in April. This would also be an opportunity to introduce Sarah to her wider family back in the UK, quite a few of whom couldn't wait to see her!

The Ringing World carried the news, stating that they were looking forward to meeting many ringing friends at the Central Council meeting at Stoke-on-Trent on Whit Tuesday 1961. In the event, George was asked to give a resume on ringing in Australia at the Council meeting which was very well received and he was elected an honorary member of the Central Council, the start of a very active association with the Central Council of some eighteen years.

In fact, George later served as the convener of the Overseas Committee of the Central Council. In that respect the communication he had established very early on with the isolated towers in Australia, via a letter writing exercise he embarked on soon after he arrived in Australia in 1956, was invaluable and helped him develop this role. Unless one has been to Australia, it is difficult to imagine the vast distances involved and the isolation of many of the towers. Not only were many of the towers isolated, but there was no guarantee that the closest towers, often several hundred miles away, would be able to provide the necessary infrastructure for them to progress, and it would not be until the '80s and '90s that electronic communication started to make things easier. For now, in the '50s and '60s, any communication would have been unusual.

Eleven peals were rung during that three month period in the UK, including Yorkshire Maximus at St Giles Cripplegate, Cambridge Maximus at Macclesfield including a number of ringers from the very well-known 'Cheshire band' and also at Audley and Broughton, the latter Pat Cannon's 500th different tenor turned-in to a peal.

Back to East Anglia, appropriately a peal at St Peter Mancroft, Norwich was rung for the marriage of HRH the Duke and Duchess of Kent and was Diana's first twelve-bell peal. A peal in a new method named after the Australian town of Springvale, Victoria, home of George and Diana, was rung with the Willesden band. Back to Grundisburgh and a peal of London Major involving five members of the Pipe family, Diana, Sylvia, Rod, George and Jim. This was Sylvia Pipe's first peal since 1949 when she injured her arm. The other three members of the band were Ernest Pearce, Roger Whittell and Jim Morley. Finally, a peal of Grandsire Caters at Grundisburgh was rung in memory of George A Fleming, a member of the local band actively involved in George Pipe's early ringing career, but also one of the St Mary-le-Tower band who took part in many first peals in the method on twelve.

Back to business, with more firsts in Melbourne

1962 was a relatively quiet time from a ringing perspective – George rang two peals during the year, both on handbells and both with the expected array of firsts, Kent Major in May and the inaugural ANZAB peal. (More of this later.) Later in the year, on 24th August 1962, Stephen Wilgress Pipe, George and Diana's son and a brother to Sarah, was born at Glen Iris, an outer Melbourne suburb

By contrast, in early 1963 things got busier! Partly this was due to George and Diana's impending departure from Australia for the UK, on Good Friday, 12th April 1963, but there were also projects to be completed! On 7th February 1963, Jack Roper's wife, Gwen, rang her first peal at St Paul's Cathedral, Melbourne, believed to be the 100th peal rung in Australia. On 25th February 1963, as part of 'a week in Melbourne', George conducted the first peal of Surprise Major (Cambridge, rung at third attempt) to be rung outside the United Kingdom, on the light eight at St Paul's Cathedral, followed on 2nd March 1963 by the first peal of Royal on tower bells by a resident Australian band, Plain Bob Royal in 3 hours 29 minutes, conducted by Tom Goodyer from Sydney.

It is significant that his farewell peal at St Paul's Cathedral on 4th April 1963, Plain Bob Major, was conducted by George's closest ringing friend in Melbourne, Jack Roper. Jack had been ringing at St Paul's since the 1930s. It was his first peal as conductor and Jennifer Murphy, Anne Cowling and Helen Pettet (née Henderson) all rang their first peal. Evidence of George's leadership and enthusiasm to encourage those with whom he rang to progress and take the next step higher.

Just before they left in April 1963 he had, with the support of the band, asked the St Paul's Cathedral authorities if they would consider sending the bells to England for refurbishment. The bells were a complete 1889 Mears and Stainbank twelve. They agreed and in July 1963 the bells were lowered ready for the journey to Taylor's at Loughborough. They were returned in good time for the Great Adventure 2 Tour of 1965. One of the reasons for the Great Adventure 2 Tour being delayed for a year was concern that Melbourne Cathedral bells would not be back from Taylor's.

Adelaide Cathedral – First peal of Major on the bells

During his visits to Adelaide in the 1950s and early 1960s, George had come to know and admire the 41 ¼ cwt Taylor eight of St Peter's Cathedral. In his view, these were amongst the great rings in the world and a peal attempt here would be a great privilege. They had been installed in 1947, but the first peal on the bells had yet to take place. While he was in Australia this became an irresistible challenge.

He eventually obtained permission for an attempt, on 15th October 1961, at the first peal on the bells. He and Diana, together with Ken Minchinton and Jack Roper came over from Melbourne to join four Adelaide ringers for the attempt – Grandsire Triples conducted by George. Sadly, after about one and a half hours the attempt was lost.

Time was starting to run out for George, and in the meantime ringing was forging ahead in Adelaide, aided significantly by other inter-city visits between Adelaide and Melbourne. The first peal on the bells, Grandsire Triples, was rung by the Sunday service band on 20th February 1963 for the visit of Her Majesty the Queen to Adelaide – 5,040 Grandsire Triples in 3 hours 32 minutes. There were plenty of footnotes, such as Enid

Roberts as the first lady to conduct a peal in Australia, and David Bleby's first peal was on the 41cwt tenor! David notes that George's enthusiasm, his previous visits and his influence on the Adelaide ringing contributed to the first peal being rung as early as it was and to the development of the ringers in the successful peal.

Time was now very much of the essence – 20th February 1963 was less than two months before George and Diana and family were to return to the UK. But, never to be deterred, George's patience was rewarded when permission was given to attempt a second peal on the bells on 24th March 1963, which he conducted from the tenor. Diana and Jack Roper were also in the band, with five locals. The attempt, the first of Major on the bells, succeeded: 5,040 Plain Bob Major in 3 hours 36 minutes, and in 98 degrees with stifling humidity. This was a wonderful achievement since at that temperature the risk of indisposition to one of the ringers becomes a possibility. Less than three weeks later, George and his family left Melbourne to return to the UK on 12th April 1963. Adelaide Mission accomplished!

George also published some articles in *Ringing Towers*, the ANZAB journal, to assist others, for example "Conducting – The first Stages" and "Conducting – The Calling Positions". He was also an accomplished artist and many of his excellent drawings of Australian and New Zealand bell towers grace the covers of early editions of *Ringing Towers*.

Were the objectives George set on the boat back in 1956 achieved? It is difficult to measure success since much is subjective in this context. However, it is fair to say standards did go up, unringables were restored and ANZAB was founded. Great Adventure 2 was successful within the ten years specified, in 1965, and George's father Jim came on the tour.

Chapter 6

Foundation of the Australia and New Zealand Association of Bellringers

The move to a national association?

When he and Diana arrived in Melbourne, George noted that ringing in Australia was scarce, Grandsire Triples and little else. The nearest change ringing tower was Adelaide, six hundred miles west, and they could only manage Doubles. There was no national ringing association, just several old state societies, mainly in Victoria and New South Wales, a result of local rivalries. These were mostly weak and fragmented. As mentioned earlier, George and Diana were loyal Guild members when in Suffolk – guilds and associations were very important as things developed after the war, there was the Guild and not a lot else besides in many areas.

The possibility of forming an Australian national association was therefore attractive to them: a very different proposition in scale to a county association in the UK and bringing fresh challenges. A small group including Bill Pitcher (Adelaide) and George, began to work on the project to create a new association, ANZAB, the Australia and New Zealand Association of Bellringers. One of the most important aspects of George's six years in Australia was his tireless pursuit of the creation of ANZAB.

At a time of change, what usually emerges is a classic mix of youngsters who are pro-change and established ringers who often are anti-change and prefer the status quo. If the case is really strong – for example, if the current situation is racked by injustice – then they will get involved. Then you have those who don't commit, sometimes called fence-sitters, who don't particularly mind what happens either way, but don't really want to get involved and certainly don't want to upset anybody else or be upset themselves. It is the proportions within all those categories that will determine whether change is possible and what it will be.

Association formed: 2/3 June 1962

Tom Goodyer is in his 90s, lives in Sydney and is still an active ringer. He takes up the story:

"The NSW Association, which was formed just after the War largely through the efforts of Bill Rowe, became big enough (50 members) to qualify for a CC representative. Ringers in other States were envious of this position, but did not have functioning associations or enough members. So those ringers wanted an Australia-wide association. But there was resistance from some of the old guard in NSW (Bill Rowe and Ralph Joyner). Perhaps they feared losing control, perhaps they thought other States should not easily get the benefits of their years of hard work. At any rate the matter made no progress."

Then George arrived in Melbourne and realised that with work it could be done. Bobby Ferris from Parramatta and Tom made a ringing trip to Melbourne where the matter was discussed. Back in Sydney, support was gathered, eventually enough to get a majority at a NSW Association meeting at which the name was changed to ANZAB. The old NSW Association became the NSW branch of ANZAB. South Australia and Western Australia applied for admission as branches and were accepted, and there was optimism at the time that Tasmania, Queensland and New Zealand would also form branches – this would represent a sea change from the situation before, where old New South Wales Association was the only ringing society in Australia. Tom believes none of those around at the time foresaw the growth of ringing in Australia that would follow, with ringers focusing on working as ANZAB, a national association.

George came to Sydney for the meeting in June 1962 at which ANZAB was born and on Sunday 3rd June of that weekend they rang the first peal for ANZAB, Plain Bob Royal on handbells at Tom's home. Phil was six years old, Andy was five and Judy four. Margaret did not ring in the peal, but she was given the job of keeping the kids clear – no easy task. Willy Watson, John Fryer and Enid Roberts joined George and Tom for the peal, which finished in gathering dark because they had not turned the light on before starting and Margaret would not risk distracting them by coming into the room to switch it on!

Laith Reynolds's view is that the Sydney ringing 'establishment' fought hard against ANZAB as they had a solid New South Wales group and were very suspicious of any moves from Melbourne to 'takeover' via an Australia-wide association. He remembers the younger Sydney ringers, some of whom had travelled to Melbourne on interstate weekends referred to earlier, to be taught by George and Diana, were all for it and eventually it went through and ANZAB was formed. Laith is one of the few who were at both the first and 50th meetings of ANZAB, both in Sydney, but

Dinner at Lansdowne Road, summer 2004. Clockwise from bottom left: Philip Goodyer, George Pipe, Tom Goodyer and Diana Pipe

he was unaware of the politics at that first meeting. However, there was undoubtedly some fallout as a number of the St Mary's Sydney ringers who were anti-ANZAB then left and went to St Benedict's Broadway.

Bill Rowe – opponent becomes supporter

Bill Rowe, from Sydney, had very strongly and vehemently opposed the idea of forming a new association and gave George a very tough time right through to the Association being formed. Of course, George wasn't helped by being a young, smart, dynamic ringer, from Melbourne, and a pommie to boot! However, many years later George recalled,

> *"One of the incidents I shall never forget was after a ring at St Benedict's in 1994 with Bill Rowe and 'the old boys', having a beer (or two) with them at Redfern RSL. Bear in mind that these were some of the ringers who had been very anti-ANZAB, but Bill shook me by the hand and said "You were right, you know, we just didn't have the vision". That was a courageous thing to say, but to me embodied the ANZAB spirit of moving on."*

Laith Reynolds – a sixty-year friendship

One of George's longest ringing friendships was with Laith Reynolds, from Perth. Laith is about five years younger than George and they first met when Laith was about sixteen or seventeen, and a highly inquisitive young ringer. It's worth remembering that Perth was the ultimate in ringing backwaters in the mid-1950s with just one tower, Saint George's Cathedral. A lot has happened since then, and Laith has been involved in much of this development.

Laith Reynolds, the driver behind the development in Perth of The Bell Tower and Swan Bells

When George arrived in Melbourne in 1956, a key objective was to visit the sales agents for Ransomes, Sims and Jefferies in Australia. There was an agent in each state, including Tasmania. One of the agents he needed to see was a company called Mortlock Brothers in Perth, and as it happened, they were just round the corner from St George's Cathedral. Laith Reynolds was one of the people George met at St George's Cathedral – this had been Laith's family church for generations and he was an apprentice in the two-way radio trade to a company in a street behind the Cathedral. He had transferred from his local parish church to the Cathedral, joined the Anglican Youth Fellowship and became an altar server at the Cathedral under George Appleton, the Archbishop of Perth. He was then invited to join the bell ringers, and quite quickly became the captain of the band.

There was no knowledge at St George's of English-style change ringing where the bells were rung full circle. Although it was obvious that the bells were intended to swing, the wheels had been tied to the frame to stop that from happening! Instead, they were chimed because the art of full swing ringing/change ringing had been lost in Perth, due to the Great Depression and the need for the church to use the money elsewhere.

Attending an Anglican Youth Conference some 4,000 km away, he saw change ringing in parish churches in rural Victoria, which inspired him to go back and see how he could revive the bells in St George's. They cleaned up the bells and with the support of the Dean, bought books specially ordered in from the church bookshop. They paid for new ropes and had the bells restored. Laith and the others started to teach themselves how to ring. Laith had been sent to another Youth Conference, a National Youth Conference, by the federal government, and he was taught to handle a bell over the weekend.

Since the start, he has viewed bellringing or change ringing as part of the mission of the Church. His international business interests mean he has lived and worked in many parts of the world and when appropriate has pursued bells projects in New York, Vancouver, Toronto, Sydney, Melbourne. He has lived in Vancouver, Singapore, Jakarta and Hawaii. He conceived and championed the Hawaii project in 1991, and, notably, the Swan Bells project in Perth over many years – this is now a leading a tourist attraction in the city. Very recently, in 2019, the bells at Singapore Cathedral were restored and augmented to form a fine ring of twelve bells, rung full-circle – his first contact with the cathedral was in 1973, so that one was a serious slow burner over 45 years!

The rescue of John Taylor and Co in 2009

Laith was one of the three people who rescued John Taylor and Co of Loughborough, a business established for 400 years, when purchasing the company when it went into administration in 2009. The Taylor family had died out and the firm had quietly collapsed. It took ten to fifteen years, maybe twenty years, for it to happen, but it was a slow wind-down. That leaves Taylors as the sole complete bell foundry in the English-speaking world. All the other foundries in England and America have gone. There were maybe ten foundries a century ago, but by 2017 there were just two foundries left, Taylor's and Whitechapel. Sadly, in 2017 Whitechapel closed so there is just one left now, Taylors, and the business is thriving. Bells and the Church's mission in bells have been a big part of Laith's life, more so than bellringing itself. His mission just happens to have been bells in English churches.

The relationship between the Reynolds and Pipe families is a very strong one, going back over sixty years or more. George went out to Perth in 2001 to ring in some of the inaugural peals on the ring of sixteen at the Bell Tower, which had previously been at St Martin-in-the-Fields in London. George and Laith were very different characters and I guess they got on well because they had complementary skills and interests – as already mentioned, George had many skills and is an excellent ringer, whereas Laith enjoys conceiving and managing bell projects which he has done very successfully in many areas of the world, as evidenced by his 45 years' endeavour with the Singapore Cathedral project. The vast distance between England and Australia was no barrier either as Laith has a home in Burford, Oxfordshire where he lives during the English summer.

Moving forward from the foundation of ANZAB

Once ANZAB had been formed in 1962, the pace of development in ringing sped up rapidly with growth over the years that could never have been foreseen. Alongside that, a great record of achievement in ringing was developed. Peal ringing statistics are still a reliable record reflecting any bellringing organisation's health. For example, at its peak, ANZAB was averaging 70 peals per year over the ten years 1988 to 1997, including over 100 different ringers per year taking part. The annual ANZAB AGM weekends focus on training to improve members' ringing. Just recently, specialist twelve-bell ringing training weekends have commenced, a recent one being in Adelaide and the plan is that this will be followed by further weekends in future, further evidence that ANZAB is in good shape, meeting the needs of its members through innovation. ANZAB has finite resources and bells; ideas such as encouraging members to apply for grants towards travel costs for these weekends are far-sighted and help the Association to punch above its weight.

Bell restoration projects

During George's time in Melbourne, a lot of pioneering and hard work went in to try and get most of the unringables going again. In 1956, there were just 25 towers, of which seven were unringable. Today, in 2018, there are 62 rings in Australia comprising just two unringables and George and Diana went back teaching three times.

Mention has already been made of the re-establishment of ringing at St Patrick's RC Cathedral in Melbourne on some very difficult bells in the 1950s and 1960s. Without that, it is most unlikely that the bells would ever have been rehung, as they were in 1988–1989. With George's encouragement, the bells of St Paul's, Bendigo were to be rehung in 1962 (unfortunately by a local contractor who managed to crack all the bells in the course of removing their canons for rehanging!). They were recast into a fine ring of eight in 1963.

Perhaps George's most significant project was to initiate the retuning and rehanging of the St Paul's Cathedral, Melbourne bells in 1963–4. While it all happened just after he had returned to the UK, it is unlikely that it would have happened at all at that time without George's initiative. There can also be little doubt that the seeds were sown by George's activities and enthusiasm for the rehanging of the bells at St Paul's, Geelong, in the early 1980s, for the augmentation and rehanging of the bells at St Peter's Ballarat in 1965–6 and for the ringing, with difficulty, in 1963 of the previously unringable bells at Adelaide Town Hall. While George may have been instrumental in inspiring these and indeed later installations and renovations, they would also not have happened without the hard work and dedication of the people he inspired.

Chapter 7

Great Adventures aplenty

A little explanation …

Until the 1930s Australia had always been uncharted territory for bellringers, apart from those who had emigrated from the UK. So when on 15th September 1934 a group of ringers from the UK commenced the 12,000 mile trip to Australia and New Zealand on a tour they named Great Adventure 1, this was seen by many as something quite remarkable. The timing of the tour was to mark the centenary of the foundation of the city of Melbourne. At least fifty ringers, including many of the ringing 'aristocracy' of the time saw them off from London's King George V Dock, in what is now Docklands. Youngsters like Jim Pipe and A Patrick Cannon, who would both go on Great Adventure 2 in 1965, were there. The tour returned to Tilbury on January 22 1935, and the party was away for approximately four months. Of course, what differentiated this tour from those before was the sheer distance involved: some five weeks on the water to get there, and having great expectation rather than firm knowledge of what would happen. They took twelve ringers, ten sound ropes and some handbells! Inevitably, the selection of the ringers was to a degree driven by financial ability as few could afford a tour of that nature, or the time. The story of the tour was seen as so significant that in 1935 it was published as a book entitled 'A Great Adventure' by *The Ringing World*, whose editor, J S Goldsmith, had been one of the tourists. It's fair to say that the book, written by W H Fussell, the main organiser of the tour, is very much of its time, but nevertheless it is a fascinating read.

I've used the 'Great Adventure' theme because of the spirit of adventure George and Diana generated during their times in Australia, and it's a useful way of differentiating their several visits. The 1934 tour is usually known as Great Adventure 1, and there was a tour in 1965 named Great Adventure 2, so I have taken the opportunity to name the various visits back to Australia by George and Diana following their residency there from 1956–63 as Great Adventure 3, 4, 5, 6 and 7, all great adventures in different ways!

Great Adventure 2 – 1965

Great Adventure 2 preceded the advent of cheap air travel and the internet and was the final of George's four objectives. It was in many respects a child of the original Great Adventure of 1934. George, once living in Melbourne could see the opportunity for a repeat of the first Great Adventure tour. He had hoped that it would be possible to

ON AUSTRALIAN SOIL FOR THE FIRST TIME.
The English Tourists on the Dockside at Freemantle, Western Australia, with ropes and spanner, ready for all eventualities.

[*Frontispiece*

A GREAT ADVENTURE

THE STORY OF A BELL
RINGING TOUR IN AUSTRALIA

Told by

J. S. GOLDSMITH
(*Editor of "The Ringing World"*)

and of

A VISIT TO NEW ZEALAND

Related by

W. H. FUSSELL.
(*Organising Secretary of the Tour*)

"THE RINGING WORLD," WOKING.
1935.

Great Adventure 1 – the first pages of a book published by The Ringing World in 1935. "On Australian soil for the first time. The English tourists on the dockside at Freemantle, Western Australia, with ropes and spanner, ready for all eventualities."

celebrate the 30th anniversary of the first Great Adventure and worked particularly with Tom Lock in England to bring this about. The collaboration later included Bill Pitcher in Adelaide, working towards a tour in 1964. In 1963, after George's departure, the planned tour was deferred until 1965 because of uncertainty as to whether St Paul's Melbourne bells, the only ring of twelve in the country at that time, would be back from the UK in time for a tour in 1964.

Nevertheless, George's hopes and aspirations were fulfilled in a very successful tour in September and October 1965, known as Great Adventure 2. The eleven ringers included Tom Lock, Pat Cannon, Tom White (Editor of *The Ringing World*), Len Stillwell, Wilfred Williams and, appropriately, George's father, Cecil W (Jim) Pipe.

Great Adventure 3 and bicentennial lecture tour in 1987

By the mid-1980s, the Australian authorities were aware of the rapidly approaching bicentenary in 1988 and the need for appropriate forms of celebration, with the benefits this could bring to the country in a cultural and economic sense. So in 1986, a consortium of the Australian Arts Council, the British Arts Council and other bodies decided to involve Britain and other countries with a strong relationship with Australia in the 1988 year-long celebrations. These would cover music, art, drama, dance, theatre and sport. Funding was made available and interested bodies were invited to make the case and bid for funds.

Planning the 1987 tour

Laith Reynolds, at that time President of ANZAB, saw the opportunity for campanology to be part of this initiative and applied for a grant, supported by ANZAB, for six ringers to visit as many of the centres of ringing as possible to encourage, enthuse, teach and generally do everything possible to give ringing a boost for the Bicentennial and the future.

A number of questions apart from funding arose: who, at what time of year, how would such a group be received by Australian ringers and could it all be done in the space of four weeks? Not all Australian ringers felt this was a good plan and that it could have been delivered by them! However, the problem of vast distances to be travelled internally was applicable to all, and how would the focus have been maintained given the need to cover a large number of centres in a short period of time? In the mid-1980s, finding people able to deliver such a programme and take four weeks off work to do it was a significant limiting factor.

Who to deliver the lecture programme?

Those invited to undertake what was a considerable challenge were George and Diana, (with very strong Australian connections), John (CCCBR President elect) and Beryl Baldwin and Bob and Ruth Smith, all high-quality ringers in their own right, also with the ability to carry out the ambassadorial part of the mission. The groundwork for this was laid during Laith's presidency – he was succeeded by David Bleby of Adelaide in the autumn of 1986, thus the organisational side was in very good hands.

A lot of work went into planning what was very much a teaching tour and the Baldwins, Pipes and Smiths all assembled at Melbourne, Derbyshire on 10th December 1986, for a day's face-to-face planning. They would offer 28 separate training modules available according to individual requirement and three people were prepared to speak on any of those topics, although there was a tendency where possible for speakers to focus on their specialist areas. Obviously George and Diana had lived in Australia for seven years, but to the others it was undiscovered territory and in prospect was truly a great adventure beyond their wildest dreams, with wonderful hospitality, scenery and, of course, lots of ringing, albeit only seven peals.

The tour covered the major centres in the southern part of the country. What emerges quite strongly is that many of the towers that today's visitors to Australia take for granted were in fact either new or in the planning phase in 1987, so the training activity they were undertaking was well-timed and very necessary. They started in Perth, Western Australia where there was no 'Swan' in those days, but it was already known that a campanile was to be built at the University, hopefully to house the retuned and refurbished twelve of St Martin-in-the-Fields, London. There was considerable excitement and anticipation about acquiring this slice of English heritage, and for bellringers, of course, new life for a historic ring. George's account of the lecture tour said 'some of us believe that with careful tuning and a first-class rehang, they could sound a very presentable twelve – we keenly await the completion of this ambitious project'.

New perspectives and sales opportunities

Bob Smith, as Head of Engineering at Loughborough College, could bring much to this particular party and delivered a lecture at the University of Western Australia's School of Music on towers, bells and their installation and maintenance. The audience was wide-ranging, engineers, musicians, architects, clergy and enthusiasts. At this stage there was a massive distance to go, since what was in effect a national bell project to mark the bicentenary would require a huge amount of work to bring to fruition, with a very large number of interest groups involved. All credit to Leith Reynolds in making this major Bicentennial project happen and also the subsequent Swan initiative.

A peal band at Adelaide, 12th January 1987. Left to right: Diana Pipe, Bob Smith, George Pipe, Ruth Smith, Richard Jolly, Brian Cox, Anne Haskard and Ian Harris

There were one or two other selling initiatives during the tour, one being at Wangaratta, where a freestanding tower 140ft high was in the process of being built, basically four steel corner posts with frequent cross bracing, but no buttresses and clad in wooden shingles, with minimal foundations and the tower showing an alarming amount of movement together with significant vibration in the steel girdering. In attendance when the party arrived were the Bishop, the Dean, the architect and others, including Henry and Elizabeth Rossell from Melbourne who were drivers on the Melbourne-Sydney leg.

This occurrence highlighted the importance of liaising with architects and bell advisers, and gaining consensus as to what is the correct way forward, and of course that applies everywhere.

A 'flagship' peal was rung at Adelaide Cathedral, Lincolnshire Surprise Major, Bob Smith on the tenor, but a disappointing aspect of the tour was that the intention to ring the first peal of Surprise Maximus in Australia at Melbourne Cathedral with a band comprising six Australian ringers and six UK ringers was foiled by a broken gudgeon.

Results of Great Adventure 3 in 1987

George summarised: 'If our efforts over four weeks have fired imagination and enthusiasm as Australia approaches its bicentennial then we shall be glad. May their bells long ring out and the art flourish down under – we are sure it will – no worries!'

The 'activity tally' is impressive. 109 talks to about 250 ringers and non-ringers in 24 ringing towers, on TV, or in universities and visited a further eleven towers destined to have bells installed shortly. They travelled 4,000 inland miles, by plane, ferry, train, bus, tram, car or foot and rang at least once, several times a day, every day for a month.

Finally, a party, some party I guess, at Jack and Gwen Roper's house involving most of the people they rang with when living in Melbourne 24 years before, 34 people in total, and back to the UK on 7th February.

Ringing in Australia really took off during the bicentennial year, with lots of parties from the UK visiting, peal ringing growing in volume and complexity and new bands starting to be taught. It is likely the work done on Great Adventure 3 made a significant contribution towards this progress.

Great Adventure 4 – Sydney 'Living city' ringing initiative

In March 1997, George and Diana were off again on an extended tour to Australia. Sydney City Council had agreed to contribute to a bellringing project based at St Mary's Cathedral. This was in connection with Sydney's 'Living City' programme, which acted as a lead in to the Olympics in Sydney scheduled for the year 2000. Sydney City Council was keen to offer financial assistance to cultural and community-based organisations in the city, and as far as bellringing was concerned, this filtered through to a seven-week ringing programme of training, peals and quarter peals and public lectures. George and Diana, well-known in Australia from their time living in Melbourne between 1957 and 1963, were invited to lead the programme and were resident in Sydney from late March until mid-June 1997. The specific targets for the programme were to train four new recruits and develop competent Stedman Caters, Yorkshire Royal and Kent Maximus teams, and the programme was seen as a success.

The focus was on Sydney for this 1997 trip, but they were able to spend two weeks 'up country' in New South Wales running schools at places such as Armidale, Goulburn, Yass, Wagga and Griffith. Having been founding members of ANZAB in 1962, they attended their first ANZAB annual festival, in country Victoria. There was the opportunity to ring some peals as well, particularly at some of the new towers which weren't around when they left in 1963, for example the new twelve in Adelaide and the twelves at St Mary's Cathedral and St Andrew's Cathedral in Sydney and another peal at Ballarat City Hall as well.

Claire O'Mahony, now in Somerset, was living in Sydney in 1997. She wrote in 2019:

"I first met George at St Jude's, Randwick and I remember being aghast at how tall he was. We had met there to combine cars to drive on for a day at Randwick Races with my parents who were visiting from England. It was 1997, George and Diana had come to Sydney initially, then on to the lecturing tour which was to include most, if not all, regional NSW towers culminating in the ANZAB Festival based in Albury, Wangaratta and Beechworth almost two months later. The highlight of the ANZAB evening was George's after dinner speech, full of hilarious anecdotes that only George can deliver. Quite befitting as George and Diana were founder members of ANZAB, and I know George keeps his ANZAB badge proudly mounted in his library at Lansdowne Road, Ipswich!

"But George and Diana were no strangers to living 'down under'. Arriving in 1956, 7 years in Melbourne, their lifelong friendship with Jack and Gwen Roper (their Australian "parents") and very happy days were spent building a band. In October 1958, the St Paul's ringers rang for the memorial service for Pope Pius XII at St Patrick's Cathedral – "an example of ecumenical cooperation" was reported in the press.

"Ringing with George and Diana makes one feel as if one is in a masterclass, whether it's rounds and call changes or Turramurra Surprise Maximus. The effort put in is just the same!

"Very, very dear friends …"

A highlight of the 1997 visit was the peal of Yorkshire Maximus at St Paul's Cathedral, Melbourne on 22nd April 1997, for ANZAB, including ten resident members, overturning 1987's disappointment when mechanical problems the day before caused the planned attempt to be cancelled. For George and Diana, the 1997 peal was something they could only have dreamed about during their time in Melbourne in the early 1960s when Cambridge and Double Norwich Major and Bob Royal were the staple diet. Not forgetting the formidable logistical effort involved in getting twelve ringers from all over Australia in the same belfry.

Great Adventure 5 (2001) – Swan Tower, Perth, and Laith Reynolds – Background to the Swan Tower and Bells Project

For many people across the world, bellringing will be characterised by the Swan Bells visitor attraction in Perth rather than the sound coming from an idyllic country church in an English village. Completed in late 2000, following what to Laith Reynolds must have seemed a catalogue of false dawns and delays (which characterise all major projects, of course) over many years since the late 1980s, things were really starting to motor in Perth by the Millennium and the Swan Tower and Bells project was on target to be completed in late 2000. Laith brought unbelievable levels of tenacity, energy, commitment and, of course, great skill to this project. Ultimately all the various elements need to line up so the project gets finished.

Whilst there was plenty of debate about the value-for-money aspects of the project (the project cost was 5.5 million Australian dollars), the Swan Bells project was one of the few bicentennial projects that came in on time and on budget and Swan Tower is now one of the top three tourist attractions in Perth, superbly marketed and communicated in the tourism mix the city offers. Some of the statistics are staggering, demonstrating a huge amount of demand for a wonderful facility.

Visit of HM The Queen to Perth

So a massive amount of expectation came to fruition when Her Majesty the Queen arrived in Perth on 30th March 2000 for a three-day visit. The itinerary was publicised in small doses so there was a sense of anticipation in those involved with the Bell Tower project and the general public of Perth as well. It was announced about a month before the visit that she would be coming to the Swan Bells site and would be viewing the installation and meeting ANZAB ringers. On the last day, over a thousand people were present at the Barrack Square site. Among those presented to the Queen was Laith Reynolds, Honorary ANZAB member and past President, proudly sporting his gold ANZAB badge, the only one ever awarded, for his work in organising new and refurbished towers in Australia during the 1988 bicentennial celebrations.

Old bells from London

St Martin-in-the-Fields, Trafalgar Square, had a ring of twelve bells dating back to the 1720s and cast by Abraham Rudhall, a noted UK founder. It was Laith Reynolds who discovered that these bells were to be melted down in 1988 and rescued them for Perth. Given that the Rudhall bells had been in central London throughout their working lives, there was considerable historical and heritage value in keeping them intact as a twelve and bringing them to Australia. In the late 1980s, the first initiative to do so failed when promised state support failed to materialise. After the bells had been shipped to Perth, they remained in a warehouse for ten years whilst the bell frame rusted in a farmyard as several attempts were made to raise $1,000,000 for a new tower.

Fundraising for the new bells

Fundraising in London (half a million Australian dollars) enabled the old bells to be exchanged for new Western Australian copper and tin for the casting of the new ring of twelve bells at St Martin-in-the-Fields. A new ring of twelve for St Martin-in-the-Fields had been cast by the Whitechapel Bell Foundry in the late 1980s when discussions about Perth/St Martins old and new bells originally took place, but stalled.

Finally, Laith Reynolds approached the premier of Western Australia and told him of his vision for the Swan bells. The government's advisers were keen to promote new attractions for visitors to Perth and saw the project as a great opportunity, in part because the scheme included the visitors gallery to watch both the ringers and the bells and to observe the magnificent river views. The new Western Australia government agreed that building a tower would provide the city with the tourist icon.

The opening of the ring of sixteen bells and the Swan Bell Tower Festival

Another significant development was that the old ring of twelve from St Martin-in-the-Fields would be moved to Perth with four new bells being added to expand this to a ring of sixteen bells, the first ring of sixteen in Australia, hung in The Bell Tower. A huge amount of activity was planned once the installation was operational, with the Swan Bells Festival, effectively a grand opening of the bells, over the Easter weekend from 14th to 18th April 2001. Eighty ringers attended a special event on Easter Saturday evening, 14th April, where the dinner was in the form of a buffet with speeches interspersed between courses. George spoke to congratulate all concerned in the remarkable Swan Bells story and to propose a toast to Laith Reynolds who had conceived and seen through the project.

Earlier, on 7th April, George rang in the first peal on Swan Bells (on the back ten), of Little Bob Royal, a real honour and recognition of his friend Laith Reynolds' sterling efforts – this included four local Perth ringers. Further landmarks were achieved over the weekend including the first peal on more than twelve bells outside Britain, Yorkshire Surprise Sixteen, by an ASCY band including George. Comment was made of the bells as being the best ring of twelve in Australia and probably the best ring of sixteen outside the UK and Ireland, with very good internal and external acoustics. Some complex logistical issues were reported in *The Ringing World*, essentially down to there being a great number of ringers expecting to be able to ring peals on sixteen (for which some had been practising hard) with a limited number of peal ringer slots to accommodate them! Rescheduling a small number of flights soon fixed this problem. Workshop sessions were held on Monday, Tuesday and Wednesday and included an open forum in the HQ hotel, chaired by George who observed that the question and answer format with its face-to-face contact could often be more beneficial than the textbook. This concluded with a showpiece course of Little Bob Maximus by an all-Perth band.

The festival then moved to Adelaide, Melbourne and finally Sydney, with eight-bell and twelve-bell striking contests. George and Diana stayed on for this part of the tour and he fixed a 'half -and-half' Australian/UK ringers peal of Cambridge Maximus at St Mary's Cathedral, a nice way to end the tour.

Change ringing on sixteen bells

The idea of installing a ring of sixteen bells for English-style change ringing is quite recent. Curiously, one of the advantages it offers is that because of the number of bells in the tower it is possible to ring on large or small numbers of bells – for example five, six, eight, ten, twelve, fourteen or sixteen – as well as rings of bells of different weights. Traditionally, rings of twelve bells had always been the maximum for English-style change ringing. Rings of sixteen bells are still relatively rare. The idea was conceived by Rod Pipe, George's brother, who spearheaded the project to supersede the existing ring of twelve bells with a new, complete ring of sixteen bells at St Martin's, Birmingham in 1990/91. Rod was a mathematician and a brilliant, highly prominent and loyal ringer in Birmingham for over

50 years. As a gifted composer and conductor of ringing, he believed that installing an English style change ringing ring of sixteen at St Martin's, Birmingham would enable the Birmingham band to innovate in the future. Although at the time ringing on sixteen bells represented uncharted territory, he believed the Birmingham band was strong enough to develop the new opportunity. It is generally agreed that the best of the three rings installed to date, and by some distance, is that at the Swan Tower, followed by St Martin's Birmingham and then Christ Church Dublin, an old, mixed ring augmented to sixteen in 1999.

Change ringing on twelve bells has been widely practised in approaching 150 locations for about 200 years. Change ringing on sixteen bells introduces new and significantly greater levels of difficulty. There are several components of 'difficulty'. One example is odd-struckness, which is about whether each bell strikes exactly when the ringer expects it to. Usually they don't! The evenness and clarity of sound to the ringers is important, but the most obvious difference is the size of the 'gap', the visual/audible gap between the bells as they strike. A three and a half hour peal of 5,000 different changes on twelve bells means 60,000 'hits' of the bells collectively, a similar 5,000 changes on sixteen bells will take maybe 20 minutes longer and will generate 80,000 'hits' of the bells collectively, i.e. 20,000 hits more. In theory, this means that ringing sixteen bells is about one-third more difficult than ringing on twelve. Many people who have rung on sixteen bells would probably judge the one-third more difficulty as definitely understated!

Great Adventure 6 – 2007 trip to Australia

In February 2007, George and Diana were off to Australia once more, this time a short trip mainly visiting friends with just one peal, Stedman Cinques on the augmented twelve at Goulburn Cathedral, conducted by Bill Perrins. This was a 'must ring' peal for two reasons: firstly, it had been specially arranged and 'rung in memory of John J F (Jack) Roper OA, a founder member of ANZAB and a fine Christian gentleman'. Jack was George's great friend in Melbourne from when he arrived in Australia in 1956, and secondly, Goulburn was George's one outstanding Australian ring of twelve bells for a peal so to a born collector, success here was most important. And the peal was successful – thankfully!

The George W Pipe Library at Adelaide Cathedral

It was a mark of the man that George's highly tangible influence on Australian ringing continued 50 years after he left. In 2012, St Peter's Cathedral, Adelaide, generously made available the second or south-eastern tower of the Cathedral for use as what is now the Adelaide Ringing Centre. On two levels it houses, on the top level, a ringing room for eight dumbbells above, with electronic equipment to enable any combination of bells to be rung with their dedicated computers and headphones, or rung together as ordinary bells with amplified sound in the ringing room. It is a first-rate teaching facility. On the lower level is a resource centre and library with facilities for small seminars with appropriate electronic and whiteboard aids. It also houses the appropriately named George W Pipe Library to which George very generously contributed from his own extensive library. He had an office full of books! This is typical of George's generosity towards the art of

St Peter's Cathedral, Adelaide

campanology in general and in particular it demonstrated his love and commitment to Australian ringing nearly fifty years after leaving. This is not the only example of his generosity towards ringing in Australia.

1963 – Back to the UK: reflections on George and Diana's time in Australia

Several pages of commendation were published in *Ringing Towers* in May 1963 when the news of George and Diana Pipe's return to the UK became known. These retrospectives, coming from respected ANZAB members in Melbourne, Sydney and Adelaide are a testament to what they achieved during their stay and how valued and appreciated they were. Today, 60 years on, it is difficult to imagine the effect a dynamic young couple moving into Melbourne, an established Australian centre of ringing, might have. George and Diana clearly settled into the Melbourne ringing community and made a very significant difference to it, but their ringing ability was just one part of it.

Jack Roper wrote the lead piece in *Ringing Towers* in May 1963. He commented on how George and Diana's house in Springvale, a Melbourne suburb, was always open house to ringing friends, how there was plenty of ringing and plenty of social gatherings of ringers, and how the St Paul's Melbourne annual meetings were noteworthy for the dedication of the latest peal boards celebrating state occasions and ringing firsts. Most noteworthy, in Jack's view, was George's leadership and conducting which led to these milestones being possible, not forgetting successful and hard earned peals at Ballarat, Yass and St Patrick's RC Cathedral, Melbourne, the latter made possible by George forging new relationships with the RC Cathedral following the death of Pope Pius X11 in 1958.

George and Diana's influence was felt in neighbouring states and frequent trips to and from Melbourne enabled many young ringers in all states to advance their ringing, learn new methods and develop new ringing friendships. In those days, ringing in Australia was largely practised in each state and there's no doubt their work in integrating some of this activity, providing individuals with real opportunities to progress as part of a wider team, stimulated the setting up of ANZAB.

Willy Watson, from Sydney, added to Jack's piece, saying it was a grand experience to have known them and how ringers felt great indebtedness to them for their services to the Exercise in Australia both in and outside of the tower. Their genuine interest in Australian ringing and their aim to utilise the best of English ringing to stimulate the Exercise in Australia led to an increase in standards and a new enthusiasm for ringing. George's brilliance as a ringer and organiser was more than an example, it was an inspiration, it was also infectious. Diana was also commented upon as an exemplary ringer who had been of great value to ringing in Australia, with her loss a great blow.

Bill Pitcher, from Adelaide, also commented on the four objectives George had set as targets to achieve during his stay in Australia, a general improvement in standards, the restoration of unringables, the formation of a national association and Great Adventure 2 taking place within ten years. Most of these had been achieved, although the Great Adventure tour planned for 1964 was delayed for a year, a disappointment perhaps. Bill commented that at the time what Australian ringing needed was a leader, and over the past seven years they had had one in George. In all his efforts, Diana supported him and together they offered their friendship as spontaneously as they did their encouragement and practical help.

On Good Friday morning 1963, when they left Melbourne airport to fly home, 25 to thirty friends were there to say farewell to the family – George, Diana, daughter Sarah and son Stephen, both children born in Australia – a very moving occasion for all those assembled. It's worth bearing in mind that George and Diana had achieved all this and yet were still only in their late twenties.

On the way back, stopping off in British Columbia, they rang at Vancouver Cathedral and Mission City, with a quarter peal of Stedman Triples at Victoria Cathedral on Vancouver Island, which was the first quarter peal of Stedman Triples in British Columbia.

Chapter 8

Back to the UK in 1963
and the challenge of severe autism

Settling back in the UK

In April 1963, George and Diana returned to the UK. Having left in 1956, and now with a young family, they were returning to a new life back in the UK. They lived initially in Grundisburgh and Nacton, prior to purchasing their house. Later in 1963, they purchased 8 Lansdowne Road, Ipswich, on the north-east side of the town, towards Woodbridge and just over a mile from St Mary-le-Tower church. George called it 'a bit of rural Suffolk in the town.' 8 Lansdowne Road is a highly individual bungalow built in 1907 with lots of space. George told me that having lived in Australia for seven years, the thing that was most important to them was space! They would have hated the idea of being hemmed in or having a house which was not large enough. The home is set in one-third of an acre and backs on to a bowls club. The garden is mostly a massive lawn, at the bottom of which is a 30ft railway cutting which accommodates the Ipswich to Felixstowe goods line, reckoned in the early days of container traffic to be the most profitable British Rail line anywhere. At one time George rented a terrace in the railway cutting to grow vegetables at a rent of £1.50 a year. Diana remains in the house they had shared for nearly 57 years, until George died in March 2020.

8 Lansdowne Road, Ipswich, a haven

This was a haven for their large family, now including great grandchildren – many of whom live locally – and their many friends. For nearly 57 years George and Diana shared this house with countless others: church people (St Mary-le-Tower is a big community) and ringers from all over the world, to name just two groups. They committed to these and other communities, to their many other friends, and they did this selflessly. They were also 'go-to' people for those experiencing difficulty in their lives. They were sympathetic, wise and positive, simply excellent people, kind, hospitable and generous. Their primary consideration was always for others. The hospitality was first-rate.

Since they came from Suffolk, they were able to renew and nurture their many friendships from the mid-1950s and before, but of course they would create many more through the children growing up, work (back at Ransomes in Ipswich), church and ringing. Most of their family was in Suffolk and a major change had been that Rod was now 23, had finished his degree at Birmingham University, and was now working at Cadbury's.

Autism – and family life

As mentioned elsewhere, Diana and George were richly blessed with three children – firstly Sarah Margaret, born in 1958, then Stephen Robert Willgress in 1962, both of whom were born in Australia and baptised at St Paul's Cathedral, Melbourne. Their younger daughter, Alison Mary, was born on 9th April 1967, a birthday present for her father, with a peal of Double Norwich at Lavenham rung to honour her birth.

A beautiful baby, Alison's physical development was normal, but she only said only a few words before all speech disappeared. She became extremely difficult to understand or manage, and seemed to be living in her own confusing and frightening world. It was feared she was on the autistic spectrum.

Back in 1971, understanding of autism was at a very early stage. On the third visit to the Maudsley Hospital in London Alison was given the final diagnosis of severe autism. She was five years old. As there was no specialist schooling locally for autistic children, who could be very disruptive and totally misunderstood, her parents were advised that she should go to a Rudolph Steiner School in Thornbury, near Bristol, where Alison would live as part of the school family, sitting round the meal table and going to lessons in one of the school houses set within a park, and where she had the same main teacher, Bob, all the time she was there. It was so hard to part with her at such a young age but there seemed to be no alternative. Alison benefited enormously from her nine years at Thornbury. She progressed hugely and seemed very happy there.

George and Diana always regarded Alison as a wonderful gift to them despite the extreme practical difficulties presented by her autism. Far from being a negative, all this would mark a huge and very positive change in their lives, with a significant future involvement in helping to improve the lives of autistic people: the Maudsley Hospital kept in contact with George and Diana and was very helpful with advice over many years, and the whole family took part in a research project looking into all aspects of autism including the impact autism had in middle age and adulthood, and on family life. Alison is 53 now and lives in supported living accommodation in Ipswich, and Diana still spends time with her whenever possible. In earlier years, holidays were at Scratby (yes really!), Norfolk. These days a static caravan at Walton on the Naze gives the family space.

Provision for autistic young adults

Autism even now is not well understood, but back in the 1970s little was known about it. Alison was diagnosed in 1971. Obviously by then George and Diana had been living with the condition and its effect on Alison for several years. It also impacted heavily on them as parents and it meant the family came under immense pressure.

Inevitably the time comes when the autistic child becomes the autistic young adult. Until the 1970s, there had been no special provision in East Anglia for autistic young people after school leaving age, and if they could not be accommodated at home, then all

The family pictured at 8 Lansdowne Road in 1970.
Left to right: George, Stephen, Sarah, Diana and Alison

too often they could be admitted to mental subnormality hospitals. These were not able to provide specialised care and attention, without which autistic young people could easily become more withdrawn, frustrated, violent, and difficult to understand and manage.

Progress was being made in certain areas of the UK in the creation of residential communities for young autistic people, as at Thornbury. As an Anglian Autistic Community Trust (Anglian ACT) flyer from the early 1980s put it, 'now it is being done for school leavers in East Anglia too!'

Fundraising and Barton Hall initiative

Cambridgeshire and Norfolk each had an autistic society but, as there was none in Suffolk, George and Diana, together with a group of family, friends and influential people, joined with Cambridgeshire and Norfolk and formed Anglian ACT. An extremely hectic period of meetings, fundraising and viewing properties ensued, and finally Barton Hall, near Mildenhall, was purchased for £125,000, all fundraised. Barton Hall catered for about eighteen young people, offering continued education, craft work, horticultural and leisure activities in peaceful surroundings with extensive private grounds. Supervision was by trained staff with the time, patience and understanding to help each autistic young person according to their own specific needs.

The hall, a Georgian building, needed to be completely modified to meet the living needs of autistic young people, so a further £200,000 was needed for essential repairs, which included significant modification and reconfiguration, refurnishing and purchasing new equipment. A huge fundraising campaign was launched. The flyer was fairly direct in that it was very clear that without raising the money it wouldn't be possible to retain Barton Hall. It is interesting to note that the sort of big-money funding we are used to these days didn't really exist in the 1980s. The flyer talked about cheques, deeds of covenant, bequests, coffee mornings, bring and buy sales, charity fundraising groups in schools, colleges and large firms, making toys, garments, fancy goods, providing jams or supplying garden produce for Anglian ACT charity stalls. 'Crowdfunding' of a different type! This was old-fashioned, traditional fundraising, very hard work, but the money was raised. And of course an Anglian ACT advertisement appeared in the 1978 Suffolk Guild of Ringers Annual Report.

The Anglian ACT ran Barton Hall for many years until it could no longer raise enough funding for the modern specifications required by the local authority. At this point the National Autistic Society stepped in and continued to run it, with some of the residents still remaining. By 2019 Middlefield Manor, as it had been renamed, was in need of another massive investment, the scale of which could not be justified, and in 2019 it was put on the market for £750,000.

George and Diana got involved in other charitable causes as well, notably George's fundraising for the Spastics Society in 1971, collecting Green Shield stamps to raise funds for a minibus. In those days local papers used to carry reports of who the successful collectors were and George was noted as 'our largest single collector with 40,000 stamps'. With the help of family, friends and work colleagues, he went on to collect 62,000: ever the collector! George recalled once being in Wilfred Williams's car travelling to Wolverhampton. They were following a car with a rear window sticker saying 'Jesus Saves'. Quick as a flash Wilfred said '… Green Shield stamps.' Wilfred was a collector for the Red Cross!

Chapter 9

Suffolk Guild and the challenge of change

Rod Pipe in Birmingham – 'Thursday night is peal night'

By 1963 brother Rod had left home, gone to Birmingham University and was one of the leading ringers and conductors in the Birmingham band which was regularly ringing peals of Surprise Maximus on Thursday nights. The band had developed and strengthened largely through the addition of local ringers coming through, such as the Insley brothers, (John and James), the Fellows brothers (Martin and Michael) and the highly talented John McDonald. Cliff Barron, John Anderson and Peter Border were already established.

Others moved in. David Purnell moved up from Somerset (and eventually back again, after which he led initiatives to augment the existing eight to twelve at Midsomer Norton, and a similar exercise later at South Petherton). Alan Ainsworth moved to Birmingham from Newcastle upon Tyne (then later to Amersham, where he masterminded firstly the augmentation of a very mediocre heavy six to eight and a few years later a complete new light Taylor twelve, before becoming master of the St Paul's Cathedral Guild). He remembers George Pipe's enthusiasm and communication skills, 'qualities not often encountered in such measure in ringers.' These ringers formed the backbone of the band that rang the long peals of 16,368 Cambridge Maximus in 1965 and 15,699 Stedman Cinques in 1966, both on the 31cwt ring of twelve at St Philip's Cathedral, Birmingham. At the time, the Birmingham Cathedral band was probably the most competent twelve-bell band ever and they were ringing on their own bells. These days ringing a long peal on a 31cwt twelve would be most unusual, but the band was young and ringing peals most Thursdays, most weeks. Some of them came down for weekends at Grundisburgh and George took the opportunity to ring with this band when he visited Birmingham.

George Fearn ran the show. He must have thought he'd got lucky – weeknight peals of Maximus most weeks! He had been ringing in Birmingham since the 1920s and was still firmly in charge of a talented group. He was an encourager of all ringing talent and, to his considerable credit, a supporter of lady ringers. A number of lady ringers started to come through and ring in Thursday night peals, for example Susan Funnell and Ann Fellows. But the most famous lady ringer at this time was Muriel Reay – she had rung in Thursday night peals at Birmingham Cathedral since the late 1940s, and later she became the first lady Master of the St Martin's Guild. A head teacher by profession, she became somewhat revered in later life. Having become the first lady to ring 1,000 peals, in 1974, the 30th anniversary of this achievement was marked with another ladies peal. This time there were around forty lady 1,000-pealers to choose from! She died in 2015.

Suffolk and new people

Ringing-wise, following the hard work that George and Diana contributed to ringing in Australia, it was time for some 'top end' ringing and personal advancement now available to them. 20 Spliced Surprise Minor with John Mayne was an advance on the typical Suffolk 'steady seven', and peals followed of Stedman Cinques at St Giles, Cripplegate and Cambridge Maximus at Great Yarmouth and Birmingham Cathedral. London Royal No 3 became popular, with peals at Stradbroke (seven resident Suffolk ringers, including six firsts) and Luton (with Wilfred Williams band). George's 300th peal, Plain Bob Major at Grundisburgh on 30th November 1963, was historically significant in another respect – it was the first peal for William E E Pye, the fourteen-year-old grandson of the great William Pye.

Quite a number of people who had arrived on the East Anglian ringing scene after George left the UK in 1956 did not know him when he returned in 1963. One of these was Joe E G Roast, who like George was born in 1935, a true contemporary. From a ringing family at Danbury near Chelmsford – his father was a baker – Joe and some of his contemporaries rapidly became prominent on the Essex ringing scene, particularly in the fields of Surprise Major and Multi Minor, the latter being practised by more than one band in Essex at that time. Joe says:

> "My earliest memory of George was a peal of Yorkshire with him at Great Waltham, the heaviest eight in Essex, on 17th September 1955. George conducted and his father Jim rang the tenor. Whilst working in Australia he gained an almost mythical reputation which was still evident when I toured the country in 2001. His ringing of heavy bells and bell handling was legendary. Back in Suffolk, a story emerged of an outing that George was on where he arrived at a rural tower to be greeted by one of the locals. Advancing on the local with extended hand he greeted him with "How do you do, George Pipe". A rather terrified looking local backed away with the words "No, no, but I wish I was ..." I cannot confirm the truth of this but it is a good story and shows the reverence accorded the man. A most likeable man, he is a person I felt privileged to have known."

Alan Barber, who now rings at Whitley Bay, learnt to ring at Fordham, Cambridgeshire:

> "When I learnt to ring as a young teenager George appeared to be the face of Australian ringing. At the time there were few towers 'down under' and George was the driving force of ringing there. Soon after his return to his beloved Suffolk, I rang a peal at Horringer, which for me was memorable as it was the first peal I rang with George, Diana and Andrew Beckwith. Over the years I have come to very much admire George. As well as being a superb all round ringer, whether as conductor, heavy bell ringer or organiser, he was also the Great Communicator. When meeting George he knew who you were, where you rang, with the history of that tower, and who you rang with. His overall knowledge was absolutely fascinating! I consider that if I only had half of George's talents then I would be a much better person."

Change, and more change

The 1960s were characterised by profound change, with established norms often being turned upside down. A youth culture we had never seen before established itself, as did pop music, the Beatles, the Rolling Stones and many more to follow. With the advent of one-day county cricket (for the Gillette Cup) even cricket changed! One detects something of this change in the bellringers' newspaper, *The Ringing World*, with less deference and more openness than before, whilst the 'governing' body, the Central Council of Church Bell ringers, was still dominated by the great and the good! The assassination of John F. Kennedy in November 1963 was marked by several special *Ringing World* supplements, recording peals and quarter peals, with the inevitable debate in the letters column about which was the first piece of ringing in honour of JFK. This was a state event in the USA, clearly commemorated by bellringers in the UK in a quintessentially English way.

The Pipe/Egglestone effect

In the almost seven years George and Diana had been away things had changed in Suffolk ringing as well. In early 1964 a new name came into George's peal book, Howard W Egglestone, who came from Essex, a multi-Minor specialist (more on this later), had moved to Claydon near Ipswich to work in the concrete industry and was teaching a young band at Henley. They were of similar age, but since George had been in Australia, he and Howard had never met. However, George was Ringing Master of the Suffolk Guild between 1964 and 1969, and Howard from 1969 to 1974. It's true to say that through their efforts, ability to work together, sharing of visions and goals, they were largely responsible for some very significant advances in ringing in Suffolk during that decade.

A good example was the Suffolk Guild's 50th anniversary in 1973, with a 24-page issue of *The Ringing World* (No 3232 dated April 6 1973). On the front page there was a collection of pen and ink drawings by George featuring some of the major towers in the county, Leiston, Beccles, Bury St Edmunds, Lavenham, Bures (where I learnt to ring), Helmingham and, of course, Ipswich St Mary-le-Tower. Inside was a little summary of those churches followed by a 5 page article, again by George, giving a whistle stop tour through those fifty years, whether good or bad, followed by a report of the Guild's special efforts to ring quarter peals in all the ringable towers in Suffolk, about 160 at the time, during the 50th anniversary year.

The '160 quarters' project was a wonderfully inclusive form of celebration, which required much co-ordination to bring to fruition. As Howard Egglestone, Ringing Master at the time, said, in the celebratory issue of *The Ringing World*, 'Many youngsters rang their first quarter, many towers which do not feature regularly in *The Ringing World* were successfully 'quartered', a lot of fun and a deal of hard work were involved and 266 ringers took part in 160 quarters. Interest was rekindled in the bells in several towns and villages and the 50th anniversary is well and truly marked.' I remember this – Howard absolutely loved it, motivating, cajoling, getting others to achieve things they didn't think possible.

The 1974 Suffolk Guild AGM at Bury St Edmunds. Attendances of well over one hundred were typical at that time, with towers open (three or four routes in) as part of the day out. George and Diana are in the front row, third and fourth from the left, Howard Egglestone (Ringing Master, wearing badge) is in the centre of the front row, and the author of this book is in the back row, fourth from the left.

The Suffolk Guild

As a Suffolk person and a committed member of the Suffolk Guild of Ringers from boyhood, it is no surprise that George became Ringing Master of the Suffolk Guild of Ringers soon after returning from Australia in 1963. His reflections on Suffolk ringing, and particularly his time as Master, are interesting. Suffolk is a rural county and once had great bands of ringers at rural towers, but those bands are no longer there. They died off and in many instances also failed to teach ringers to succeed them. One wonders if this is a problem inherent within ringing, which is a high skill, relatively slow progress pursuit that happens in a team environment. We have 21st-century mobility, commuting to work, living lives which are more about dormitory than community, and of course people are living these lives at an increasingly fast pace. Is that just a given, or can we overcome it and use it to our advantage? Perhaps the bands at Ipswich, St Mary-le-Tower (the old pre-war band), Lavenham, Bures, Debenham, Framsden/Helmingham, Leiston, Beccles and Henley would have died or contracted anyway. The Suffolk Guild has invested very significantly in bell restoration (including a lot of DIY) for the last forty years or so such that the bell stock is now in much better condition. Perhaps the focus on training and developing ringers needs to be beefed up? How?

George saw something of a polarisation between ringers at the top and those at the bottom, which he felt reflected in limited opportunities to learn conducting, which can often be a 'closed shop'. District meetings used to be an important part of ringing, but had become poorly attended and less regular than they used to be, though newer and more varied programmes have worked quite well and meet members' needs. He felt striking competitions could be better supported, particularly by the better ringers, as could Guild training days. He acknowledged that there are issues with geography in Suffolk, Norfolk and Cambridgeshire. Suffolk is a large rural county, but the Guild is, and always has been, as good as the sum of its resources. He believed the best period for the Suffolk Guild in his seventy years of membership had been during the fifteen years from 1979 to 1994.

27 years of continuous office in the Suffolk Guild

George served the Suffolk Guild in a variety of capacities for the majority of the period since 1964, as Ringing Master, Chairman, Vice President and Life Vice President. He valued the Guild and what it does very highly and contributed to its quality of ringing and restoration focus throughout. He had a phenomenal ecclesiastical knowledge of Suffolk, including ringing.

Ringing Master of the Suffolk Guild, 1964–1969

In the summer of 1964, George was elected Ringing Master of the Suffolk Guild of Ringers, a great honour for someone who has always valued the work done by territorial associations. Change was overdue – by 1964 plenty of work needed to be done in Suffolk. He served for five years, handing over to Howard Egglestone in 1969 and in those ten years the two of them effectively reshaped the Suffolk Guild into an organisation fit for purpose moving into the 1970s and beyond. The Suffolk Guild had until then only had two masters, Charles J Sedgley 1923–1956 and Leslie G Brett 1956–1964, so the longstanding members were used to having one of their own age as Master.

It would be wrong to assume that the change to a young dynamic new Ringing Master would be totally smooth, or that being a Suffolk person would mean he would be accepted into the role with open arms. After all, to some he'd been away for years, making a name for himself in Australia and Washington, nothing to do with Suffolk and they weren't going to have him order them around and introduce fancy ideas into their Guild. In the 1960s and 70s meetings were characterised by a culture of heated, sometimes raucous debate. He needed to show strength of character to counter some of the views of the older members – and they could be vociferously negative and change-averse: 'Who do ['Suffolk', not an error] he think he is coming back from Australia and telling us what to do?' George's reply: 'I can only do my best.'

This true anecdote, indicating the value of both over- and understatement, was delivered just after George's election as Ringing Master at the 1964 AGM, one to be there to hear; his competition was Harry Clarke! Shades of what he'd encountered on becoming Ringing Master at Melbourne Cathedral? George reached out to people like Harry – they supported the Guild, they were its grass roots, they were entitled to their view and they should be listened to. George had a wonderful ability to build rapport, often through charming others, in order to resolve these issues, and everything concluded amicably later with a couple of beers, always. Worth noting too that it was George Pipe who provided a board for Harry's 'in memoriam' quarter at Hawkedon.

George's first annual report for 1964 stated that Guild membership was diminishing at around 300 and the ringing scene in Suffolk was in a quite a sorry state. Although 70 peals were rung in 1964, including a number of firsts, these involved only 70 of those 300 members. In about a dozen centres real progress was being made, beginners being taught, quarter peals being rung, usually under good enthusiastic leadership, but there had been a lack of teaching and bell maintenance. The situation at that time was mirrored by other counties. In October, a peal of 7 Surprise Minor was rung at Tannington to mark the arrival in Suffolk of J Barry Pickup, a teacher who had moved to Lowestoft and remained in Suffolk thereafter, becoming a significant contributor to ringing, particularly in North Suffolk. Later in October, James Bennett, an early thousand pealer and once a regular ringer with William Pye's band, rang his 1,300th peal, at Grundisburgh.

Signs of improvement

Winston S Churchill died in early 1965 and an appropriate contribution to his memory was a half-muffled peal of Doubles at Winston, Suffolk, in which George rang, 'partnered' by a peal at Churchill, Somerset. This was just a small part of the ringing across the country to mark his death, 'the greatest Englishman probably of all time', as *The Ringing World* put it. A half-muffled peal of Stedman Cinques was rung at St Paul's Cathedral on the day of his funeral. The tribute on the front cover of *The Ringing World* of 12th February 1965 and the peals and quarter peals rung occupied some 25 pages over several weeks.

In terms of the Suffolk Guild, 1965 showed improvement, with 19 first pealers alone. George was a well-travelled Ringing Master in what is a big county, 37 towers visited in 1964, and 51 in 1965. Areas requiring improvement were the Western half of the county, historically always the weaker area, and the highly rural Central District, which was eventually absorbed into the other four districts.

Away from strictly Suffolk Guild business, but nevertheless warranting considerable celebration, July saw George Symonds's 90th birthday peal at Grundisburgh, which also marked George and Eva Symonds's 58th wedding anniversary. George Symonds would reel off many more great achievements in the years to come including a BBC Blue Peter appearance at 95!

The message for 1966 was positive, with membership increasing and 500 members by 1970 a realistic target. George attended 15 of the 22 Guild meetings in 1965. Astonishingly when compared to today's attendances, 200 people attended the 1966 Guild AGM at Lavenham with its now restored historic ring of eight. And there was the small matter of six Suffolk Guild members setting a new multi-Minor record of 148 methods under Howard Egglestone's conducting expertise: more on this later.

1967 saw a drop in peals to 63. By 1968 membership had reached 448, but the maintenance imperative had not been properly addressed – only 145 towers out of 240 with rings of five bells or more were described as fair or better in the Guild report. The 1968 peal total was 109, including a couple of tours to the county. With grants totalling £60 being awarded and a restoration fund totalling just over £300 this funding was clearly ineffective. George's final report for 1968 made a clarion call for subscribing to *The Ringing World*, 'our only national printed link within the exercise'. Clearly the critical faculties George might display in Melbourne ('Keep it going, I think I heard a good change then', in case readers may have missed it earlier!) had not been dimmed by his return to England.

'One cigarette a week'

John Girt – more on him a bit later – and I both remember a subscriptions increase at an AGM sometime in the early 1970s. Income was down, finances were stretched with inflation at around 20%. We remember George 'softening' the proposal in his own inimitable way, 'ladies and gentleman, the increase equates to one cigarette a week, we really must pass this motion', and the meeting did. John remembers Guild Management Committee meetings too – at the vote following an often contentious discussion many of those present would quickly look up and then raise their hands following the way in which George voted. George was by then not in the Chair!

Canon Lawrence Pizzey has been a Suffolk churchman for fifty years, a regular officer (now an Hon Vice President) of the Suffolk Guild since 1969. He has worked with George at Guild and Diocesan level over that time. Lawrence says:

"George might be described as ringing's greatest name-dropper; and deservedly so because he always had a wonderful recall of a huge number of ringers who he had met and rung with over six decades, with a great fund of stories about many of these. He had the good fortune, throughout his ringing career, often to have been at the right place and at the right time, to be invited to take part in notable ringing achievements; but he was never boastful about these, nor the many bell restorations and augmentations to which he gave endless organisational skill and tireless effort. He was always happy to share knowledge gained from his tremendous collection of ringing books, pamphlets, paraphernalia and artefacts. However, leaving aside all this, above all there stood the huge personality that was George. The warmth of his greeting and his friendliness with ringers of great or little ability; encouraging all to achieve the best of which they are capable and always insisting on good striking! – that was George Pipe."

Dennis Knox

George first met Dennis when they were both on the 1954 Suffolk tour mentioned earlier. In 1970 Dennis moved from North London to work at Martlesham, Suffolk with the Post Office, later BT labs, its dedicated research function. A number of other ringers from BT have moved to Suffolk since. Dennis learnt to ring in Bedfordshire and rang 125 peals, some of which he conducted, with the famous Willesden band (packed with high quality performers – think of people like John Mayne, Bill Critchley, Richard Speed, Joan Beresford), often firsts in the method. He was a composer of some note whose compositions are still rung today.

Dennis was a quiet, modest character and a very good ringer who participated fully in Suffolk ringing. From George's perspective Dennis became a very supportive and highly valued member of the St Mary-le-Tower band in the years before the new twelve were installed.

Lavenham – an iconic village and tower

Lavenham is a Suffolk village noted for its Guildhall, Little Hall, stunning fifteenth-century church and half-timbered medieval cottages, during which period it was among the twenty wealthiest settlements in England. Considered to be Britain's best preserved medieval village, it was one of Suffolk's most important wool towns. The church, particularly its tower, nave and chancel, are an ecclesiologists' delight. The church is regarded as one of the finest examples of Late Perpendicular Gothic architecture in England. 1966 saw the restoration and retuning of the historic 21cwt eight at Lavenham, with its famous Miles

Graye tenor, dated 1625. The mediaeval oak bell frame (dating to 1553) was replaced with a new cast iron frame before it became really dangerous. Few old-fashioned 21cwt eights give a ringing experience quite like that of Lavenham, with its massive ringing room with huge recessed windows (with seating), long draught and very clear acoustics – some call them 'old growlers'! In the 1960s for local youngsters like me it was one of *the* places to ring in Suffolk, Saturday evening practice with strict-but-kind mentors and the visit to the Swan afterwards, where handbells were kept behind the bar!

George rang 22 peals here, one of his favourite towers. He called the final peal on Lavenham bells before the work was carried out in 1966, to Heywood's peal composition of Double Norwich, also marking the visit of the Archbishop of York to the diocese. In the peal were two people he was to ring with regularly over the next thirty or forty years, Ken Hesketh and Phil Rothera. They both came from the food industry, Ken from the food processing industry and Phil a dairy farm manager for Lord Rayleigh's farms in Essex. The three of them had much in common since George sold high-value agricultural equipment into that industry for his firm, Barlow Handling. Ken would later organise a significant number of George's twelve-bell peals over many years.

A new multi-Minor record in 1966

1966 was marked by a series of peals leading up to the successful peal in 148 Minor methods at Ashbocking on 13th July, conducted by Howard Egglestone, the greatest number of methods rung to a peal at the time. This was stimulated by Howard's enthusiasm – he had led one of several multi-Minor bands operating in Essex prior to moving to Suffolk in 1962. The particular reason for this happening in 1966 was that Joe E G Roast's band in Essex had rung 145 multi-Minor on 25th March 1965 (in which Dennis A S Symonds, who originated from Lavenham, was one of the band). Anthony R Peake's Wiltshire band was also very active.

Peals by the Suffolk band were rung in 16, 26, 40, 66, 100, 134 and finally 148 methods. There were eighteen attempts in total and plenty of practising of extents when peals were lost. Apart from Howard Egglestone, none of the ringers had any experience of multi-Minor. George Pipe had previously indicated an interest in multi-Minor and joined the band at the 40-method stage when one of the band was relocated to Bedfordshire. The band was fortunate to have someone keen and able join them at this stage. In an excellent write-up, it was hailed as a remarkable achievement. George thanked Howard for his efforts, not just with this project but in being leading peal ringer (just 23) and conductor for 1966, besides considerable teaching and work on the social side (including famous pre-Christmas 'socials'), a strong overall contribution.

An interesting postscript is that the original idea when starting out was for Bob Lester, tower captain at Barking, where two of the peals were rung, to ring a peal of Minor in 14 methods in early 1966, but the initiative was shelved for eight months or so in favour of other matters! He eventually achieved this on 30th August 1966. A note of congratulation from Joe Roast to the Suffolk band appeared in *The Ringing World*. Joe also commented that:

> *"George was capable of learning and ringing unlimited methods as demonstrated when he rang in the record peal of 148 Minor methods at Ashbocking conducted by Howard Egglestone in 1966. I had conducted the previous record of 145 methods in 1965 and was not surprised when this was surpassed a few months later."*

From 1935 – a family peal that wasn't! All named Symonds, six of the band were from Lavenham and two from St Mary-le-Tower Ipswich. George and his son Harold, from Ipswich, are second from left and sixth from left. Dennis A S (who rang in Joe Roast's 145 Minor band in Essex) is fourth from left.

Early days and a youthful perspective on ringing 148 methods

It was at about the time of the 148 Minor that I learnt to ring, at Bures, which is near Sudbury in the Stour valley. Leslie Mills taught me to ring in the mid-1960s. It was probably in mid-1966 although, strangely, I'm not sure when or where, a rather odd admission from a biographer. However, I do remember the name 'George Pipe' from when I started to learn to ring, and years later George told me that he used to come to Bures to stay with the Mills family during school holidays in the late 1940s. A little earlier I referred to George's rather difficult relationship with his father, Jim. The Mills family, among others, in what we today would call a support network, were very helpful to George, although Leslie disliked Jim! Leslie was 'old school', spoke his mind, always had a project and was very dynamic. The first project was the restoration and augmentation to eight of Bures bells in the early 1950s and the final project was to save the then-redundant church of St Peter, in a wonderful position overlooking the market in Sudbury town centre, and to regenerate it as a thriving arts and community centre in the late 1970s. Leslie's contribution was in fundraising to get the old eight (unrung since the 1950s) rehung in a new frame and augmented to ten, something he never expected would happen. Not surprisingly, given the history and the very recent efforts to install a modern twelve at St Mary-le-Tower, Leslie and George had huge respect for each other and their work.

I remember as a twelve-year-old reading the Suffolk Guild report for 1966, cover to cover of course! I was lent this by one of our other ringers as it wasn't until 1967 that I joined the Guild and had my own copy. I couldn't quite believe what I was reading, about a peal

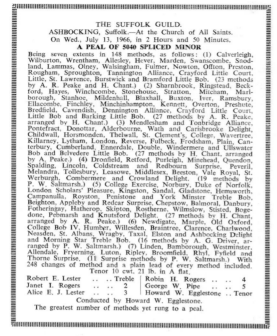

THE SUFFOLK GUILD.
ASHBOCKING, Suffolk.—At the Church of All Saints.
On Wed., July 13, 1966, in 2 Hours and 50 Minutes,
A PEAL OF 5040 SPLICED MINOR
Being seven extents in 148 methods, as follows: (1) Calverleigh, Wilburton, Wrentham, Allesley, Hever, Marden, Swanscombe, Snodland, Lammas, Olney, Walsingham, Fulmer, Nowton, Offton, Preston, Rougham, Sproughton, Tannington Alliance, Crayford Little Court, Little, St. Lawrence, Burstwick and Bramford Little Bob. (23 methods by A. R. Peake and H. Chant.) (2) Sharnbrook, Ringstead, Beckford, Hayes, Winchcombe, Stonehouse, Stratton, Mitcham, Marlborough, Stanhoe, Mildenhall, Blaxhall, Buxton, Iver, Ramsbury, Ellacombe, Finchley, Minchinhampton, Kennett, Overton, Preshute, Bredfield, Cavendish, Dennington Alliance, Crayford Little Court, Little Bob and Barking Little Bob. (27 methods by A. R. Peake, arranged by H. Chant.) (3) Mendlesham and Tonbridge Alliance, Pontefract, Donottar, Alderbourne, Wath and Carisbrooke Delight, Childwall, Horsmonden, Thelwall, St. Clement's, College, Wavertree, Killarney, Lytham, London, Reverse, Fulbeck, Frodsham, Plain, Canterbury, Cumberland, Ennerdale, Double, Windermere and Ullswater Bob and Belvedere Little Bob. (27 methods by H. Chant, arranged by A. Peake.) (4) Dronfield, Retford, Purleigh, Minehead, Quendon, Spalding, Lincoln, Coldstream and Redbourn Surprise, Peveril, Melandra, Tollesbury, Leasowe, Middlesex, Beeston, Vale Royal, St. Werburgh, Combermere and Crowland Delight. (19 methods by P. W. Saltmarsh.) (5) College Exercise, Norbury, Duke of Norfolk, London Scholars' Pleasure, Kingston, Sandal, Gladstone, Hemsworth, Campanulla, Royston, Penistone and York Minster Treble Bob, Beighton, Appleby and Redcar Surprise, Chepstow, Balmoral, Danbury, Fotheringay, Hatherop, Skipton, Rostherne, Wilmslow, Stisted, Bogedone, Pebmarsh and Knutsford Delight. (27 methods by H. Chant, arranged by A. R. Peake.) (6) Newdigate, Marple, Old Oxford, College Bob IV, Humber, Willesden, Braintree, Clarence, Charlwood, Neasden, St. Albans, Wragby, Taxal, Elston and Ashbocking Delight and Morning Star Treble Bob. (16 methods by A. G. Driver, arranged by P. W. Saltmarsh.) (7) Linden, Bamborough, Westminster, Allendale, Fryerning, Luton, Ripley, Broomfield, Rhyl, Fyfield and Thorne Surprise. (11 Surprise methods by P. W. Saltmarsh.) With 248 changes of method and a plain lead of every method included.
Tenor 10 cwt. 21 lb. in A flat.

Robert E. Lester	.. .. Treble	Robin H. Rogers	 4
Janet I. Rogers	 2	George W. Pipe	 5
Alice E. J. Lester	 3	Howard W. Egglestone	.. Tenor

Conducted by Howard W. Egglestone.
The greatest number of methods yet rung to a peal.

The record multi-Minor peal

in 148 methods (as I later found out, proper old-fashioned Minor in the days when a band had to ring seven extents, each containing all 720 changes, none of this soft stuff!). I only knew about three or four methods and at the time I mostly rang the treble. At home we rang Plain Bob Doubles or Triples, Kent Major (if there were sufficient people) and if the all-stars turned up, Stedman Triples, which often fired out! Reading about this peal gave me perspective on what could happen in ringing and showed me the variety and the scope available. As a keen youngster I wanted to progress and ring at this level myself. The stuff of dreams?

Rapidly up, and then down

George made a major impact on me when, as Suffolk Guild Ringing Master, he wrote to me in February 1968 to congratulate me on my first peal. It was my first experience of that handwriting – I had no idea anyone could have handwriting like that irrespective of what they were saying! The message was simple and direct – 'well done' – and the Suffolk Guild in future would badly need the involvement of youngsters like me. This was inspirational stuff to a twelve-year-old. I knew George was a very good ringer; clearly he was also a good chap, kind and considerate as well. With the Suffolk Guild producing twelve or more first pealers annually, he must have written plenty of letters of congratulation.

My first peal on eight bells, Kent Treble Bob Major at Bures in August 1968, provided a different experience, something of a nightmare in fact. Leslie Mills, my mentor, overrated my ability and experience and the result was a fairly consistent 'commentary' from George on my performance. No one had ever called me 'Johnny' before. George delivered it late on with a massive sigh and I was gripped by shock rather than fear. You either sink or swim as a result of such an experience. I would swim, of course. We never went to the pub at Bures – I guess I wasn't old enough anyway – so I dashed home for a spot of confidence bolstering from my mother, she of much common sense. All was soon well again!

First peal at St Mary-le-Tower

Our next peal together was four years later, on 17th September 1972, at St Mary-le-Tower, Little Bob Maximus by a Suffolk band. I was seventeen at the time, glad to get the invite, the first time I'd rung at St Mary-le-Tower. It would have been so easy for George to include a few experienced people from outside to bolster the band a bit, but the objective was to ring it with a resident Suffolk Guild band. At the time of George and Howard Egglestone as Ringing Master the policy was always to 'bring people on'. That meant growing your people in the local environment, and creating opportunities for a wide selection of ringers, not merely ones with great potential.

So in what some might see as a rather risky approach, George invited three people who had not rung a peal on twelve. Adrian Knights was one. He became an accomplished twelve-bell ringer and was a St Mary-le-Tower ringer for many years, taking part in most of the 'modern' band's achievements. There was Sam Twitchett, pushing 70 with little experience on twelve. Sam suffered from phlebitis, which makes standing difficult, so he would need to minimize that for the day, or just ring through it. Plenty of determination and sheer nerve was in evidence, but of course he was going to be there, added to which George had known Sam since he was a boy. The other was Frank Gilbert, and he and Sam were both from Clare. These chaps were out teaching ringers in West Suffolk most evenings so they got minimal decent ringing. It was a humid afternoon and the tower was very stuffy, and Sam in particular was soaked by the end, but very chuffed that George had invited him, and he'd rung a peal on twelve. Christine Knight, who learnt to ring at Clare at this time, recalls Sam talking about the peal on many occasions afterwards – he could talk! This was a perfect example of George's kind and considerate style of organization giving new people an opportunity to progress, very special to witness. This happened countless times in a ringing context and there are further examples elsewhere in this book.

Always 100% commitment

Thereafter college beckoned, so I always lived some distance from Ipswich, and George and I rang relatively few peals together. Many of those were twelve-bell peals, including 25 at St Mary-le-Tower over many years, but only 73 in total. Nonetheless, he came to be a good friend to me for the next forty years. As a ringer, his consistently high level of performance, whether he rang at the heavy end, in the middle or round the front (where he was top class), always reinforced and enhanced the band. Peter Sanderson put it very aptly: 'you always get more than just George in a band, he adds to it.' This applied to his ringing, where the high standards he always set himself never diminished.

Of course, the enthusiasm and commitment we associated with him in all aspects never waned. Very late in his ringing career he realised it might be possible to achieve a notable ringing target, to ring 500 twelve-bell peals. I and a number of others were pleased to help him with this initiative and in 2010 and 2011 he joined us for peals at several new twelves (another interest): Hursley, Bitterne Park, St Magnus the Martyr, Ripon and Portsmouth Cathedral. He was not in great shape by then, but those ringing were impressed by the level of commitment he showed – if you elect to do these things then you do them properly. These were not easy trips for him, driving West to link up with us, and overnight stays. Despite his protestations of no longer being up to it, the end result was as good as ever! He ended on 481, a valiant effort.

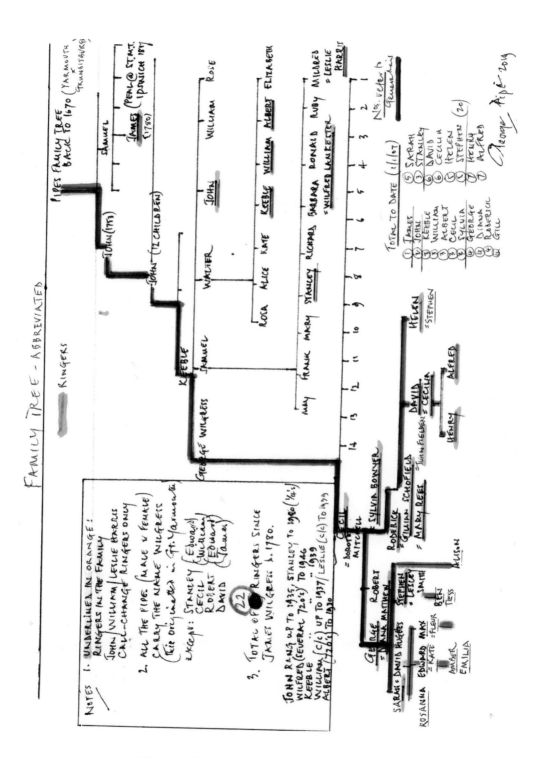

The Pipe family tree in George's hand (2019)

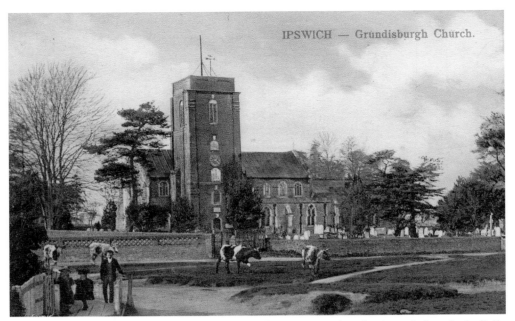

*A colour postcard from George's collection of St Mary's Church, Grundisburgh, Suffolk.
The family had connections with the village for 250 years before George's birth. George's
father, Jim, grew up in Grundisburgh, learned to ring and was buried at the church,
and was involved in augmenting the bells from eight to ten.*

*Forty-eight years and over five thousand peals after they learned to ring together in 1944 –
Rod Pipe, John Mayne and George Pipe after George's 1,000th peal in 1992.*

Back from Australia for a three-month extended holiday in the UK, July 1961. In the garden with the family at Easta, Grundisburgh (clockwise from bottom right): Jim, Sarah, George, Sylvia, Rod and Diana.

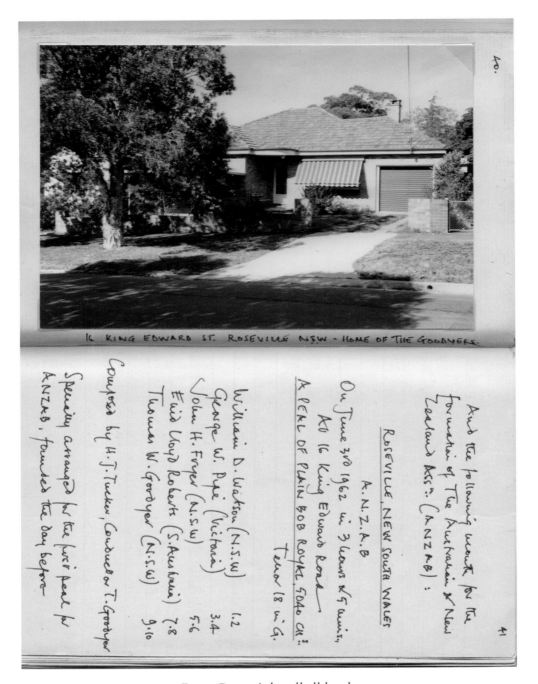

16 KING EDWARD ST. ROSEVILLE N.S.W - HOME OF THE GOODYERS.

And the following work for the formation of The Australian & New Zealand Assn. (A.N.Z.A.B):

ROSEVILLE NEW SOUTH WALES

A. N. Z. A. B

On June 3rd 1962 in 3 hours & 5 mins,
At 16 King Edward Road
A PEAL OF PLAIN BOB ROYAL 5040 CH.s

Tenor 18 in G.

William D. Watson (N.S.W)		1.2
George W. Pipe (Victoria)		3.4
John H. Finzer (N.S.W)		5.6
Enid Lloyd Roberts (S. Australia)		7.8
Thomas W. Goodyer (N.S.W)		9.10

Composed by H. J. Tucker, Conducted by T. Goodyer

Specially arranged for the first peal for A.N.Z.A.B., founded the day before.

From George's handbell book:
The first peal for the Australia and New Zealand Association of Bellringers,
rung in 1962 at 16 King Edward Road, Roseville, New South Wales (pictured)

The Bell Tower, Perth, Western Australia, which contains the ring of sixteen known as the Swan Bells. (Photo courtesy The Bell Tower)

St Peter & St Paul, Lavenham, Suffolk, a wonderful wool church in an iconic village. George went to the annual Lavenham Ringing Festival throughout his life. A classic 21cwt ring of eight bells of great character hang in the tower. (Photo courtesy Nigel Gale)

George and Eva Symonds's Diamond Wedding Anniversary, 1967.
A course of Double Norwich Court Bob Major was rung by (left to right):
George Pipe 1-2; Charles Sedgley 3-4;
George Symonds (aged 92) 5-6; Cecil Pipe 7-8

An image by Jill Jackson used as the cover of the first of a series of
'Fen peals' CDs. Clockwise from left: Frank Price, John Loveless,
David Brown, Gareth Davies, Bill Jackson, Lesley Boyle

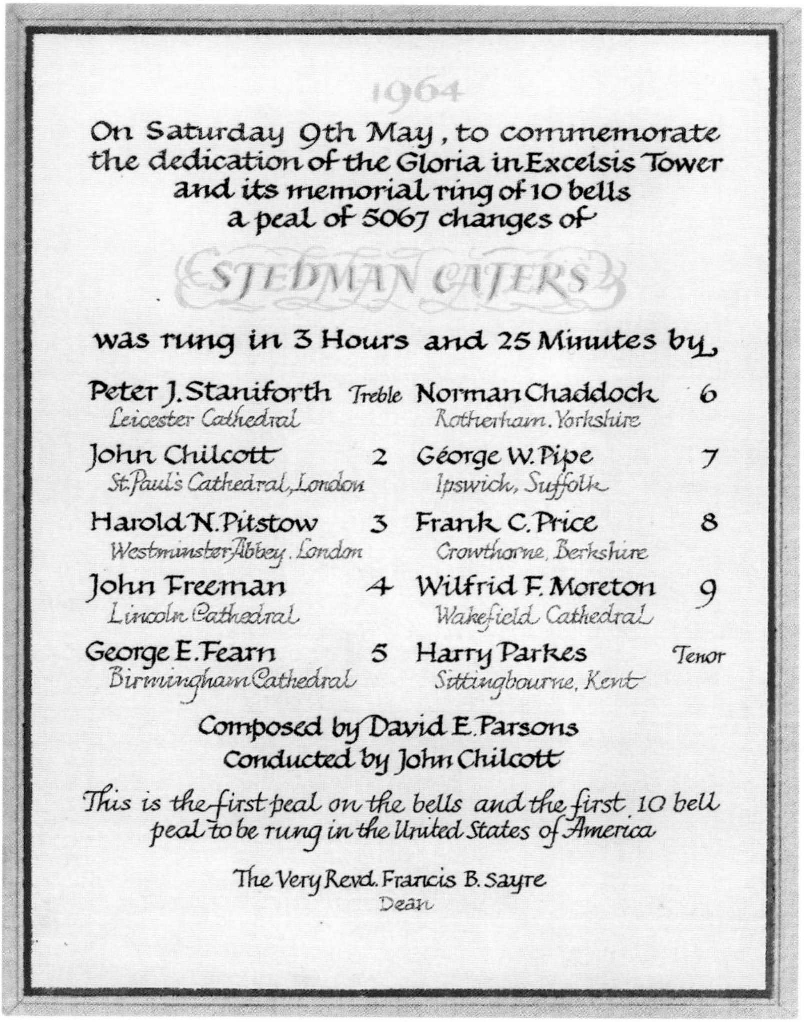

1964

On Saturday 9th May, to commemorate
the dedication of the Gloria in Excelsis Tower
and its memorial ring of 10 bells
a peal of 5067 changes of

STEDMAN CATERS

was rung in 3 Hours and 25 Minutes by

Peter J. Staniforth	Treble	Norman Chaddock	6
Leicester Cathedral		Rotherham, Yorkshire	
John Chilcott	2	George W. Pipe	7
St. Paul's Cathedral, London		Ipswich, Suffolk	
Harold N. Pitstow	3	Frank C. Price	8
Westminster Abbey, London		Crowthorne, Berkshire	
John Freeman	4	Wilfrid F. Moreton	9
Lincoln Cathedral		Wakefield Cathedral	
George E. Fearn	5	Harry Parkes	Tenor
Birmingham Cathedral		Sittingbourne, Kent	

Composed by David E. Parsons
Conducted by John Chilcott

This is the first peal on the bells and the first 10 bell
peal to be rung in the United States of America

The Very Revd. Francis B. Sayre
Dean

*The 1964 peal at Washington Cathedral, the first peal on the bells
and the first ten-bell peal rung in the United States of America*

WASHINGTON NATIONAL CATHEDRAL

presents to

GEORGE W. PIPE

On the occasion of the

35TH ANNIVERSARY

of the DEDICATION *of the* GLORIA IN EXCELSIS TOWER

WHEREAS *the ringing of church bells in the tradition of* ENGLISH CHANGE RINGING *was virtually unknown in the United States in 1964; and*

WHEREAS, *the band which came from England in 1964 to ring for the Dedication of the Cathedral's tower and 10-bell ring, through their patient and skillful instruction, established a strong foundation for the ringing programs developed at the Cathedral and at the National Cathedral School; and*

WHEREAS, *members of the Dedication Band have continued to provide generous hospitality and strong encouragement to Washington ringers visiting Great Britain throughout the ensuing 35 years;*

The undersigned wish to express our deepest gratitude for the extraordinary talents, generous support and Christian example of those men whose service to the Cathedral in May of 1964 has so greatly enriched our community ever since:

May 1999

RICHARD S. DIRKSEN
DIRECTOR, THE WHITECHAPEL GUILD

QUILLA ROTH
TOWER CAPTAIN, WASHINGTON NATIONAL CATHEDRAL

AGNES UNDERWOOD
HEADMISTRESS, NATIONAL CATHEDRAL SCHOOL

THE VERY REVEREND NATHAN D. BAXTER
DEAN, WASHINGTON NATIONAL CATHEDRAL

THE RIGHT REVEREND RONALD H. HAINES
BISHOP OF WASHINGTON

Washington Cathedral shows its appreciation for George's continuing commitment

ANCIENT SOCIETY OF COLLEGE YOUTHS

founded 1637

A.S.C.Y.

50 Years Membership
of
The Society

by

_____

_____ Master _____ _____ Secretary

_____ Master _____ _____ Secretary

A certificate by George for those who achieve fifty years
as members of the Ancient Society of College Youths

St Leonard, Shoreditch, London E1

Christ Church, Spitalfields, London E1

St Martin in the Fields, Westminster

25. St Mary, Market Weston, Suffolk
by George Pipe. Pencil on paper

26. St Mary, Happisburgh, Norfolk
by George Pipe. Watercolour on paper

27. Roof Tops and Towers of Ipswich *by* George Pipe. Ink, watercolour and collage

28. St Nicholas Bedfield, Suffolk *by* George Pipe. Ink on paper, watercolour and collage

Some of George's pen and ink drawings and watercolours, displayed at the
'Inspired by Bells' Ringing World Centenary Exhibition in 2011

George and Diana's silver wedding anniversary, 1981

Silver wedding anniversary celebrations, 1981.
The boys – George, David (Sarah's husband)
and Steve

Silver wedding anniversary celebrations, 1981.
The girls – Alison, Sarah and Diana

Diana and George at grandson Ben and Fleur's wedding.
Kingston Lacy, Dorset (2018)

Siblings' eight-bell peal at Wicken, Northamptonshire.
Back left to right: Rod Pipe, Frank Price, George Pipe, Peter Randall, Geoffrey Randall;
Front: Alan Paul, Graham Paul, Richard Price

Siblings' twelve-bell peal at All Saints, Worcester. Pictured in ringing order clockwise
from front right, 1–12: Geoff and Peter Randall, Linda and David Garton, Alan and
Graham Paul, David and Philip Rothera, Rod and George Pipe, Robert and Adrian Beck

The Norman Tower campanile and the Millennium Central Tower
of St Edmundsbury Cathedral – nearly one thousand years between them

The band for the first peal on the twelve at St Edmundsbury Cathedral,
25th August 2012. Clockwise from front left: Diana Pipe, Paul Stannard, Joan Garrett,
George Pipe, David Potts, Alex Tatlow, Ian Holland (Conductor), Christopher Movley,
Jed Flatters, Christopher Munnings, Timothy Hart and Phillip Wilding

*George in his study at Lansdowne Road, preparing for an exhibition
of his bellringing memorabilia at Felixstowe in 2015.
A print of Great St Mary's, Cambridge, where in December 2012
he rang his last peal, is on the door behind him.*

Chapter 10

A little book on handbell ringing ('A minimalist handbell life')

Just a little book

In 2004, George pulled together all the documentation he had about handbell ringing and wrote it up in an 85-page, approximate A5, hardback notebook. There's an immediate 'George' element to it in that on the spine reads 'GEORGE W PIPE * HANDBELL NOTES' in gold plate, classy! Adrian Knights and Brian Whiting had always shown an interest in George's ringing exploits and he thought they might enjoy the book. George also thought it would be a pity to simply dispose of the various pieces of documentation. Well it would have been, but it's a treasure trove! I had been anxious to find interesting material for this book and handbell ringing is one of the gaps. I'd not had a lot of material, there usually isn't a lot of material, it can be – well – almost a bit private – and I wasn't very clear about George's handbell ringing exploits. I knew he had rung a small number of handbell peals in total, mainly in Australia, and a couple of peals of Stedman Cinques, and also some sampling of the simple stuff as a kid, as many of us do, but that was all I knew.

George described the book as 'probably the most inconsequential book you will ever read.' Not at all! It covers handbell ringing in all its forms, peals, quarter peals, exhibition ringing at dinners, media appearances and AGM's, and from the age of seven when he used to be allowed a go at ringing handbells on a Sunday morning at St Mary-le-Tower, where there were some good handbell ringers and they could ring Treble Bob Maximus. The book covers the sixty years of history from 1944 when he first rang handbells, up to 2004, with everything recorded, down to the shortest touch at a meeting, the method rung and usually by whom and on which pairs!

Early days of handbell ringing

It's clear that George never considered himself a handbell ringer and over the whole of his ringing career rang very little on handbells. Since boyhood he always looked upon handbells as a quite different art form to tower bells for many reasons, a view shared by many: respect while keeping a distance! Equally though, he always had the greatest admiration for those who can ring handbells well.

Limited parental interest

His parents were not interested in handbell ringing, although both could ring elementary methods. Jim was a rhythmic tenors ringer. They had a good ring of eight handbells in the house, but even when Rod was old enough to ring handbells they never rang with any regularity. George's earliest recollection of handbells was in the ringing room at St Mary-le-Tower just before the outbreak of war in 1939, when he was four, and then during hostilities when there was a ban on tower bells. At that time, the St Mary-le-Tower band would meet for handbells on Sunday mornings, presumably in order to keep together as a band. Jim would take George there, first from Woodville Road, where they lived until 1939, and then from Grundisburgh, after they had moved back to the family home at Royal Cottage. They travelled into Ipswich on the Eastern Counties 210A, a camouflaged bus, as they all were at the time.

The Mayne family

In 1944, George's interest was rekindled a little when the Mayne family moved to Grundisburgh: Cecil C Mayne, employed at Debach Aerodrome, Phyllis (who was the first lady to call Holt's Original), and John R Mayne, two years older than George. It was from the Mayne family that George picked up the rudiments of elementary change ringing on handbells. Eventually the Mayne family moved back to Harrow Weald and that was really the end of any serious handbell ringing for George and it became peripheral once again.

Interestingly, many years ago when I was starting out, Howard Egglestone told me that John Mayne once said that handbell ringing is principally about opportunity and practice (assuming there is ability as well I expect!). George's personal view on handbell ringing was one that echoed the views of many otherwise talented people who never really fulfilled their true potential on handbells, and it remains true for some young ringers today. George was not alone in that view, and that is why I have developed this theme more than might be expected in this biography. He was a wise, perceptive chap.

Handbell ringing in Suffolk after 1945

Since 1945, Suffolk has never really been a strong handbell county. There was one small, keen group – George Fleming, Frank Fisher, William Wightman and Willoughby Maulden – but they were getting old by the 1950s. George rang Grandsire Triples and Bob Major regularly with his tower bell mentors, people like George Symonds and Frank Fisher, both of whom conducted Holts Original Grandsire Triples from every bell on tower bells and every pair in hand! George Symonds, despite his great age – in 1954 he was 80 – was always keen to ring handbells, but his pre-war band had finished – people like Frederick J Tillett (Bill Pye was once heard to say that of all the handbell ringers he had met, none were better on the tenors to twelve than Fred Tillett), Charles J Sedgley, William P Garrett, Hobart E

Smith, William J G Brown and Percy May. These names festoon the peal boards at St Mary-le-Tower and of course these men were all from the St Mary-le-Tower band which generated so many 'firsts' between the wars.

The Bailey brothers from Leiston were very talented. They rang many family peals, including Stedman Cinques in 1921, but apart from ringing for the odd occasion, handbell ringing in Suffolk had virtually ceased by 1960. Some new ringers moved into Suffolk in the 1960s and '70s, but there were not enough of them to form a band that could develop regular handbell ringing, and it was more about who was keen enough to come and ring.

So from 1944 through to 1953, George's little book records plenty of handbell ringing for local festivals, church services, Christmas and for seven successive years they were invited to ring at the Royal William pub in Woodbridge at Harvest Festival time. There were some highlights around this time, between 1951 and 1953:

George Thompson,
drayman and bellringer

In 1951, Rod Pipe rang his first peal as conductor, Kent Royal on tower bells at Grundisburgh, to his own composition. His father Jim, ever adept at squeezing local publicity and mobilising a little poetic licence when necessary, arranged a feature in local papers, *The Suffolk Chronicle*, *Woodbridge Reporter* and *Wickham Market Gazette*. Rod & George and Jim & Sylvia were in the photo which showed all four of them sitting in the house (I think) ringing handbells. The family were billed as 'handbell ringers'. It worked!

William Dye, mentioned in the first few pages of this book, an old ringer who had an impact on George as a youngster, died in 1951 and handbells were rung at his funeral. He had been a gardener on the Tollemache estate at Helmingham, rang in George' first 720 in 1944, and had conducted Holt's Original as early as the 1870s. The funeral of George Thompson from Hasketon in 1952 may be of significant interest to only a few, but he had been a drayman for Cobbold's brewery in Ipswich and apparently used to drink between fifteen and twenty pints every day!

Unexpected opportunity knocks in 1953

1953 was a bittersweet year for George regarding progress on handbells, some unforeseen, and it involved a stroke of luck. The Beamish family from Chilvers Coton, who were very kind to him, invited him over to stay for two weeks in July 1953. They arranged various ringing for him, but the highlight was a peal at Loughborough Parish Church. He recounts saving hard for weeks to be able to afford the train fares. Sadly, they met one short for the peal. Harold J Poole, Detective Inspector with Leicester Constabulary, a great motivator and one of the leading conductors in the country, made a rapid executive decision, saying 'we can't let the lad go back to Suffolk with nothing – you, you, you and you meet at Peter and Jill's flat in an hour'. The others went home, and George wondered what was happening, and what was going to happen!

Peter and Jill Staniforth, 2003, friends of George and Diana for over fifty years. George spoke at each of their funerals.

Anyway, out came twelve handbells. Poole was inspirational: 'We'll ring Stedman Cinques, George you ring the tenors', and 3hrs and 1min later the bells came round. This was George's first attempt for a handbell peal, it was on twelve bells, it was unscheduled and it was successful – he was over the moon! The band sat:

LEICESTER DIOCESAN GUILD
LEICESTER, 126A London Road
On Wednesday, July 29 1953
in 3hours 1 minute

A Peal of 5019 Stedman Cinques
Tenor size 15 in C

Brian G Warwick	1-2
Margaret E L Beamish	3-4
Jill Staniforth	5-6
Peter J Staniforth	7-8
Harold J Poole	9-10
George W Pipe	11-12

Composed by Frederick H Dexter
Conducted by Harold J Poole
First handbell peal – 11-12

In those days, it was quite common to have umpires, or at least someone present, for handbell peals, and John A (Jack) Acres, originally from Newmarket, an excellent handbell ringer himself, was the umpire for this peal.

Rosie Mason (née Staniforth), daughter of Peter and Jill Staniforth, recounts an amusing anecdote in connection with this peal:

"The 1953 handbell peal of Stedman Cinques – above – was rung at 126A London Road, Leicester. This was the flat where my parents, Jill and Peter Staniforth, lived when they were first married. As you may know, George likes to take a photograph of every place where he has successfully rung a peal to accompany the entry in his peal book. On this occasion for some reason George was not able to do this. The flat

belonging to Jill and Peter was over a butcher's shop. Many years later, after my parents had moved out, and George was in Leicester, he went to photograph the flat, however the shop was not now a butcher's, but an Ann Summers shop, quite different. He wondered if anybody had rung a peal above a sex shop!"

A disappointing end to 1953

George returned to Suffolk in the autumn of 1953, full of enthusiasm – no one in the family had ever rung a handbell peal – and persuaded Messrs Symonds, Sedgley and George Fleming to practise Double Norwich Major. They had about six practices in St Mary-le-Tower belfry and then attempted a peal which was lost after about an hour and a half, and lost again a week later after about an hour. The year

George and Eva Symonds' Diamond Wedding, 1967. A course of Double Norwich: George 1-2; Charles Sedgley 3-4; George Symonds (aged 92) 5-6; Cecil Pipe 7-8

finished rather disappointingly and George wonders if this was the reason why he never got enthusiastic again about handbells. They rang two peals of Treble Bob Major, Oxford on 25th October and Kent on 6th December. Sadly the compositions for both peals, by Henry Dains, who was somewhat prone to composing false peals, were indeed later found to be false!

To Australia in 1956

Soon, in June of 1956, he was sailing to Australia, where in addition to valuable media work referred to elsewhere, four handbell peals were rung during their six years there, usually for special occasions and involving firsts or firsts in the method. These are covered elsewhere. The final one was the first peal for ANZAB, Plain Bob Royal, conducted by Tom Goodyer. This was rung the day after ANZAB's formation, quite a 'prize' and well worth celebrating.

A 74th anniversary handbell peal. Clockwise from bottom left, Howard Egglestone (cond) 1-2, George W Pipe 5-6, Barrie Hendry 3-4, George E Symonds 7-8

Back in the UK in 1963

George and Diana returned to the UK in 1963 and in terms of handbells it was really a case of George resuming where he had left off, with sporadic opportunities, particularly in Suffolk, and great difficulty in finding a regular band to ring with, although into the mid-1960s and it was clear that George remained very capable, if unfulfilled. Plenty of handbell ringing was done in Washington in 1964 and again the 1967 Central Council meeting at Truro provided a forum, with Jill and Peter Staniforth, Bob Smith, John Jelley and George ringing Cambridge Royal for an hour – until George's 9th clapper came out! Stedman Triples is usually tough, but it was lost after two hours later in the year with Jill and Peter Staniforth and Alf Ballard, all competent and regular exponents at that time.

George E Symonds – an unlikely TV star at 95

In 1967, a party was organised to mark George and Eva Symonds' Diamond Wedding anniversary, they were 92 and 90 respectively. All their family attended, including their son Harold, a pre-war ringer at St Mary-le-Tower who had rung in the first ever peals of Yorkshire and Pudsey Maximus, and who flew over from Toronto, Canada. After tea George Symonds requested a course of Double Norwich in hand, the band as follows: George Pipe 1-2, Charles Sedgley 3-4, George Symonds 5-6, Cecil Pipe 7-8.

George (Pipe) wrote:

"This was still an early time in the growth of TV and there was scope to do more on the PR front, given that George Symonds was now, at 95, the oldest ringer in the country as well as being in very good shape. In 1970 he was invited to appear on Blue Peter and I took him to BBC TV at Teddington studios where we had a grand day out. George Symonds was interviewed and was quite amazing with his powers of recall and lucidity. We were asked to ring handbells. Since this was known about in advance, Bill Cook (St Paul's and Westminster Abbey) and Michael Moreton were lined up and joined us for a course of Stedman Triples: Bill Cook 1-2, George Pipe 3-4, George Symonds 5-6, Michael Moreton 7-8.

"This quality act was followed by an elephant being brought on to the set for a different type of quality act – it promptly defecated all over the floor! ('Cut! Take 2!!')"

In August 1972, a handbell peal was rung with George Symonds, then in his 98th year and on the 74th anniversary of his first peal in hand.

A much more stressful experience must have been ringing handbells for George Symonds at the great man's funeral in August

SUFFOLK GUILD

IPSWICH, Suffolk, 57 Mornington Avenue

On Wednesday, August 2nd, 1972
in 2 hours and 29 minutes

A Peal of Plain Bob Major 5184 changes

Tenor size 15 in C

Howard W Egglestone	1-2
Barrie Hendry	3-4
George W Pipe	5-6
George E Symonds	7-8

Composed by J M Hadley Hunter
Conducted by Howard W Egglestone

Specially arranged as a 97th birthday compliment to George E. Symonds, being rung on the 74th anniversary of his first handbell peal.

1974. He was a few months short of his 100th birthday. His funeral was at All Saints Church, Ipswich, where he was a chorister (bass) for over forty years. Grandsire Caters was rung with Hilda G Snowden, Edward P Duffield, Howard Egglestone, George and Jim Pipe.

Charles J Sedgley

Charles J Sedgley died just before George Symonds, in January 1973, aged 85. He was twelve years younger than George, but the two of them were a compelling partnership at St Mary-le-Tower over many years. In many ways it was they who helped make the difference between St Mary-le-Tower and other twelve-bell centres. He moved to Ipswich from King's Lynn in 1909 to work for the *East Anglian Daily Times* as a printer and bookbinder.

From a ringing perspective, his progress was rapid once he had arrived in Ipswich and he rang in only the second peal of Cambridge Maximus, in 1910. He became the first Master of the Suffolk Guild when it was founded in 1923 and held that position for 33 years. He was on the Central Council for 29 years as well. His greatest contribution was probably in the field of composition, especially in Surprise on all numbers and also Stedman, as George Symonds observed to George Pipe after his funeral. His compositions are still rung today. His life was not just bells and he was a man of many interests, encompassing spoken and written French, sport, philately, church architecture, history, heraldry, and many other subjects.

Suffolk Guild Handbell Days

J Barry Pickup and Barrie Hendry had moved to Suffolk by then and were active handbell participants. 'Handbell days' became popular in the 1970s, with Roger and Rosemary Palmer, excellent on handbells, from Fordham, and the Pipes each hosting one.

Saturday 16th September 1972 – the day before the peal of Little Bob Maximus – was an example of a Suffolk Guild handbell day. The programme for the day, a masterpiece of regimentation (not surprisingly) was put together by Howard Egglestone, Suffolk Guild Ringing Master, and a copy was kept by Christine Knight! With eighteen participants indulging and regular room changing it must have come across as a slightly bizarre activity to some, but at this time there was something of a resurgence of handbell ringing in Suffolk. At this stage, the resurgence had not spread as far as the author – that happened later, and I suspect he declined the offer because he was worried he couldn't do it!

This was an insight into the enthusiasm that was so typical of this era, with plenty of purpose for each participant and great things being achieved. Look at the 1974 AGM photo – packed with young ringers. These handbell days were well-organized, characterised by the dynamism and energy of George and Howard, and by the Pipes' incredible hospitality. They crossed age boundaries. Christine remembers this as the event that confirmed her as someone who would pursue ringing in a very serious way. At fourteen, she was the youngest person there, but every session contained something for her, and she got to ring

Shake my hand

HANDBELL DAY. SEPT 16ᵗʰ 1972.

PARTICIPANTS.
1 G.W. PIPE
2 S. TWITCHETT
3 F. GILBERT
4 W. PERRY
5 CHRISTINE
6 J. GIRT
7 B. HENDRY
8 B. REDGERS
9 L.R. PIZZEY
10 G. SYMONDS
11 R. HEATH
12 R. PALMER
13 MRS. R. PALMER
14 R. ROGERS
15 MRS. R. ROGERS
16 J.B. PICKUP
17 T.N.J. BAILEY
18 H.W. EGGLESTONE

FIRST SESSION.
ROOM A   1. 2. 3. 4. 5. 6
     B   7. 8. 9. 10. 11. 12
     C   13. 14. 15. 16. 17. 18.

SECOND SESSION
ROOM A   1. 2. 3. 4. 7. 8.
     B   5. 6. 9. 10. 17. 18.
     C   11. 12. 13. 14. 15. 16.

THIRD SESSION
     A   1. 2. 7. 8. 13. 14.
     B   3. 4. 5. 6. 17. 18.
     C   9. 10. 11. 12. 15. 16.

FOURTH SESSION.
     A   3. 6. 9. 12. 15. 18.
     B   2. 5. 8. 11. 14. 17.
     C   1. 4. 7. 10. 13. 16.

FIFTH SESSION.
     A   3. 8. 9. 18. 13. 16.
     B   2. 6. 7. 12. 15. 17.
     C   1. 4. 5. 10. 11. 14.

SIXTH SESSION
     A   2. 13. 4. 10. 15. 17.
     B   1. 3. 6. 8. 9. 12.
     C   5. 7. 11. 14. 16. 18.

SOME SUGGESTIONS!

MAJOR.	TEN	TWELVE
TOUCHES PLAIN BOB.	BOB ROYAL.	GRANDSIRE CINQUE
TOUCHES GRANDSIRE TRIPLES.	LITTLE BOB ROYAL.	BOB MAXIMUS
SPLICED PLAIN.	TOUCHES GRANDSIRE CATERS	LITTLE BOB MAXIMU
DOUBLE NORWICH.	STEDMAN CATERS	TREBLE BOB
TOUCHES STEDMAN TRIPLES.	TREBLE BOB.	
CAMBRIDGE.		TREBLE BOB FOURTEE

The programme for a Suffolk Guild handbell day in 1972

with 97-year-old George Symonds too! Sam Twitchett, a mere seventy, was no longer old! Defining experiences also for the author, in that a further result of declining this offer was that the he never rang with, or even met, George Symonds: the folly of youth.

Recent Maximus on handbells

George commented favourably on some of the more recent Maximus ringing on handbells in the 1990s, by David Brown's band and particularly some of the recordings of the Fen series of methods as we pursued the alphabet to previously unrung Surprise Maximus methods named after Fens. The recordings were created by Bill Jackson, one of the band, and his assistant, Linda Harris, who made a cameo appearance on the cover of the final CD produced. Bill produced firstly cassettes which were superseded by CDs. He recorded most of the ringing we did, and he was a brilliant editor. The setting up of the equipment each time we rang was accomplished with military precision. Sadly Bill suffered from multiple sclerosis and died in 2009, having been unable to ring for the last ten years or so, but he retained a very keen interest in ringing. It was a privilege to have the opportunity to ring in these peals and be on the CD cover, which was the work of Jill Jackson, Bill's wife. For the record, we were ringing at 5 St Mary's Walk, Fowlmere (our house) that evening, Jill was sketching Euximoor Fen Surprise Maximus, and the ringers on the CD cover were, left to right, Frank Price, John Loveless, Lesley Boyle, David Brown, Gareth Davies and Bill Jackson. This was one of at least thirteen CDs produced by Bill and Linda.

Handbell ringing and unrealised potential?

David Brown is a fine all-round ringer and brilliant on handbells. When I asked David to comment briefly on George for this book, it was interesting that he focused on a specific achievement of George's on handbells:

"Since I first rang a peal with George in 1972, this larger than life character has been interwoven with my ringing life and I rang many memorable peals with him and shared many enjoyable times. But I achieved with him something which few other ringers have, in that I rang a handbell peal with him. I note that he has only ever rung eight peals in hand, but he is one of those ringers that can turn their hand to anything. Before he went to Australia, he had only rung one handbell peal – Stedman Cinques with the Leicester band in 1953. What a talent just to be able to go and do that as your first handbell peal!

"In the 1970s, when I was regularly ringing handbells at Bottisham near Cambridge, we had a phase of ringing peals of Stedman Cinques and George fancied a reprise of his 1953 performance and asked if he might come along to attempt a peal one evening. So after 26 years, during which he had only rung a handful of peals of Plain or Treble Bob methods, he came and joined us on 9-10 for a peal of Stedman Cinques. His delight afterwards was boundless and over the years he recollected this performance numerous times when we have met. Maybe the experience was as traumatic as it was satisfying but, whatever the reason, he never rang another handbell peal!"

George recalled that he was particularly pleased to ring a peal with Marj Winter, who as Marjorie Batchelor was one of the early Washington Cathedral recruits in the mid-1960s and became one of the most celebrated lady ringers in North America. She had settled in Cambridge and married another talented ringer, Alan T Winter.

In summary, George was very good on handbells and he had the potential to become even better. He demonstrated his ability on several occasions when the opportunity arose to do so. There are scores of people participating in team pursuits who fall into a similar category, richly talented, but lacking the opportunity to really progress. It happens in many places, not just Suffolk. As John Mayne said, handbell ringing is primarily about opportunity and practice. Reading the little blue book, George performed in public many times, bringing our skill of bellringing to the attention of many people, and he would often be the one who would answer questions put to the handbell group. That's really adding value to ringing.

Chapter 11

The opening of Washington Cathedral bells in 1964

The privilege of a lifetime

Ringing in the United States was very much in its infancy at this time. There were very few ringable towers, just Kent School and Groton (replaced with a new ring in 1962) and consequently very few ringers. However, at Washington Cathedral things were changing, with a new 100-ton Taylor carillon installed in 1963. George, because of his ecclesiological interests, was aware of the completion of Washington Cathedral and the impending installation of a new 32cwt Mears and Stainbank ring of ten in 1964, but little did he realise that he would be one of those invited to go across to Washington to open the bells! Nevertheless the prospect of bells in Washington National Cathedral, at the heart of the United States capital city, was incredibly exciting.

The Cathedral is massive, 301 feet high and Gothic-style – the Dean in 1964, Dean Sayre, a grandson of Woodrow Wilson, pointed out, 'a Cathedral must stand not for 30 or 300 years, but 3,000 years, a symbol of Christianity and tribute to the building of the 14th century.' So there we have it! The bells were to be hung in a circular bell frame similar in design to Liverpool Cathedral, fabricated in steel. Looking back, the installation of bells at Washington was the single biggest influence on the growth of ringing in North America.

The bells and early ringing

The ring of ten bells for Washington Cathedral was cast by Mears and Stainbank at the Whitechapel Bell Foundry, London, in 1962. There was little publicity until the ringing population learned through *The Ringing World* that they had been shipped over the Atlantic to Baltimore, arriving in June 1963 prior to installation in the Cathedral's 'Gloria in Excelsis' central tower in the autumn of 1963. Wayne Dirksen, Associate Organist and Choir Master at Washington Cathedral (also father of Rick Dirksen, who would prove to be an influential leader of ringing over many years) was an important figure from the start and it was he and Ronald Barnes, Carillonneur, who visited England to approve the carillon at Taylor's in Loughborough and also to view the work on the ring of ten bells for the Cathedral at Whitechapel Bell Foundry.

The 'Gloria in Excelsis' Tower, Washington Cathedral
from the S.W. (The belfry windows and gallery are im-

*A newspaper photo of the 'Gloria in Excelsis
Tower of Washington Cathedral
(Washington National Cathedral Archives)*

Washington Cathedral Ringing Room – the peal band's first try-out of the bells

The first ever ringing at Washington Cathedral was on the weekend of 19th–20th October 1963, when some of the boys from Groton School and their ringing tutor, Russell S Young, came down to Washington – this was effectively the 'try-out'. At that time, the only change ringing towers in the US were Groton School and Kent School, so trained ringers in the US were at a premium. Most of the Groton School ringers on the Washington weekend had gained experience and reached a reasonable standard, some to Stedman Doubles and Triples, when visiting the UK on an organised tour in the summer of 1962. Without this Groton School influence, one wonders where ringers would have come from.

The reports from Russell Young and Rick Dirksen of the October weekend make really encouraging reading. The main purpose of the two and a half hours of ringing on the Saturday was rounds and call changes on ten to enable acoustics experts to make tests of volume in various parts of north-west Washington (with no history of ringing and uncertainty how loud would the bells be), as well as to measure tower vibrations with the seismograph. The final hour and a half of that time was given to ringing Stedman Doubles and Triples with about a hundred people in the ringing chamber!

Teaching plan

Washington was a 'greenfield' ringing site at this time with no history at all. What is obvious is that even before the dedication of the bells, the ringing and the ringers were generating a huge amount of interest locally and the confidence already built came through in *The Ringing World* reporting, with Russell Young stating that 'the Cathedral already had more candidates for a Guild than it needs.' Rick Dirksen was soon appointed Bellmaster and, on 12th October 1963, presided over the first meeting of all those interested in learning to ring, followed by what appears to have been very intensive tied-bell 'preliminary ringing instruction'. Shades of the Singapore Cathedral installation 56 years later and the need to import tutors to develop bell handling. Consideration needs to be given to the need to 'package' training into wider projects.

Harry Parkes's contribution

The job of hanging Washington Cathedral bells in the autumn of 1963 was assigned to Harry Parkes, one of the Whitechapel Bell foundry bell hangers. Because of America's stringent labour laws at the time, Harry's input was largely of a supervisory nature. However, he was a very important figure during the early stages of the training efforts aimed at developing something of a band at the cathedral before the dedication and as part of the dedication itself in May 1964, and of course he was in the inaugural peal of Stedman Caters. Indeed, the contract with Whitechapel stipulated that the bell hanger should be a ringer and capable of teaching ringing.

Harry was a very popular chap and Rick Dirksen lauded 'his superb teaching ability and boundless patience with such a group of novices as ourselves, we shall ever be most grateful.' Harry left Washington on Saturday 2nd November 1963, having had his stay extended by two weeks (with thanks to Whitechapel), and thereafter progress slowed a little. But he was delighted to hear respectable rounds on ten and rang Stedman Doubles on handbells with four of the American ringers before leaving for the airport.

Dedication Day – 7th May 1964

Washington Cathedral bells were dedicated, along with the tower itself, with a quarter peal of Stedman Caters to mark the occasion, on Ascension Day, Thursday 7th May 1964, greeted at the end by an enthusiastic audience of two hundred in the ringing area, ably managed by Rick. This was followed later that day by the first handbell peal in the United States, Plain Bob Major, rung by Messrs Staniforth, Price, Freeman and Moreton as a compliment to the hosts and hostesses to the band in Washington. The first peal on the bells, Stedman Caters, was rung two days later on Saturday 9th May 1964. There is a rich and interesting history behind the story of the dedication of Washington Cathedral bells. It was not all plain sailing – these things seldom are – and this was a complex initiative to bring to fruition.

Douglas Hughes – Whitechapel Project Manager supreme

Alan Hughes talked of how hard Douglas Hughes, MD at the Whitechapel Bell Foundry, worked on the Washington project. It is important to acknowledge the huge contribution he made over many months preceding the dedication to make sure everything ran smoothly, much more than designing a frame and installing the bells. He was the person in charge of the UK side of the Washington project and he did all the design work in the Cathedral architects' offices in Washington. This included resisting suggestions from the architects for the frame to be timber – ultimately a radial arrangement was recommended to eliminate torsional forces on the tower, a very tall structure standing on four legs, albeit 26 feet in diameter. A project of this scope, with Douglas working exclusively on just one project for several months both at the design stage and then with the selection and financing of the opening band, put pressure on the Whitechapel Bell Foundry infrastructure. All the other current projects were handled by Bill Hughes and Dennis Langdon. These were busy days, with Gillett and Johnston not long gone. It was a slog for all involved.

Team manager role

One of Douglas's key tasks was to invite John Chilcott, secretary of the Ancient Society of College Youths, to select the band of ten to go to Washington. This was quite a tough assignment since these ringers, as well as being high quality exponents of the art of bellringing, would effectively be 'Ringing for England', and the inaugural peal at Washington Cathedral would be the most important ringing of their lives. Most had not been to the United States – only four had flown before! Interest was high, reflected by *The Ringing World* coverage which carried about 25 separate updates on the whole Washington event over the period June 1963 to September

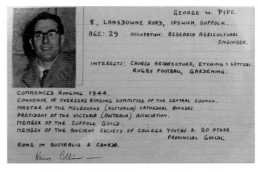

George's Washington ID card

1964, plus a four-page supplement reporting the story of the dedication written by George Pipe and published in the *RW* of 12th June 1964. A man to cover everything, Douglas Hughes sent ID cards for each of the ten ringers to Washington Cathedral shortly before the dedication. It was a good idea since all were previously unknown to their hosts.

Funding the journey 'across the pond'

There were some interesting financial aspects to the trip. Washington Cathedral by late 1963 had developed a contingency of around £1,000 ($1,600), to help fund air travel for the ringers from the UK and back. Douglas, ever the gentleman, felt that there needed to be a similar contribution, also of £1,000, coming from the UK side. After all, the Washington people had had their hands full with major Cathedral-related fundraising for a massive build over many years and we needed to do our bit.

£2,000 doesn't sound a huge sum by today's standards but the dedication happened well over fifty years ago and £2,000 then equates to more like £25–30,000 today, a considerable sum which was treated very seriously. So Douglas Hughes put an advertisement in *The Ringing World* during February 1964, headlined 'Ten ringers wanted for Washington dedication – appeal for £1,000' and signed off, 'I trust we shall not fail him (Dean Sayre) for lack of financial support', making clear that no final decision would be taken on whether the venture would proceed until it was safe to assume the total cost would be within reach.

Douglas obviously lived this project for a very long time and genuinely felt that the ringing exercise as a whole should be proud that the Dean had asked for a band from England to take part in the dedication. The Dean had advertised in *The Times* on 31st January, his rationale being that the local Washington ringers were inexperienced and felt they would be unable to do justice to the occasion when the cathedral's Gloria in Excelsis tower was dedicated on 7th May, therefore he would need the assistance of English ringers.

Douglas communicated with ringers regarding progress on the £1,000 target via *The Ringing World*, but it was clear that raising the money was very difficult. The *RW* in late February disclosed that £300 had been raised, clearly deemed not to be great progress, and Douglas reinforced that the Washington event 'is contingent upon worthy contribution towards the expenses being forthcoming from this side of the Atlantic', even at one stage expressing doubt about whether the venture would actually take place – or perhaps there was a little gentle bluffing going on.

Douglas clearly felt he needed to communicate the message to the ringing fraternity to stimulate more funding. In the *RW* of 6th March, with funding at still little over £300, he held back on stating the names of the band that would be going 'as final approval has not yet been received from Washington'! In the *RW* the following week, the band was announced even though additional funding was still required. Donations had been received from just two county associations, a number of private individuals with no obvious connection with ringing, and from Westminster Abbey, total contributions to date £370 and then up to £450 by 10th April. This sum would fund three return airfares and was deemed by Mr Hughes to be a fair contribution. The rest was secured from friends and well-wishers in the United States.

The Washington Band, photo taken at Westminster Abbey in March 1964, left to right: Wilfrid F Moreton, Frank C Price, Harold N Pitstow, Harry Parkes, John Chilcott, John Freeman, Norman Chaddock, George E Fearn, Peter J Staniforth, George W Pipe

Final preparations

Meanwhile, the band all received their invitations from John Chilcott (handwritten as was the way at that time), all accepted and the band met in London on Saturday 14th March 1964, had lunch together at Three Nuns, Aldgate, hosted by Douglas Hughes, and received their instructions for the trip. Some of the ringers had not rung together before so it was an opportunity to get to know each other. After lunch, they rang on the back ten at St Giles, Cripplegate and then moved from the City to have their photographs taken in front of Westminster Abbey. These photos would be used by the Washington Cathedral authorities for their preliminary publicity purposes. *The Ringing World* of 10th April headlined, on the front page, 'The Ten for America – special photograph': the shape of stardom to come?

The teachers

John Chilcott chose his people wisely and led his band well. He needed the right mix of ringers to do the job, and he needed other attributes than just pure ringing ability. There would be a programme of regular and pretty onerous teaching commitments (they were there for a week, during which there were teaching sessions of two to four hours on most

*English ringers for the Washington Cathedral dedication arrive on
Saturday 2nd May 1964 at Washington's Dulles Airport.
Left to right: Harold Pitstow, Norman Chaddock, Harry Parkes, Frank Price, John
Chilcott, George Fearn, George Pipe, Wilfred Moreton, John Freeman, Peter Staniforth*

days) and Norman Chaddock, Wilf Moreton, Peter Staniforth, George Pipe and Frank
Price were well-qualified in this area. Norman and Wilfrid had pioneered ringing schools
and courses in the UK, for example the Hereford course, which Wilfrid had founded.
Frank Price had spent time in the past teaching beginners at Groton School. The interest
in handbells was such that Douglas Hughes donated the set of handbells he had brought
over for demonstration purposes to the Washington High School, a fine investment
marking the start of a culture of change ringing on handbells in Washington.

Band selection and response

John wanted the party to be representative of the UK rather than just a line-up of the
great and the good from the Exercise, and he therefore elected to choose ringers from ten
different dioceses. He happened to choose nine College Youths (well, John's invitation from
Douglas Hughes to organise the band had come to him in his capacity as Secretary of the
Ancient Society of College Youths) and one Cumberland, Harry Parkes, the Whitechapel
bell hanger, at the request of the Americans and in recognition of his assistance in training
new ringers.

   Criticism rained down in certain quarters when this was announced in *The Ringing
World*! Some suggested a lack of balance in the band, others that there were better ringers
who were not being utilised. No women had been selected to ring, as Olive Barnett,
president of the Ladies Guild, observed. Herbert G Andrews called for Joan Beresford

*Washington dedication 7th May 1964. Evensong procession. Left-hand row from front:
Rick Dirksen, John Chilcott, Frank Price (top of head), George Fearn, Harry Parkes;
Right-hand row from front: Douglas Hughes, John Freeman, Peter Staniforth, William
Hughes, Norman Chaddock, George Pipe, Harold Pitstow and Wilfred Moreton (hidden)*

(Summerhayes) to be included and for Peter Staniforth to step down from the band in favour
of Jill Staniforth. Frank Hairs felt the Washington authorities should not be expecting the
ringers from this country to be funding £1,000 for their glorification and they should have
raised it from their own people. £1,000 could be used to far greater effect in this country.
Mrs J R Little from Derby said she would support funds of her choice and not allow Mr
Hairs to dictate how she disposed of her money. She told her American cousins they should
take no notice of Mr Hairs – his warped view was not representative of English ringers!
Ken Croft of Southampton expressed a calmer, approving view: 'are my wife and I the only
ones to think that the Washington venture is a good idea and feel satisfied with the band
that Mr John Chilcott has invited?'

The ringers left England from Heathrow (then London) Airport on Saturday 2nd May,
seen off by their families and friends. Meanwhile *The Ringing World* gave them a great
send-off, Tom White (the Editor) gently unruffling some of the recent issues regarding
band representation and choice, and pointing out that this was a glorious era for change
ringing, meaning it would have been possible to select these ten people many times over
from elsewhere. He noted, too, that women were to be found 'in the front rank of Surprise
bands'. But as *The Ringing World* noted, 'it is the calibre of the men as ringers and
instructors and their ability to represent all that is best in English ringing that counts. They
are representative of the best we can offer.'

A high profile event

There was huge coverage for this event and the week was packed with an intensive programme of receptions, presentations, dinners, a TV appearance, radio coverage, visits to the British Embassy, the White House (including meeting Robert F Kennedy and family), the New York Opera Company, the Capitol Building, not to mention social events with their many hosts. Peter Staniforth was a keen amateur photographer and had a cine camera. In addition, it was important to have an enthusiastic scribe, George Pipe! The combination of Frank Price and George was a good choice to take part in a TV interview during the week.

Being involved in the opening of the bells during a marvellous week of celebration in Washington, each member of the band staying as valued UK visitors at some of the wonderful residences of the Cathedral community, made it one of the great ringing events of all time. A bit later when George Pipe talked to George Fearn, the most prolific peal ringer in history by 1964 (with over 1,900 under his belt) about his memorable ringing experiences, George remarked that Washington was without question his highlight.

First ringing

The opening touch on the first Sunday morning, three courses of Stedman Caters (followed by applause) was witnessed by about two hundred people in the ringing room, which fortunately is very expansive – it needed to be, given the size of audience! The lifts up to the ringing room were also kept busy. This was the introduction to what, for some, would be their second home during the week, spending three or four hours per day teaching people to ring on tied bells.

An LP record of the celebrations was put together and there are still people with copies today. This too was masterminded by Douglas Hughes, who also provided the commentary. English and American listeners would have felt this was being delivered by an English gentleman with an excellent speaking voice, ideal for the job! The covers featured a brief history of the project, cost $4,500 for a ring of ten bells, profiles of each of the ringers and interviews, the dedication ringing on Thursday 7th May and the inaugural peal on Saturday 9th May. The celebrations inside the tower at the end of the peal are recorded. The record sleeve stated 'the ensuing acclamation is included in this record from which the listener can gauge the enthusiasm and interest of the audience which throughout 3 ½ hours of continuous ringing was said to exceed 1,000 people.'

The peal – Saturday 9th May 1964

The inaugural peal itself was rung to a standard fixed-treble composition, relatively simple by today's standards – but it was hardly a time to experiment! David's composition 'The Washington peal' remains the only composition I know of to be solely associated with a tower. This was also the first peal on ten bells in North America. It was extremely hot and humid, with the temperature in the ringing chamber during the peal at around 92°F!

Shortly after finishing the peal, the band was bidding its farewell to their many friends from the week's activities and made a fairly hasty retreat from Washington in order to arrive at Groton at a reasonable time: catching the 8pm flight up to Boston, a mere 500 miles or so, arriving at 10pm to be met by two of the teachers and then driven back to Groton! Sunday service ringing with the boys, followed by lunch and then a peal of Cambridge Surprise Royal rung at the school chapel in the afternoon, followed by a quick snack and back to Boston Airport, then back to the UK overnight, arriving at London airport at 7am.

Establishing a band for the future

Eventually ringing-related matters in Washington calmed down and returned to normal. The decision was taken to teach two bands of ringers. The Whitechapel Guild, drawn from the National Cathedral Girls School and St Albans Boys School, grew rapidly and rang very regularly together. Teaching the adult Cathedral Ringing Society ringers, by contrast, meant progress

Washington DC, United States of America
National Episcopal Cathedral of
SS Peter & Paul
On Saturday, May 9, 1964
in 3hrs 25mins

A Peal of 5067 Stedman Caters
Tenor 32cwt 4lb in D

Peter J Staniforth	Treble
John Chilcott	2
Harold N Pitstow	3
John Freeman	4
George E Fearn	5
Norman Chaddock	6
George W Pipe	7
Frank C Price	8
Wilfrid F Moreton	9
Harry Parkes	Tenor

Composed by David E Parsons
Conducted by John Chilcott

was slower, with many more broken stays! There was never a shortage of ringers – for example, when Fred Price arrived in October 1964, he had 63 students in total and after four weeks they could raise and lower the bells, ring rounds and stand at either stroke. Indeed the girls rang the touch of Grandsire Triples as a farewell in February 1965. They were the core group who formed the basis of the band. Further ringers have been consistently developed and many have continued to ring at Washington over the years. Continuity of ringing in Washington has been assisted by a number of people moving to live in the city or for a more temporary stay, who have had the time to help teach ringing at Washington Cathedral and also at the Washington Old Post Office Tower. Tony Kench's name comes to mind also – he rang at Washington Cathedral for several years in the early 1980s, calling a number of peals and quarters as the local band progressed. There were plenty of others too.

Ringing World reprint

The 12th June 1964 issue of *The Ringing World* featured 'Ten Men Went to Sow', a Washington Supplement written by the scribe for the trip, George Pipe, and a great read it is too. He captured the spirit of the occasion from the band leaving London Airport on Saturday 2nd May waved off by families, through an exhausting, though fulfilling, week of engagements, the dedication itself and the inaugural peal through to the rapid visit to Groton and then flying from Boston back to London to be greeted by families again. As George put it 'thus ending the greatest of Ringing Adventures'.

It wasn't the end as far as *The Ringing World* readership was concerned! In the issue of 4th September 1964, the journal advised that 'in view of the interest on both sides of

*Ringing at Washington Cathedral, Christmas 2019. The ringers span the generations.
All are Whitechapel Guild Alumni, all having learnt to ring at Washington
Cathedral, and the photo shows the spacious Cathedral ringing room.
Left to right: Quilla Roth, Beth Sinclair, Ann Martin, Rick Dirksen, Cecily Rock and
Haley Barnett. In the background on the left is Becky Joyce and Rick's wife Libby,
seated next to their daughter-in-law, Lucy*

the Atlantic in the dedication of Washington Cathedral bells there has been a reprint [these were unheard of] of the issue of 12th June and also the supplement. Usual price. With supplement 3d.'

At the end of March 1965, the Washington band reconvened and rang a peal of Stedman Caters at Leicester Cathedral. This, by invitation of Peter Staniforth, was by the same band standing in the same order, with the Washington composition conducted by John Chilcott. Even the time of the peal was the same, three hours and 25 minutes!

Back again in 1990

Peter Staniforth, Frank Price and George, all from the 1964 band, returned to Washington in September 1990 for a weekend of celebrations associated with the completion of the Cathedral. Many ringers from the UK and elsewhere outside of the United States had contributed to the development of change ringing in the United States during the first 25 years since the dedication and they all came for what was a massive celebration. Matters commenced on the Thursday with a National Cathedral Celebration dinner attended by 900 people including the ringers with an audio visual presentation 'A Dream Realised' covering the 83 years of the construction of the Cathedral. On the Friday, a Festival Evensong and a Litany of Thanksgiving for the Founders and Builders was held, attended by 700 people, followed by a peal of Grandsire Caters. On the Saturday, the final stone was set in the presence of President George Bush, with peals of Yorkshire Royal at the Cathedral and Plain Bob Royal at the Old Post Office Tower.

Finally, on Sunday was the service of consecration of the completed Cathedral in which the ringers participated fully. George recalled a particularly stressful element in the visit to Washington in 1990 to celebrate 25 years since the bells were dedicated. For the Sunday Service Choral Mattins there was to be a course of Stedman Caters on handbells rung from the crossing, a nerve-wracking experience. Frank Price and George were keen on ringing Grandsire but the three Washingtonians said they were more comfortable with Stedman. Stedman it was! Frank Price, scribe on this occasion, observed that 'to be part of such a marvellous and unique service can do no other than leave an everlasting impression in everyone's mind'. Both Frank and George did their bit over the years, making a significant contribution to the development of ringing at Washington by hosting parties of young ringers from the Whitechapel Guild (Washington National Cathedral School) every summer and arranging a programme of ringing for them in the UK.

The 50th anniversary in 2014

A wonderful account of the 50th anniversary of the dedication of the bells at Washington Cathedral can be found in *The Ringing World* of 5th September 2014 (issue 5393), one of the best accounts of a major occasion in the world of bells and bellringing I have ever read. Sadly, George was not well enough to make the trip, but he was involved in a discussion panel in the Cathedral's lecture hall to discuss the dedication ceremony and early days of ringing at the Cathedral. Before the panel, the group was treated to a telephone call from George, one of the only two members of the original dedication band still alive, the other being John Chilcott. 'If you can't be there then be important'! George was disappointed that his health prevented him from being in Washington in person, but he lucidly recalled his memories of 1964 and congratulated the Washington ringers on the achievements since then.

That 12th June 2014 issue of the *RW* was filled with good things and great historical perspective. Rick Dirksen, who led the Whitechapel Guild for over forty years, wrote about the very early days before the dedication in May 1964 when most of those who were learning to ring knew nothing about it, the inspiration provided by 'the ten' who came over from the UK, with their diverse skills, noting that 'by the time they left, Washington ringers had heard world-class ringing, but through intensive media coverage the entire community had gained a real understanding of the significance of this new addition to the cultural life of the city'.

'Ten Men Went to Sow' lives on as **the** definitive account of Washington. Rick refers to 'the ebullience, humour and enthusiasm of Frank Price and George Pipe'. Richard Offen recalls reading the article, and in particular George's account of the first Sunday morning touch, capturing his imagination:

> *"The first touch was a somewhat nerve-racking experience but John Chilcott took everything quietly and organised us with the minimum of fuss. The three course touch of Stedman Caters went like clockwork and the applause at the end was tremendous, the first time any of us remember being clapped after tower bells."*

No doubt many others on both sides of the pond have been inspired by his article. The value of the work done by 'the ten' in 1964 is appreciated and lives on.

Some Washington ringing history

Rick Dirksen, whose father Wayne held senior roles at the cathedral back to as far as the 1940s, commented of George Pipe:

> *"All of us knew and loved George for many, many years, and, to the extent that the Tower Dedication Band was singularly responsible for bringing ringing into our lives and supporting us ever since, we remain deeply indebted to him for the thousands of hours of joy (including well over 1,000 peals between us) that ringing has brought into our lives."*

Three Washingtonians – Quilla Roth, Ann Martin and Rick Dirksen – were there at the start in 1964 and are still practising ringers. Quilla has been a regular ringer all the way through and was in the inaugural group of Washington CG girls who began learning on tower bells under Fred Price in October 1964.

Washington should be proud of what has been achieved since 1964. For example, more than 400 high school girls have been introduced to ringing through the Whitechapel Guild (WCG), the change ringing organisation started at the National Cathedral School in 1964 and named after the foundry which cast the bells. The NCS is a girl's school associated with Washington Cathedral. Many of those who learnt to ring went on to ring quarter peals and 27 of them have rung peals. Their collective peal total as a group is over 1,500. This is commendable and represents a very strong teaching record.

The Washington Ringing Society (WRS) was created in 1983 when the Old Post Office Bells were installed, superseding the Cathedral Ringing Society, so that both towers would be rung by the same ringing organisation, with close coordination of ringing between the two towers. It is sometimes referred to as "the adult band" when talking with WCG girls about it, but it's open to all ages.

Chapter 12

Outside the belfry

A lover of the arts

Perhaps understandably, most people connected George with bellringing only. The reality is he had many other interests. He didn't stand and watch, he got involved. His younger brother Rod was keenly interested in astronomy (witness Orion, Rigel and other names given to particularly difficult methods), photography and gardening. George, by contrast, was always a lover of art in many of its forms. At school, he was able to study the history of art, majoring in church architecture – he confessed to being an ecclesiological 'nut'. Of course, this artistic interest was a marvellous adjunct to ringing and the two complemented each other in many instances. He counted himself very fortunate to live in East Anglia, which has a tremendous density of ancient churches, and to have had the opportunity to visit all its churches, some 1,150 of them, as well as 3,000 churches worldwide.

He was adept in a variety of mediums, pen and ink, pencil, pastels and watercolour combined with illuminated lettering. Many people, the writer included, have work by George in their towers or homes, nearly always as gifts – he was very generous with his artistic talents, not to mention his time. He was also an avid book collector, especially books on Norfolk and Suffolk, the City of London, the work of Victorian architects, sport (particularly cricket) and topography.

He was a lover of poetry too, particularly the war poets, A E Housman and Sir John Betjeman (a great lover of bells), whom George was privileged to meet two or three years before he died. Church postcards were a big collecting category for him. Although much of the collection had been given to other people over time, he had what was regarded as the largest collection of postcards of East Anglian churches, over 3,000, with some in duplicate. My mother was born at Hindringham, Norfolk, and he once gave me a postcard of the church, a duplicate I guess. And of course he was a stamp collector, as one might expect!

At one time, George's collection of church postcards numbered 22,000. With the exception of those of Suffolk and Norfolk churches, most of these were given away during his lifetime to libraries or people. One collection of which he was particularly proud was the 514 Suffolk and 661 Norfolk postcards of church exteriors, over 100 of which are of ruined churches and thus a little more difficult to obtain. These collections took 51 and 57 years respectively to complete and are believed to be the only complete sets in existence.

Artistic talent – the written and spoken word

George was well known for his calligraphy/pen and ink work, which enabled him to undertake commissions for peal and memorial boards. He was a member of the Ancient Society of College Youths since 1955 and in recent years a tradition has been established whereby members with 50, 60 or 70 years' service are presented with commemorative certificates at the Society's annual dinner in November, with the relevant name beautifully written on the certificate by George. This is a new and much valued part of College Youths membership, which attracts many out of London members to annual dinners – nothing better than recognition from one's peers!

Andrew Wilby, a former Hon Secretary of the Ancient Society of College Youths (1982–92), commented in 2019:

> *"George inherited his love for the College Youths from his father Jim, who would have been Master had World War 2 not ordained otherwise. He has rung many peals over the years with the Society, made a number of very generous donations to the Library and Archives and of course in recent times, become the scribe for the 50 years membership certificates that are presented every year. He has become an ASCY national treasure!"*

George's artistic talent, the results of which he shared so generously, meant he completed over one hundred pen and ink drawings and fifty watercolours, mostly for presentations or gifts and sometimes commissions, the latter usually not chargeable. He did plenty of calligraphy, typically with illuminated drawing, either for peal boards or framed records, often for friends. For example, Linda and I have a pen and ink drawing of Great St Mary's Church, Cambridge, which was a wedding gift, and a wonderful framed record of three significant peals. I treasure these, further examples of George's remarkable generosity and a rare skill, so freely given to me and to many others as well. I know we are not alone in this. There were the congratulatory phone calls and letters or cards, scores of them – such a prolific letter writer. Then, of course, there were his speaking and writing skills, which people commented upon for decades. These always caught the mood and spirit of the occasion and are mentioned elsewhere. We keep talking about these skills!

Paul Mounsey and David Dearnley, prominent London ringers, develop this theme in their tribute:

> *"George was someone whose name we have known from early on in our ringing lives, and he and Diana were always a continuing inspiration and loving friends. Ringing with George the bell-ringer was always a pleasure, his performance rarely less than immaculate. George the friend was characterised by his kindness, embracing people for who and what they are, his encouragement, and his wise words.*
>
> *"We very much share George the historian's interest in the events, personalities, and connections which have made ringing what it is today. Indeed we are privileged to have prints and watercolours by George the artist, gifts over the years: a daily pleasure to see and often admired by visitors.*
>
> *"On a recent visit to St Edmundsbury Cathedral we found the south aisle occupied by an exhibition of post-cards and photographs of all the churches in the Diocese. The captions were beautifully hand-written and the pictures carefully grouped by Deanery. It was no surprise that George had created and curated it.*

"This encapsulated George perfectly: his love of the Suffolk landscape and its historic churches, their towers whether magnificent or meagre, with or without bells, his eye for the visual image, and his generosity, all in a historic Christian place."

Cumberlands pen-and-ink anniversary sketches

When the Society of Royal Cumberland Youths, of which Diana is a member, celebrated its 250th anniversary in 1997, George was asked to design a trio of pen and ink sketches of St Martin-in-the-Fields, Spitalfields and Shoreditch to mark the occasion (*see the central pages*). These were very popular and raised a considerable amount of money. When you live in Ipswich, popping down to London for some sketching requires some preparation and considerable commitment. Once again George gave of his time freely and generously.

... and some 'Tales'

Michael Uphill's 'Tales from the London County Crypt', at times a seriously irreverent though never unkind review of The London County Association, was first serialised in *The Ringing World* back in 2007–8 and the book was released in September 2010. Michael comments on George:

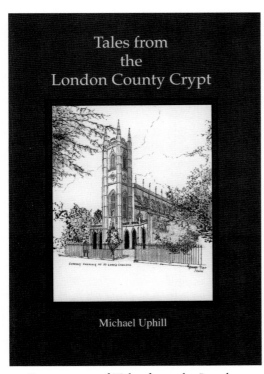

Front cover of Tales from the London County Crypt, *with George's drawing of St Luke's, Chelsea*

"Some of us who have been about in ringing for a long time (I've just completed sixty years) may have rung with several thousand ringers. Some of us are lucky enough to remain in touch with some of them, perhaps just by bumping into each other on the odd occasion over the years (sometimes searching one's brain forlornly for a long-forgotten name!), sometimes by ringing regularly together for long periods in local, quarter peal or peal bands; but, possibly in many cases, meeting up in something arranged by them or by a mutual friend at something rather less than regular intervals.

"Some of them we are lucky enough to be able to count as friends. One such was George Pipe, who I met and rang with probably on only a few dozen occasions over fifty years or so but yet always seemed to find the time to greet me as an old friend, with an extraordinary knack of knowing exactly what I have been up to since

we last met. That he would be so interested in me is truly humbling. I give just one example of his generosity of time and talent which is self explanatory. It was partially through George's encouragement that I went ahead with the publication of "Tales" which raised nearly £2,500 for the Surrey Association Bell Restoration Fund. George also very kindly gave me the original (now much-treasured) drawing complete with mounting instructions, etc!

"At the time 'Tales of the London County Crypt' was appearing as a series in The Ringing World, *George rang me up and very kindly offered to produce a pen and ink drawing of my choice, in the event of the series being published as a book. I chose St Luke's Chelsea as this was the first 'London County' tower I visited in January 1961. The front cover of the book, drawn by George in August and September 2010, is the result. I'm immensely indebted to him for his generosity. Every now and again I'd get a letter in the post with George's distinctive handwriting on the envelope, immediately buoying me up for what I knew was going to be a lovely little message!"*

Always speaking for bells and ringing

George was a first-class public speaker. Joe Roast notes he has witnessed some of George's many talents including his artistic skills and believes him to be the best after dinner speaker he has ever heard, with an easy style and thorough knowledge of his subject. He uses minimal notes and has given some two hundred talks on the history of bells and bellringing, usually in a fundraising context. Suffolk is still a land of mediaeval churches, mostly with old wooden bell frames, and since the end of the Second World War has developed a proud record of bell restoration, approaching two hundred restorations. George made a considerable contribution to bell restoration work in many parishes. For example, he valued the work of Revd Harry Edwards very highly. 'Harry must hold a record of some sort, having restored five rings of bells in his parishes, Marlesford, Parham, Hacheston, Campsey Ashe and Reydon-by-Southwold'.

A love of writing

George wrote countless articles for all sorts of publications. For *The Ringing World*, he wrote two front-page articles in recent years, one on the one hundredth anniversary of the first peal of Surprise Maximus at St Mary-le-Tower, Ipswich, the other a wonderful review of Maureen Cubitt's excellent book 'The Bells Told – celebrating 300 years', regarding the ringers and ringing at St Peter Mancroft Norwich in conjunction with the first ever peal, rung there in 1715. He co-authored *Suffolk Bells and Bellringing* (with Roy Tricker) and *Bells and Bellringing in Suffolk* (with Ranald Clouston) and written some 22 book reviews covering the Johnston family (of Gillett and Johnston fame) and other 'County' books on ringers, clocks, bells, towers, etc.

George's writing always had character, unmistakeably 'him' rather than anybody else as the author. As well as having the ability to paint the picture via several media (as outlined elsewhere in this book) he had the priceless ability to paint the picture in words in his own individual style.

Freemasonry

As a youngster George knew nothing about Freemasonry. When he went to Australia, he didn't even realise that four of the St Paul's Melbourne band belonged – Jack Roper, Howard Impey (Essex), Cecil Pearson (Oxon) and Tom Bennett (Surrey) – but he sensed that there was something special about these men and in 1961 he was proposed by Jack Roper, seconded by Ray Minchinton, Ken Minchinton's father. Ray was originally from Bendigo, Victoria, and was a past master of Caulfield Lodge.

Following election, George's Lodge was Syndal No 822, in the province of Victoria, and he remembered clearly entering the temple for the first time and seeing two fine framed photographs: Pietro Annigoni's painting of HM Queen Elizabeth 2 and another of Lord Stradbroke, Grand Master of Victoria. Stradbroke is 20 miles from Grundisburgh in Suffolk, which made George feel at home!

On George and Diana's return to England in 1963, he joined St Luke's Lodge number 225, Ipswich, and later the Lodge of Wisdom number 8333, in Ipswich, with his boyhood friend Frank Price. George very much enjoyed his Freemasonry, which he said strengthened his Christian faith while his Christian faith enhanced his Freemasonry. Under the Provincial Grand Mastership of Robert Tile, who interestingly was George's

Head of House at Woodbridge School in the 1940s, he was made a Provincial Chaplain, given Grand Lodge honours by the Marquess of Northampton and held the post for thirteen years. As well as being a great privilege, he found the role very fulfilling. He was also a past Prelate of the Rose Croix Lodge and a member of the Royal Arch. Through these connections, he met and worked with some fine men from all walks of life.

George commented that there is a lot of misunderstanding about Freemasonry. It is not a secret society but a society with secrets based on the principles of brotherly Love, relief of the poor and needy and speaking the truth. Its tenets are faith, hope and charity and all that can and does mean. Freemasonry, as essentially a benevolent society, gives millions of pounds worldwide to needy causes. Masons admire and share the same motto as the Rotarians, 'service before self'.

Some readers will know there is a Ringers' Lodge, Clavis Lodge 8585, formed in the 1970s. Clavis ensures close contact with parish churches and

Freemasonry – George as Provincial Grand Chaplain for Suffolk and Past Assistant Grand Chaplain of England
(June 2004)

cathedrals. The National Autistic Society, with which George and Diana have had a significant involvement since the 1970s, when their daughter Alison was diagnosed with severe autism, has benefited from Masonic giving and George in turn had the opportunity in open Lodge to give talks on this and many other topics.

Chapter 13

The loss of Bristol Maximus, the Beresford family and 'Wilfred'

'Loss' of Bristol Maximus at Ipswich in the 1930s

By coincidence, George had a little connection of his own with Bristol Maximus. The St Mary-le-Tower band up until the outbreak of World War 2 had rung peals in twelve different Maximus methods. The band's main conductors were George E Symonds and Charles J Sedgley, a mantle they had inherited from the earlier St Mary-le-Tower band going back to the first ever peal of Cambridge Maximus rung in 1908. The conductors at that time were James Motts and William L Catchpole.

Their next new method at Ipswich was to have been Bedford Surprise Maximus, but George Symonds, ever the innovator, was fascinated by the challenge of Bristol Maximus, having been sent a blue line of it by George Baker of Brighton. Sadly, at around this time there was a disastrous chimney fire at George and Eva Symonds' house in Ipswich and nearly all George's ringing papers were destroyed. However, of the little that was left there was a letter from George Baker with a blueline of Bristol Maximus already annotated by George Symonds, but the rest of the Baker/Symonds letters had gone. War was imminent and by 1945 the St Mary-le-Tower band was either too old or members had passed on. Bristol Maximus with a local band at Ipswich would not be a realistic possibility until some forty years later.

Found again

The first peals in the method were achieved at Leicester Cathedral on 22nd May 1950, followed by another, also at Leicester Cathedral in 1951, both under the conductorship of Harold J Poole, the leading twelve-bell conductor of the time. It wasn't until the late 1960s that Bristol Maximus would be practised again. No one quite knows why it took so long, but from *The Ringing World* in the 1960s it is clear that most peals on twelve were still Cambridge or Yorkshire Maximus or Stedman Cinques. Certainly peals in 'Londinium-over' methods were rung from the very early 1960s and these were followed in the mid- to late 1960s by multi-spliced (up to 110 methods) peals of Maximus.

Presumably Bristol was deemed to be too difficult until it was rediscovered and practised in 1968/9 by the Reading/High Wycombe band under David Hilling and the Cumberlands under Dennis Beresford and Derek Sibson. The take up of the method was slow and it wasn't until the mid-1970s that it really became an established method.

The Beresford family

George and Diana's relationship with the Beresford family was a very strong one from the late 1950s. In some ways it was strange and certainly unlikely that the relationship would develop because they were members of 'opposing' societies in London who, for the most part, had little to do with each other. Both were prominent members of these societies, George from the Ancient Society of College Youths and Dennis from the Society of Royal Cumberland Youths. Most importantly, they were from a newer breed, visualising a future unfettered by old fashioned ideas from the past that would no longer work.

Strangely, it wasn't until 22nd October 1966, at Coggeshall, Essex, with an otherwise Society of Royal Cumberland Youths band, that George

Dennis Beresford is considered to be the principal architect and leader of the Society of Royal Cumberland Youths' resurgence as a modern progressive ringing society in the 1960s and mid-1970s, when he was Master for fourteen years. He was the driving force behind the Shoreditch restoration in 1968 and also the initiative in 1970 where the fine Gillett and Johnston eight from Clapham Park were transferred to Christ Church, Spitalfields.

and Dennis rang their first peal together. (Despite becoming very good friends, over their lives they rang just ten peals together.) One wonders why that first peal hadn't happened earlier, since the two already knew each other through Central Council membership and had built a strong relationship. But both were family men of similar age, leaders, both energetic types who led from the front. Both were fine ringers who got things done and also had other priorities – Dennis with Shoreditch and Spitalfields, George with several initiatives in Australia and, later, Suffolk Guild and St Mary-le-Tower. The Suffolk Guild, for whom George held various offices including Ringing Master for five years, was undergoing a significant rebuilding and resurgence. Dennis was Master of the Society of Royal Cumberland Youths for much of this time and masterminded during the 1960s and 1970s what is generally acknowledged as one of the great rebuilding jobs in ringing, creating high quality bands of ringers, but also leading the largely DIY projects at Shoreditch and Spitalfields.

*Past Masters of the Society of Royal Cumberland Youths, at the Society's 250th
anniversary dinner at the Middle Temple on 6th September 1997.
(left to right) Back row: Graham A Duke (1980–1), Stanley Jenner (1977–8),
John S Barnes (1979), Simon J Davies (1993–4), Douglas J Beaumont (1995),
Ian H Oram (1984), Derek E Sibson (1969–70); Front row: Stephanie J Pattenden
(1982–3), Alan Regin (1987–9 and 1996–7), Dennis Beresford (1960–8 and 1972–6),
Edwin A Barnett (1971), Linda M Garton (1990–2)*

Modernising *The Ringing World?*

George and Dennis's compelling desire to modernise *The Ringing World* in the late 1960s
caused considerable controversy; some Central Council members almost came to blows
at one meeting and the two subsequently resigned from *The Ringing World* committee
in 1968. No doubt they were seen by the old brigade who had sat on the committee for
years and resisted change as 'enfants terribles'. They were ahead of their time, young
men impatient for change generating some interesting reactions from the old guard who
wouldn't embrace change sufficiently quickly, or at all! Both served nearly twenty years on
the Central Council, throughout most of the 1960s and 1970s, so were very serious, and
committed change would come, but not quickly enough, and the establishment who'd
been running *The Ringing World* for years was averse to change.

Ian G Campbell, then from the Beverley area, recalls:

*"I first came across George at a CCCBR meeting in about the late 1960s. Although
not a member of the Council at that time, just a spectator in the public gallery, I
witnessed the most fearsome argument taking place concerning* The Ringing World.
*George and Dennis Beresford wanted some radical changes and set about the then
Convenor of* The Ringing World *– a Mr R S Anderson. It was so heated that the then*

President of the Council, Revd Gilbert Thurlow, called for an early lunch in an effort to avoid a "war"! I realised then what a formidable and forthright character George was in stature, passion and expression."

The Beresford family came from the Midlands. Dennis, his twin brother Peter, and his sister Joan were taught to ring at Lichfield Cathedral. All moved south to the London area and all joined the Cumberlands. Dennis married Mary Ward and they had four children. Dennis found the Cumberlands at a very low ebb and set himself the task of rebuilding the Society. A number of others were involved in assisting him, but he was the prime mover and leader of the largely DIY restorations at Shoreditch and Spitalfields in the late 1960s and early 1970s and established the high standard of ringing that was demanded. Not averse to upsetting people either, if this was what had to happen to the benefit of the cause. However, Dennis was comfortable getting involved in the upsetting, much more so than George was! Dennis's reputation for being difficult was overstated. He was very able, single-minded and focused. He knew the best way was Dennis's way and how he wanted to achieve it. He understood the need to develop his people, to whom he was intensely loyal.

Under Dennis there were major innovations on the ringing front, involving many members of the SRCY both in London and elsewhere through what we today call 'theme' days – for example, six peals of 'Pitman's 9' in a day in 1968, two peals of Bristol Maximus by different SRCY bands in a day in 1969, and a further two peals of Bristol Maximus with a mixed SRCY/ASCY band, George, John Mayne and ten Cumberlands. The latter gave George Pipe and Howard Egglestone the opportunity to ring their first blows of Bristol Maximus. George recalled the somewhat nervous train journey from Ipswich to London on the morning of the peal as he and Howard polished up the method! It hardly seems possible now, but this was over fifty years ago.

Dennis saw the value of co-operation and working with others. He was a big builder of bridges between the Cumberlands and the College Youths in the 1960s, at a time when relations were often fractured with one society refusing to allow the other to ring at its towers – this seems impossible now. The result of this co-operation was the 1972 Central Council meeting in London, jointly hosted by the two societies – the previous Central Council meeting in London had been in 1948.

A much shortened ringing career

Sadly Dennis's ringing career was cut short in its prime. In 1976, at the age of 42, he contracted a mystery virus and subsequent surgery to correct the complications reduced him to a wheelchair for the rest of his life. As a man of many interests – business, current affairs, classical music, politics, the church, fine wine and of course ringing – he kept busy. Having retired to Devon in 1991, he was able to further develop his church interests at local, deanery and diocesan level. From a ringing perspective, he ran practices from his wheelchair from where he helped teach – successfully – some of his grandchildren to ring! Alison Waterson and Hilary Beresford, Dennis and Mary's daughters, are very active peal ringers. Nick and Tom, Alison's sons, have both rung peals. Tom has rung several peals on Exeter Cathedral tenor, one a few months before Dennis died, and he has turned it in to

Maximus. George was close to the family, not just Dennis, and gave memorable eulogies at the funeral services of Norman Summerhayes (husband of Joan) in 1998 at Egham, Joan in 2007 at Worcester Cathedral, and that of Dennis himself in 2011 at Huish.

Some notable twelve-bell peals and a great friendship

On a hot afternoon, 23rd July 1966, the College Youths rang three peals of Stedman Cinques in the City of London for the City of London Festival. George rang in the peal at St Mary-le- Bow, Cheapside, his first peal there. Another College Youths peal, again Stedman Cinques, in March 1967 was George's first peal at Waltham Abbey. It's worth noting that while such peals are commonplace these days, in the 1960s ringers were less mobile and there was less opportunity. Travelling from Ipswich to Waltham Abbey and back and including a 3½ hour peal was a very full day. For George, the mid-1960s through to the 1970s was a golden period for ringing twelve-bell peals, some highly noteworthy, for example the first peal of Belfast Surprise Maximus at High Wycombe in September 1970, Londinium Surprise Maximus rung silent and non conducted (a serious undertaking) at London St Giles Cripplegate in February 1972, Lincolnshire Surprise Maximus at Shoreditch in March 1977, and 14 Spliced Surprise Maximus (top end of the range at the time) at St Mary-le-Tower Ipswich in October 1980.

When the band for the peal of Cambridge Surprise Maximus (Bob Smith on the tenor) assembled at Worcester Cathedral in October 1972, a fearsome prospect would have awaited them. Since 1928, when the modern Taylor twelve, tenor 48cwt, were installed, they were hung in an 1869 oak frame which also housed the pre-1928 ring. This sits on top of a pitch pine structure called the 'wigwam'. It meant that in terms of practical ringing many of the bells were at the upper end of the difficulty spectrum with few bells going as well as one might expect for bells of their weight. In recent years some DIY efforts by the ringers have been made to improve the go of the bells.

Wilfred Williams ('Himself')

The name Wilfred Williams became prevalent in George's peal book between 1968 and 1978 with quite a number of mostly twelve bell peals in new towers. Wilfred was born in 1905 and grew up on a hill farm in South Wales, the eldest of six children. At the age of twelve he was driving a horse-drawn milk float before going to school; later he worked as a pipe fitter. The farm could not support eight people and this led to his leaving South Wales, where he was already an established ringer capable of conducting peals to go to London in 1929. Initially, he worked on the docks in Deptford, later for the London Electricity Board and then on the

Diana Pipe, Wilfred Williams and Gillian Pipe (now Fielden) at Wilfred's 80th birthday

London to Brighton railway electrification. During the war he worked in the aircraft industry in Cheltenham, joining Cheltenham Chess Club while he was there, before moving back to London.

Wilfred was a ringer at St Paul's Cathedral for many years and also served as Master of the Ancient Society of College Youths, whom he represented on the Central Council of Church Bell ringers for sixteen years. Although from a very humble background, he was an able man and a real achiever, creating many different records during his long ringing career, the *piece de resistance* of which was ringing peals on all (at the time 76) twelve-bell rings, including a total of 20 peals on the big twelves: Liverpool Cathedral, Exeter Cathedral, St Paul's Cathedral and York Minster. He also travelled extensively and rang peals in Canada and the United States. He took part in Great Adventure 2, to Australia and New Zealand in 1965.

He was undoubtedly *the* character in London ringing for much of that time: broad Welsh, sometimes difficult to understand, witty and the master of the one-liner. He was a very capable ringer and for many he was one of those people they wanted to keep on the right side of. George's peals

ANCIENT SOCIETY OF COLLEGE YOUTHS
CITY OF LONDON EC4
At the Cathedral Church of St Paul
On Wednesday, July 1, 1969
in 3 hours and 56 minutes:

A Peal of 5042 Cambridge Surprise Maximus

Tenor 62cwt in B flat

Wilfred Williams	1
Tudor P Edwards	2
Albert M Tyler	3
Basil Jones	4
Andrew N Stubbs	5
Kenneth J Hesketh	6
George W Pipe	7
Alan R Patterson	8
George E Fearn	9
Wilfrid F Moreton	10
John A Anderson	11
Peter Border	12

Composed by Roderick W Pipe
Conducted by Wilfred Williams
For the investiture of HRH Price Charles as the Prince of Wales
Rung by members of the Ancient Society of College Youths.

with Wilfred were mainly in the ten year period 1968 to 1977, and many of these broke new ground for him, for example those at Liverpool Cathedral and St Paul's Cathedral.

In the 1960s opportunities to ring peals on the 'big four' rings of twelve – Liverpool, Exeter, St Paul's Cathedral and York Minster – were very rare. The Liverpool Cathedral peal was followed less than nine months later, in July 1969, with a peal at St Paul's Cathedral, a real treat since at the time very few people apart from St Paul's Cathedral Guild members had rung peals there.

Wilfred also organised peals of Stedman Cinques at York Minster in 1969, at London St Martin-in-the-Fields in 1972 (a Central Council peal, of phenomenal rarity value at the time), and Sheffield Cathedral in 1974; and Cambridge Surprise Maximus at Worcester Cathedral in 1975 (Tim Collins on the tenor) which was George's 500th peal. By all accounts Wilfred's 80th birthday celebrations in London were memorable!

When Wilfred died in June 1986, Phil Corby quoted this extract from The Dean of St Paul's July notes: "Wilfred Williams died at his Lambeth home last month, a faithful bellringer since 1929, a witty individualist Welshman, a real original. He was remembered at the Eucharist on St John the Baptist day and will be cherished with a twinkle by his fellow

**ANCIENT SOCIETY OF
COLLEGE YOUTHS**
LIVERPOOL
At the Cathedral Church of Christ
On Saturday, October 12, 1968
in 4 hours and 14 minutes:

A Peal of 5019 Stedman Cinques

Tenor 82cwt 11lb in A Flat

Tudor P Edwards	1
John Chilcott	2
Albert M Tyler	3
Basil Jones	4
Edward P Duffield	5
George W Pipe	6
John S Mason	7
Kenneth J Hesketh	8
Wilfrid F Moreton	9
Clifford A Barron	10
Peter Border	11
Wilfred Williams and	12
Walter Allman	

Composed by Charles W Roberts
Conducted by John Chilcott
The first peal of Stedman on the bells, the heaviest
ring of bells in the world, tenor 82 cwt.

ringers." I never rang a peal with Wilfred, but I was privileged to ring in the peal in his memory, Stedman Cinques at St Mary-le-Tower. A measure of Wilfred's popularity was that after he died his anniversaries were invariably remembered by his ringing friends in London and further afield, with footnotes often referring to 'himself'.

(Thanks to Bill Butler, who acts as a consultant to the CC Biographies Committee, for his very useful article on Wilfred Williams in *The Ringing World*, 23rd September 2016 p.967.)

Chapter 14

The remarkable story
of St Mary-le-Tower, Ipswich

Background and history

Apart from Diana and his family, the love of George's life for some sixty years was St Mary-le-Tower, which is the civic church of Ipswich. This is where they worshipped. This is where George first saw change ringing practised, and to the highest standard, by the pre-war St Mary-le-Tower Company, an experience which so influenced him. George served two spells as churchwarden. He and Diana were ringers here since 1963, over 55 years, and she is still a member of the band. The place was very close to their hearts. But when they returned from Australia in 1963, the ringing at St Mary-le-Tower was down to Minor on the middle six and occasionally Triples or Major on the back eight. To make matters worse, the church had a seven-point restoration plan and the restoration of the bells was bottom of that list! There seemed little hope of getting the bells restored, until Canon Geoffrey Tarris arrived in 1972.

Canon Tarris had been at Bungay, North Suffolk, and George already knew him from his diocesan connections. There was no time to be wasted – George went up to Bungay to see him to explain the bells situation at St Mary-le-Tower before too many other priorities landed in his in-tray. Canon Geoffrey Tarris would prove to be an important player. When George went to Bungay to share his dilemma with him before he arrived at St Mary-le-Tower he was told, 'of course we will get the bells restored', with some caveats given the seven-point plan, and eventually it happened. Despite the glorious history of ringing at St Mary-le-Tower, particularly from 1880 to 1939, the installation by the 1960s was effectively worn out – 330 peals had been rung on them, a candidate for one of the poorest twelves in the country. They were a mixed lot that had been progressively augmented from five in 1553, from eight to ten in 1845, and from ten to twelve (with a new tenor and treble!) in 1866 and virtually untouched since then. The need for restoration was critical.

Thirteen years of commitment

George decided to take on the restoration challenge at a time when the likelihood of success was not particularly favourable. It turned out to be a thirteen-year commitment, but it did eventually come to fruition in 1976, with the installation of the excellent 35cwt ring of twelve that ringers enjoy today. He did something which at the time (or, for many of us, even today) would have been considered by some as almost reckless – he made a donation of £1,000, cheque on the table, accompanied by a little theatricality and passion no doubt! Anyway it helped get things moving forward and later, much later, in 1976, the job was completed. Progress was assisted by a large legacy to St Mary-le-Tower which was to be used for the seven–point restoration plan, leaving a manageable amount to be raised. Canon Tarris advocated that this sum be used for the bells project. And George was still only halfway through his 25 years as St Mary-le-Tower as ringing master!

1976 and a new 35cwt Taylor twelve

The dedication of the new twelve at St Mary-le-Tower, Ipswich in 1976 represented the culmination of thirteen years of effort for George and his fellow fundraisers. The task then was to build a new generation of twelve-bell ringers over the next few years. George's view was that the only way to develop a truly local band for Ipswich and the area that would ring largely as a band on Sundays and practice nights, would be to train new and existing ringers who had not previously had the opportunity to ring on twelve. This plan was very successful indeed as the town's ringers got behind the initiative and were willing to learn new skills. In the late 1970s George noted that Ipswich, after so many years in the twelve-bell wilderness, was becoming one of the centres in East Anglia.

The new ring created a light eight, the front eight of the twelve, which has been very well utilised, with around 125 peals rung in the forty or so years since the restoration. Most of these have enabled local ringers to expand their repertoire, with new names coming into the peal records and many 'firsts', which are always good for the health of ringing in Suffolk. There has been considerable growth in twelve-bell ringing at St Mary-le-Tower over this time as well.

More to be done

For financial reasons, the 1976 project did not provide a completely new modern Taylor twelve, so in 1999 some further Millennium-focused work was carried out. Following a generous bequest by Dr Ronald Jones the 5th was recast, and the 8th retuned. Bells 9, 10 & 11 were replaced with bells cast to a heavier weight. The old 9th went to Australia to form the Tenor of a ring of eight in the key of F#. The old 10th is hung in the tower as the 'passing' bell and the old 11th is also hung in the tower as the Sanctus bell.

Acoustics

Most twelve-bell towers with modern bell installations (there are now around 130) have the bells hung at one level in the bell frame. Sometimes in a tower of smaller dimensions most of the bells will be hung on a lower tier with some of the lighter bells hung above the rest on an upper tier. Without getting too technical, the new installation at St Mary-le-Tower reversed this! In terms of acoustics and ease of ringing it means that the lighter bells, being lower in the tower, are much clearer than in many other installations. On twelve bells clarity bell-for-bell is everything and a key factor in generating good ringing. The heavier bells are much more resonant because of their weight and they too remain clearly audible to the ringers.

This was George's idea and after some discussion with Paul Taylor, whose last twelve-bell job this was, they decided to take this route. There was always a possibility of something being sacrificed by taking this action and at St Mary-le-Tower it was the ability to hear all twelve bells clearly outside the tower, still a work in progress.

Creating a new twelve-bell centre

As noted above, George firmly believed there was scope to return the tower to its glory days of pre-1939 and he was determined that this could be done by building up a local band and establishing St Mary-le-Tower as a major centre of

A man on a mission – again! George outside St Mary-le-Tower with the new bells for the Millennium

ringing that people in the area would aspire to. So a key imperative was to get the right people on board, and these wouldn't necessarily be those with significant experience of ringing twelve – he was tapping potential. The initial menu would include Grandsire Cinques, Plain, Little and Treble Bob Maximus. George's eventual target method was Bristol Maximus, but most of all he wanted to ensure that high standards of performance could be set whilst the tower remained a welcoming place for those who wished to develop their skills on twelve bells.

A great example of that policy of welcoming people and tapping potential is Tina Sanderson (née Cooper), who remembers learning to ring as a youngster at Ipswich in the 1970s:

> "George Pipe became my ringing teacher and mentor when my father became organist of St Mary-le-Tower, Ipswich in 1971. George was delighted to have a connection between the internal and external choirs of the church! George had exacting standards and expected the same from his pupils. We lived in Colchester at the time, so every Tuesday evening while my brothers were at Tower choir practice, I would stay to tea with George and Diana and then go ringing at St Clement's, where I learnt to plain hunt. For ringing outings, I would stay with the Pipes to be ready for the early start. I was treated like a member of the family, creating a bond which continues to this day.
>
> "When I went to university, George introduced me to Frank Mack and I was welcomed into the Exeter Cathedral band. After graduation, I moved to York and was similarly introduced and welcomed at York Minster. A talented artist, George

gave me a pen-and-ink peal board to mark my first twelve-bell peal, with a lovely sketch of St Mary-le-Tower Church. This was followed by a beautiful pen-and-ink drawing of Huntington Church when I married Peter. Peter received one of George's famous handshakes too!

"George was never one to ignore an injustice and was absolutely outraged in 2016, when we were barred from ringing at the Minster. George wrote to Dean Faull to petition on behalf of the former Minster band. George kept a fatherly eye on me for most of my life and it has been my privilege."

Negatives and positives on the people front

In 1976, not everything in the St Mary-le-Tower garden was rosy. Jim Pipe, still active at seventy and a competent twelve-bell ringer over many years, should have played a part in the development of the new band, but sadly that didn't happen. Jim didn't believe it would be possible to build a competent local twelve-bell band in Ipswich. He had been part of the wonderful St Mary-le-Tower band of the 1920s and '30s. He had seen that band, most of whom had learned their craft either in Ipswich or the surrounding villages, achieve a multitude of firsts previously not thought possible. Jim had also seen that band die rapidly, after the war. His view, strongly expressed, was that St Mary-le-Tower should become a centre of twelve-bell ringing, but that the focus should be on inviting competent ringers from outside to come along regularly, with this the focus of developing twelve-bell ringing on the new twelve. Competent local ringers could then develop as twelve-bell ringers from that situation. Unfortunately, with Jim and George both being strong-willed people, it led to a serious split and Jim ceased supporting the tower. With Jim's death in 1980, this rift was never really healed.

George led from the front again and attracted people into Ipswich from the surrounding area. Take John Girt, for example: an established Ipswich ringer of many years standing and of similar age to George, who was Suffolk Guild Secretary from 1974 to 1989, a period which covered George's terms as Guild Chairman from 1974–77 and 1980–82. Both were pretty strong characters but they knew how to manage each other, I'm sure! John began ringing at St Mary-le-Tower after the new bells were installed and between 1977 and 2012 rang well over fifty twelve-bell peals, mostly at St Mary-le-Tower.

John summarises:

"When St Mary-le-Tower bells were restored and re-hung George asked me (then quite a novice ringer) to help build a band. I knew nothing of twelve-bell ringing, but that invitation opened a vast new field of ringing, culminating in being part of the Ipswich band that competed in the National Twelve Bell contests. It also progressed my abilities to Bristol Maximus and Spliced Maximus ringing – chances and skills for which I'm ever grateful to him. He was very generous with his time for anyone who showed interest. I have copious notes from him explaining various methods. He exuded complete confidence in his ability to chair meetings but underneath it all he could be very nervous – "how do I deal with this, what shall I say about that, who will speak to this item?" and so on. George's knowledge of Suffolk ringing and people will never be surpassed and his generosity in arranging social events was huge. I once met Charlie Sedgley, a pre-war ringer at St Mary-le-Tower, at such an event. When

my wife Shirley and I returned from a visit to Perth, W.A. in the late 1990s, George was delighted to know that some mowing equipment he had sold to the local council thirty or so years previously was still in constant use!"

Peals on all the 40cwt rings of bells

At the risk of getting a little overly esoteric, we bellringers are great collectors. Readers shouldn't be too surprised that big bells hold an irresistible attraction for some of us. There are 22 towers in the world with rings of bells with the tenor bell weighing over 40cwt. Four of these towers have additional bells weighing 40cwt or more as part of the ring. These towers are Liverpool Cathedral, Exeter Cathedral, St Paul's Cathedral and York Minster, known as the 'big four' because they have the heaviest tenor bells. This means there are 26 ringing bells in total weighing over 40cwt.

When, in July 1983, George rang a peal at Yeovil to complete peals on all the rings of bells in the world with a tenor of more than a 40cwt, he became the first person to achieve this. For some there are other targets, such ringing peals on all the *bells* of 40cwt or more, and four people have achieved this. Although these are personal achievements they require liaison with the tower, securing a very strong band for heavy rings that may be very tough, ensuring the ringers get there, and ringing for some four hours with no human or mechanical failures. I know George fixed some of these peals himself. The key factor that can make or break such ambitions is location! George had a head-start here because one of the over-40cwt towers was Adelaide Cathedral, where he rang a peal in March 1963 just before Diana and he returned to the UK.

Plenty more new twelves followed the same year, and his first peal on the ring of twelve at Exeter Cathedral, where he had rung a celebrated peal on the back eight with its 72cwt tenor back in 1954. He noted it was 'a great privilege to have opportunity to ring on the UK's rings of twelve, numbering well over 100.'

And where are these wonderful heavy rings of bells located? Well, I've listed six above.

In the South East we have: St Mary-le-Bow (Bow bells) and Southwark Cathedral.

In the West: Bristol (Redcliffe), Buckfast Abbey, Yeovil, Wells Cathedral, Sherborne Abbey and Worcester Cathedral.

In the North, Scotland and Eire: Manchester Town Hall, Liverpool Cathedral, Liverpool (Pierhead), Leeds Minster, Beverley Minster, Edinburgh Cathedral, Inveraray, Dublin Christ Church Cathedral and Dublin St Patrick's Cathedral.

Finally, in Australia: Adelaide Cathedral.

'Mission England' and significant 'firsts' in Suffolk

June 1984 marked the 70th anniversary of the Diocese of St Edmundsbury and Ipswich, coinciding with Mission England led by Billy Graham, the American Evangelist, who packed out Portman Road, the home of Ipswich Town FC. In September, George joined an illustrious band at St Martin-in-the-Fields, London in a peal to celebrate the silver wedding anniversary of Dennis and Mary Beresford.

In 1984 and 1985, George took part in peals at some Suffolk towers that are seldom pealed, such as Haughley, Cretingham (home of the famous Wightman family), Old Newton (1663, first ever peal), the restored and augmented ten at St Peter's Sudbury,

Wattisfield (1685, first ever peal), Coddenham (completing peals on all the ringable eights in the diocese) and Ipswich, St Lawrence (a pre-reformation ring of five). Some 25 years later George would be active in the restoration of this historic ring. Another noted first was the peal at Dalham in August 1984, the first peal on the bells, a ring of five since 1627, the peal rung on a very hot day, with the tenor man's discarded shirt falling 'like a wet dishcloth' to the floor. A few years later the bells were restored and augmented to eight by Frank Price and his local team.

At All Saints, Newmarket, a peal was rung to mark the launch of the All Saints parish stewardship mission and the 'Forward in Faith' initiative. This was only the second peal on the bells in seventy years and some felt the peal should never have been rung at all. A peal in December 1990 on the seventeenth-century ring of six bells at Cratfield, in North Suffolk also generated comment. This was the sixth peal on the bells and the first for sixty years.

There were occasional accusations of elitism regarding George's selection of ringers from outside Suffolk, rather than locals, for 'special' peals, and for some of the rare towers pealed. However Suffolk is a welcoming place that takes its ringing and its fellowship seriously. It is to the Suffolk Guild's credit that its members have never felt moved to introduce restrictions on visitors in peals accredited to the Guild, a practice favoured by some territorial associations.

Ipswich team enters National 12-Bell Contest

Ringing at St Mary-le-Tower prospered with Ipswich entering the National 12-Bell Contest for the first time in 1985 and reaching the final in 1988, 1989 and 1991, hosting the Contest final in 1991, coming fourth, with Cambridge winning the contest. I recall some rather strong opinions being expressed over BBC Look East taking about fifteen minutes to record bellringing at St Mary-le-Tower. It just happened that the band selected by Look East to carry out this exercise first thing in the morning was the winning Cambridge band from 1990, the band that would win the contest later in the day! Each band gets approximately thirty minutes to complete their practice and test piece, so an additional fifteen minutes for the Cambridge band was deemed to be advantageous in the opinion of some!

Amanda Richmond was elected Ringing Master of the Suffolk Guild in 1990, the first lady to serve in this capacity. These days she rings at St Mary-le-Tower – when not in the Himalayas climbing big peaks. Not surprisingly her four years as Ringing Master were full of activity and innovation. These are her observations about George now:

> *"From the days of George up in the tower, to more recent ones, when he would probably be sitting outside in the car, he ALWAYS had an effect on our striking at St Mary-le-Tower. 'Concentrate everyone, George is listening.'"*

First local peal of Maximus since 1939

Something predicted, perhaps a little bullishly, by George in 1982, was that the first peal of Maximus by a regular practice night and Sunday service band since 1939 at St Mary-le-Tower was imminent. In May 1984 this was achieved, less than ten years on from the 'standing start' following the restoration. It represented the culmination of a huge amount of hard work by George and the band to re-establish twelve-bell ringing in Ipswich. The

St Mary-le-Tower band was now strong enough to visit other twelve-bell towers to ring peals. It is always a great feeling, and tremendously gratifying, when you know your local band is good enough to go out to other towers and perform to a high standard. A number of 'awaydays' were organised during the 1980s.

Policy of welcoming visitors

Over the years some six hundred peals have been rung on St Mary-le-Tower bells, with very large numbers of visiting ringers participating. George was always at pains to point out that the tower is a 'no strings' tower. People could bring their own bands or local assistance was available. He particularly valued the support of the priests at St Mary-le-Tower over many years. When Ringing Master at St Mary-le-Tower, George had a policy of inviting visiting ringers, often coming from a distance away, to ring peals. Geoffrey Tarris, Keith Jones (later Dean of Exeter and then Dean of York) and Peter Townley (who became Archdeacon of Pontefract in the Diocese of Wakefield), have all been keen on bells and ringing. George understood the importance of those relationships and keeping them productive and

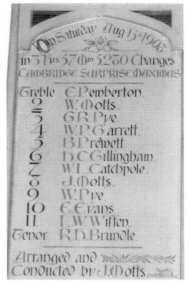

Peal board for the first ever peal of Surprise Maximus, rung on 15th August 1908 at St Mary-le-Tower

meaningful, for example with prayer ministry in the tower. Keith Jones, who wrote part of this book's foreword, attests that he did.

Commemorating the first peals

Since George was steeped in the history of St Mary-le-Tower, there were regular anniversary peals to mark the many first peals in the method rung in the tower: Cambridge Maximus every ten years, and 50th anniversaries celebrated of the first ever peals of Yorkshire Maximus, Superlative Maximus, Pudsey Maximus, all rung at St Mary-le-Tower. The ringing room is an atmospheric place – all the history is there on the walls at St Mary-le-Tower and this helps keep it fresh in the mind!

George made an outstanding contribution at St Mary-le-Tower over 25 years. It's easy to talk about the need for restoration of the bells as being obvious, particularly with a very poor, worn-out installation. But it's never easy to lead a really challenging initiative, even less so when at the outset there's no guarantee of success, then raise what always seems to be a lot of money and secure an excellent result. And to top that, lead the ringing to Bristol Maximus standard in a town which is not at the centre of the universe. A remarkable achievement!

Personal achievements

There were some notable personal achievements on twelve over the years as well for George; these include a peal of Orion in 1989 (in his mid-50s, no 'walk in the park') and the first peal of Snow Tiger in 1999. Significant peals rung elsewhere for George included Rigel at St Mary-le-Bow, Cheapside, City of London, in 1995 and 106 Spliced Surprise Maximus at St Paul's, Bedford in 1989. When George had to stop ringing in 2012, he had rung 251 peals on St Mary-le-Tower bells, considerably more than anybody else. His first peal on the new bells was in January 1977 and his total on these new bells ended at 234, with over one hundred on the 11th. Ringing the 11th to twelve-bell peals in many towers became something of a speciality of his.

… and his successor?

Simon Rudd was a ringer at St Mary-le-Tower from the late 1970s and succeeded George as Ringing Master at St Mary-le-Tower in 1989: quite a daunting prospect following a restoration and the building of a local twelve-bell band in Ipswich in quite a short period of time. Simon comments:

> *"My twelve-bell ringing was non-existent at that time and a ring of twelve was like 'a forest of ropes', as a colleague once put it. The bells were a newly installed peal of twelve with beautiful tone, often overlooked on the lists of good twelves. Many of us can trace the beginnings of our twelve-bell ringing journeys to those days at St Mary-le-Tower and the peal of bells which George's vision and drive created, with him instilling in us the need to always strive to do better.*
>
> *"Visiting for a practice, whilst being a daunting prospect at first, did however introduce to me that fierce insistence on getting things right. It was George's desire to ensure this which underlaid everything and was expressed in a variety of ways of course. A good bellow from the tenor box, a loud tut or sharp intake of breath from the 2nd or head in hands behind the 8th on the bench. We were never in doubt if we had fallen short of his expectations of us.*
>
> *"The important thing about this is the respect we had for George. His presence in the ringing room was enough to add that extra 10% of effort required to transform an average piece of ringing into a good piece of ringing in the same way that his father Jim had done before him. There was also immense appreciation for the stalwarts of ringing at St Mary-le-Tower who in the '60s had kept the old bells going when down to ringing on five on a Sunday, before George and Diana returned from Australia. Jimmy Wightman from Otley, for example, always had a warm welcome and his support was always appreciated.*
>
> *"A passion for St Mary-le-Tower in all of its facets, a passion for ringing in Suffolk and a passion for its many colourful characters and an unparalleled knowledge of their unique roles, combined with amazing powers of recall, mean that any conversation with George on these topics resulted in one learning something new."*

The present Master of the Ringers is David Potts. He took over as Master in 2009, succeeding Richard Munnings (2007–2009), Owen Claxton (1991–2007), Simon Rudd (1989–91) & George Pipe (1963–1989). The Pipe connection is a very long one – George Pipe's Great, Great, Great Uncle James Pipe rang a peal at St Mary-le-Tower in 1817!

2015

A gathering (? Holy) at St. Mary le Tower practice by all who attend regularly or fairly, Summer 2015

L-R standing: Rosemary Caudle, Ruth Munnings, Sean Antonioli, Kate Eagle, Owen Claxton, Richard Munnings (& the new tenor ringer!), Ian Culham, George Salter, Colin Salter, David Stanford, Don Price, Ralph Earey, Melvin Potts, Stephen Cheek, Amanda Richmond, Michael Whitby, Michael Burn, Alan Munnings, Paul Bray, Helen Price

Seated: Peter Davies, Ann Bray, George Vant, Diana Pipe, David Potts (Master of the Ringers), George Pipe, Enid Roberts, Sally Munnings & Mandy Shedden.
Emily & Isobel

(Missing: Rowan Wilson, Ted Flatters)

photo = Peter Davies

The St Mary-le-Tower Sunday service and practice night band, 2015

Chapter 15

The roaring '80s

The first 600 peals

When he rang his 600th peal – Cambridge Maximus at Gloucester Cathedral in July 1981 with Ken Hesketh's ASCY band – George wrote a wonderful summary of his 35 years' ringing. In some ways it almost makes the present writer's efforts a little redundant – it certainly makes life easier! He commented on what a privilege it had been to hold all the main offices of the Suffolk Guild. The seven years in Australia was an unforgettable experience too. In George's early days just after the war, peals were hard-won and many more were lost in those days than now. There was more effort in organising them and of course fewer people had cars in those days. He took the view that peals since 1963 were of a better quality and he wondered what 1981 would bring. He thought that another bells 'job' would at some stage arrive, following those at St Mary-le-Tower, Melbourne Cathedral and Bendigo in Australia. He was proud of being one of only five people to have rung peals at the six heaviest rings of twelve. This was achieved by 1981, at a time of much more limited opportunity than now. Move forward to the current time and I suspect that figure is more like several dozen people.

A purple patch in 1981/2

1981 was marked by a purple patch: peals at St Mary-le-Tower for the wedding of HRH The Prince of Wales and Lady Diana Spencer, at the Queen's Tower, Imperial College and peals of Maximus at Southwark Cathedral and York Minster, with John Mayne on the tenor to both peals, and soon York Minster again, this time with Jeff Brannan on the tenor. For George to ring two peals of Surprise Maximus at York in four months was some achievement. He was clearly rated as a top-class ringer. David Potter and his York team would raise their performance level over a number of years, maintaining a team of mixed ability and experience, eventually ringing local band peals of Maximus, a considerable achievement.

January 1982 saw the departure of Canon Geoffrey Tarris from St Mary-le-Tower after nine years of ministry, and a Suffolk band marked the occasion with a peal of Stedman Cinques. Geoffrey had been very supportive to the ringers during the fundraising for the restored twelve, dedicated in 1976. February saw George ringing the tenor to Cambridge Surprise Major at Sherborne Abbey (completing what at that time was a rare double, peals on the tenors at Adelaide Cathedral and Sherborne Abbey, the two heaviest rings of eight), and later Grantham, Leeds Parish Church and Edinburgh Cathedral tenors. If that wasn't enough, there were further peals at Wells Cathedral, Beverley Minster, Oxford Cathedral, Buckfast Abbey and Christ Church, Dublin. A busy time!

Some weighty success

In 1982, the St Mary-le-Tower band was photographed together for the first time since 1927 and local band peals of Stedman Cinques, the first since 1939, were rung, accompanied by the observation that a local peal of Surprise Maximus at Ipswich was likely to happen in the next couple of years. The St Mary-le-Tower band won the Suffolk Guild six-bell striking contest for the third time. The year developed an increasingly weighty focus, with a peal at Edinburgh Cathedral and later one at Beverley Minster, followed by Buckfast Abbey. Finally, he went to Christchurch Dublin,

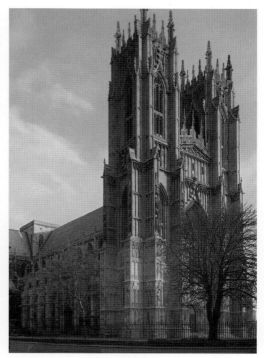

Beverley Minster – George's favourite ecclesiastical building, and a fine 41cwt Taylor ring of ten

Peter Border ringing the tenor to Royal. 1984 saw a lot of twelve-bell activity with another peal at Exeter Cathedral, Stedman Cinques, towards the end of the year. There was further development of the St Mary-le-Tower band in 1985 with nine firsts in a peal of Lincolnshire Maximus in January and then Wilfred Williams's 80th birthday later in the year.

Grandparents

In 1983, there was a slight diversion from normal activity with a grandfathers' peal, rung at St Mary-le-Tower by resident members of the Suffolk Guild as a welcome to Rosanna Hughes, granddaughter to George and Diana Pipe. The eight ringers in the band had a total of 21 grandchildren and the average age of the band was 61 and a half years, George being the youngest. A slightly different type of welcome to Rosanna!

Clare tenor and redundancy

In June 1983, I was invited to Clare, Suffolk for a peal of Bristol, with George ringing the tenor. Some thirty years before, he'd conducted a peal of Double Norwich at Clare from the seventh with his father Jim on the tenor. That day, according to Leslie Mills, my

The St Mary-le-Tower Society in 1927: (Left to right) Back row: W Woods, P May, B Tillett, C Woodcock, H Shemming; Centre: W Tillett, C J Sedgley, H C Gillingham, H E Smith, G A Fleming, A A Fleming, R H Brundle; Front: H R Roper, C A Catchpole, W P Garrett, G E Symonds, F J Tillett

The St Mary-le-Tower practice night and Sunday Service band, 1982. (Left to right) Standing: Richard, Sally, Christopher and Alan Munnings, Peter Saunders, David Culham, Diana Pipe, Stephen Pettman, George Pipe, Christina Cooper, Bevan Wilgress, Mark Ogden; Seated: Mike and Alison Whitby, Shirley and John Girt, James Smith, Rachel Lee, Christine Pegg, Simon Rudd

mentor, 'the boy rang round the old man a treat'. I was really pleased to have been asked in the peal as Clare was a tower I had rung at quite regularly before leaving the area in 1973, but I'd never attempted a peal there. I thought it unlikely that I'd be doing too much ringing round the tenor that day, however!

The peal at Clare was well rung. They are a challenging 28cwt eight rung then from the ground floor, but I wasn't the only one who was surprised when George announced that he'd been made redundant the previous day from his firm after many years in the materials handling business. A new young sales director had arrived and made it clear that the business needed to bring new, young, dynamic people on board, and because that was the chosen avenue for the future, those over the age of 45 might consider themselves finished. George was 48. After 33 years in engineering, materials handling, capital sales and two redundancies, George, by 1983, was looking for fresh employment and if it represented a change, so much the better.

Little did I realise at the time that I would myself be made redundant eight months later, at 28, but it was clear that adapting to changing circumstances would become increasingly important in the future and there would certainly be no jobs for life in materials handling or fast moving consumables roles! As is so often the case, this situation created new opportunities for George for the rest of his working life in roles, many church-based, that suited his abilities and aptitude, enabling him to make very meaningful contributions to these operations over some years.

Career change and working for the Church

The Bishop of the Diocese of St Edmundsbury and Ipswich, John Waine, was aware George was looking for employment. Following conversations over the 1983 Christmas and New Year break, George was offered an opportunity to become the Diocesan Christian Stewardship and Resources Adviser and later a director of the Church Urban fund, Archbishop Robert Runcie's initiative for helping with inner city deprivation. George really loved this work and made over two hundred visits to clergy and parishes who were receptive to the objectives the diocese was looking to achieve and welcomed his assistance. Bishop John also arranged theological training for George at St Mary's College, Selly Oak, Birmingham and later at Whalley Abbey in the Diocese of Blackburn. But George's work for the church was rendered complete by Bishop John Dennis of the Diocese of St Edmundsbury and Ipswich appointing George his Chaplain and PA. The lay chaplaincy was a new concept at the time and George was only the third appointment in the UK.

Bristol Maximus by a local band

After the installation of the new ring in 1976, several peals of Bristol Maximus were rung by visiting bands. As the local band became stronger they started practising it and finally, a peal with a regular Sunday/practice night band was rung in December 1986 at first attempt, a remarkable achievement, which gave George immense pleasure. It was proof also, given the major disagreement with his father ten years earlier when the new bells were installed, that ringing high-quality Maximus in complex methods could be done by developing a band locally rather than via an importation programme.

I received an invitation to go to St Mary-le-Tower for a peal of Bristol Maximus in early 1987. The band comprised eleven local Sunday/practice night ringers plus myself. This was one of those real privileges that ringing can generate, because some of my early twelve-bell opportunities had been at St Mary-le-Tower with George back in the early 1970s. There were three firsts of Bristol in the peal and some very good ringing. Thinking back to my first peal there in 1972, the odds on achieving this sort of progress would have been very long. George and all the supporting ringers at St Mary-le-Tower deserve a lot of credit for this.

Significant achievements rarely come in isolation, so along the way peals in the simpler methods – Cambridge, Yorkshire, Superlative, Lincolnshire, Albanian, Spliced and Stedman Cinques – were rung, as well as others on the front eight. Stephen Pettman, a talented young ringer from Grundisburgh and a very good conductor, conducted many of the early peals by the local and area band after the new bells were installed. Stephen was George's second leading peal ringer after Diana. He has given significant service to the Suffolk Guild over more than forty years, including eleven years as Ringing Master over two spells, and he has rung over 1,400 peals for the Guild, conducting just over 1,200. Stephen is a very talented composer and conductor across the full range of methods.

The invitation arrived to go to Australia to be part of a lecture tour in early 1987, reported in some detail elsewhere. George also left his diocesan post after four years to work full-time for the East Anglian Autistic Trust. In terms of ringing offices, he was approached regarding possibly taking up the role of Central Council President, but declined.

Catchpole and Beodricsworth Surprise Royal and Maximus

Beodericsworth is an ancient name for the town of Bury St Edmunds. In November 1985, a peal of Beodricsworth Surprise Royal was rung at Bury St Edmunds. The method is the old version of London on ten composed by William L Catchpole, one of the old St Mary-le-Tower band before World War II, but never rung. This was followed in 1988 by a peal of Beodricsworth Surprise Maximus, an extension of Catchpole's method to twelve bells, but again never rung because of the war. The writer was privileged to be in the peal and remembers the Maximus being a very challenging method, with 4-5, 5-6 and 6-7 dodges to add interest!

Ill health – 1989 and 1990

1989 was a bad year work-wise, proving what George had heard many times: that working for charities, such as the Anglian Autistic Community Trust, can unearth some great uncharitableness! This time it was redundancy, as the AACT became part of the National Autistic Society. He stated that had it not been for Diana's support and strength and that of his family, he is not sure what would have happened, as he suffered the worst depression he could recall. His back pain became more acute together with breathlessness and the first worrying signs of heart palpitation, leading him to wonder if a heart attack might occur, all very unpleasant. Nevertheless this was an active year, particularly with restoration projects and PR efforts for the Suffolk Guild, for example Boxford, Worlingworth, Horham, Framlingham and Hoxne, three of which projects subsequently came to fruition.

The ill health mentioned above continued into 1990. George rang a peal at Ufford 45 years after his first peal and stayed busy with Suffolk Guild activity, but he had bouts of feeling very unwell which he didn't disclose to Diana and the family. He stated in these notes that 'as I write this I honestly do believe that I shall not ring my thousand, but it's no great matter.' Thankfully, he was well enough to go to Washington for the 25th anniversary celebrations, one of three of the original band who were able to make it. He celebrated the marriage of brother Rod to Mary in December 1990 and also the marriage of Gill and John Fielden the following year, wishing both couples every happiness.

Ringing with many different ringers

George rang peals with some 1,505 ringers, some of whom made a major impact very quickly, and one of these is Alan Regin, who was awarded his MBE in 2018 for services to ringing (see Ian Campbell's piece later).

Alan talks of George:

"I first met George in the mid-1980s, he made a big impact on me, a treasure trove of knowledge about all things ringing and a fine person to spend time with. I am surprised to find I have only rung 21 peals with George, but what memories they bring back, sixteen of them on twelve, including at St Mary-le-Bow, St Peter Mancroft, Norwich, Evesham, St Martin-in-the-Fields and, of course, Ipswich. Peals I much value are those rung on the same day in November 1996 at Southwold and Wrentham, Suffolk, the towers where Bertram Prewett rang his 952nd and 953rd peals, his last peals before being killed in action – a very special day out! Another thing that remains in my memory is that good old George Pipe handshake, very warm and very firm; one's hand remained "shook" long after the event!"

Kingsley Mason is a well-known Leicester ringer who knew George as a man of many talents and interests, setting very high standards as a bellringer of the highest calibre, with an ability to ring any bell in the circle with 100% effort. Kingsley, like George, has rung peals on many of the fine heavy rings in the UK. Their first peal together was in fact Cambridge Maximus at Worcester Cathedral in October 1972.

Kingsley talks about several of these:

"In August 1982, when I rang the tenor at Beverley Minster to Cambridge Royal, George rang one of the very tricky front bells with his usual accuracy, a great support. Then in March 1987 George secured the bells at York Minster for a peal attempt and liaised with the late Ken Hesketh to complete the band. It was my thrill to be included and asked to ring the tenor. When we tried the bells for rope adjustment, George said "We are not going to ring them that fast, are we?!" A good peal of Stedman Cinques was rung in 3 hours and 46 minutes, which is fast, with George as 'Pacesetter' on the second. Some time after the peal, a parcel arrived at my home and inside was a framed facsimile of the peal, beautifully calligraphed by George, an item I treasure. It has been displayed on our sitting room wall ever since. A further demonstration of one of George's many talents and skills.

"George loved to ring peals at rare towers, one of which was a peal of Bristol at the Roman Catholic Church, Cambridge in November 1998, when he rang the 7th and I rang the tenor. This was another Ken Hesketh arrangement and all who

*rang in Ken's peals greatly miss Ken for everything that he was and did. George was
a great contributor of articles in* The Ringing World, *full of fact and interest, and
the obituaries he wrote made fascinating reading. My wife Rosemary and I were so
grateful for his input after the death of her parents and, on a brighter note, for his
'write up' of our wedding in Leicester in 2002."*

100th peal at Grundisburgh and augmentation

The spring of 1986 saw George's 100th peal at Grundisburgh, where he had learnt to
ring in 1944. The significance of Jim Pipe's 1948–9 project to restore the original eight at
Grundisburgh and augment to ten cannot be underestimated. It gave George and many
other Suffolk ringers the opportunity to ring on ten, an opportunity which didn't exist
anywhere else in the county. As the bells were available for ringing at virtually any time,
there was scope to ring peals of Major and Triples as well, so there was a lot of ringing
and a lot of beneficiaries. May 1986 saw a peal at Stonham Aspal, a thanksgiving peal for
the completion of the rebuilding of the upper timber stage of the tower, a very significant
component of the tower. Ringers rate the bells as an 'interesting' peal of ten that are quite
difficult to ring! A marvellous day, I expect, with the dedication evensong and supper
following the peal. For clarity, the very well-known Aspall cider is actually produced at
Aspall, near Debenham, a few miles away.

In July 1990 the last peal was rung at Grundisburgh prior to augmentation to twelve,
an initiative which attracted a lot of sometimes forthright comment at the time, and still
does: for example, the claim that it would spoil a reasonably good light ten which had
been a valuable resource to Suffolk ringers for forty years. Early 1990 saw a peal of Bristol
Maximus with a mainly Birmingham band
on the new twelve at Leighton Buzzard,
followed by Chester Cathedral in May.

Clifford A Barron and friends

George made further progress with
peals at new twelves in 1986, with peals
at East Grinstead, Newcastle Cathedral
and Shrewsbury. The latter was Stedman
Cinques, Cliff Barron's 1,000th peal,
in the tower where he did much of his
early ringing, and Alan Ainsworth recalls
this as one of his best ever peals. Cliff
was a very old friend of George's, going
back to one of George's early peals of
Stedman Cinques at St Philip's Cathedral,
Birmingham in 1953. Cliff was a very
fine ringer, widely acknowledged as one
of the best – he rang in the long peals of
Cambridge Maximus, Stedman Cinques

*Cliff Barron and Henry Fearn, pictured
in Paris! One of George's favourite
photographs (1968)*

and Glasgow Major rung in Birmingham during the mid-1960s, but he was happy with simpler methods for less capable bands, particularly if this provided opportunity for others to progress. In his younger days, he used to ring tenors incredibly fast, and incredibly well.

Cliff was also a highly capable beer drinker, who believed that the pub was the place to go if the ringing had not been good, no recriminations or post-mortems. He was versed in the law, in which profession he made his living in Birmingham city centre. He had a number of preferred drinking companions, the best known of which was John N Lindon, a truck driver and well-known Birmingham ringer, also known as 'Bleeding Jack', because 'bleeding' seemed to be Jack's favourite word! However, George Pipe and Cliff had much in common since Cliff was knowledgeable across many topics – he was a traveller, a good conversationalist (shyness allowing) and a raconteur. He had a command of politics, sport, the Church, Shropshire, Stedman Triples, Birmingham ringing, books, poetry, the Armed Forces and railways. Essentially Cliff was a quiet, shy and modest chap who suffered from bouts of depression.

Henry H Fearn, George Fearn's younger brother, was a popular character in Birmingham. Whereas George took his ringing very seriously, particularly in amassing the greatest peal total by anyone to date (2,667 when he died in 1974), I always thought Henry was put on this earth to have fun! George owned some property and Henry being his tenant was a mixed blessing (for Henry), since Thursday night was rent night, the idea also being that Henry would 'make one' if they met short. Henry once told me that he'd rung over 800 peals without really wanting to ring any. Henry loved his beer, was witty, very well-read and great fun to be with, a prominent Birmingham ringer from the 1920s through to the 1980s. He was also a close friend of Cliff Barron's, meaning he had contact with 'Bleeding Jack' as well! The photograph of Henry Fearn with Cliff Barron in Paris was one of George's favourites. Cliff might have been contemplating the quality of the beers or reds just sampled, or those to come. I expect Henry would have been liberally supplying one-liners to the photographer.

12-Bell Contest Judge

In 1987 there were peals at three new twelves: Birchington (Quex Park), Peterborough Cathedral and Trowbridge. On April Fools' Day at St Mary-le-Tower, the first peal of Erin Triples with no bobs or singles was rung, 388 calls rung as quick sixes, composed by Nigel Newton, the peal rung at first attempt, and in May a peal to mark the renovation of Monewden bells, previously silent for forty years. Subsequently, a number of attempts were made at Monewden for long peals of 30,000 changes, so this was clearly a successful restoration project. A number of new ten-bell towers were visited during 1987, such as Ripon, Lichfield, Wisbech, St Lawrence in Thanet, St Margaret's Westminster, and West Ham.

In June 1987, at Great St Mary's, Cambridge, with Rod as chief judge, George and Roger Baldwin judged the National 12-Bell Contest. This was won by the local Sunday Service band at Great St Mary's, the first East Anglian team to win the contest, and they went on to win it again in 1990, 1991 and 1995. Later, in August, peals were rung at St Mary Abbots, Kensington, Tewkesbury Abbey, Cheltenham, St Stephen's, Bristol, and Cirencester, with his 100th peal of Stedman Cinques rung at Southwark Cathedral in October.

A very long day

It could be said that George didn't do things by halves, as was proven when in August 1988, we went to Painswick and Midsomer Norton for peals on the same day. George drove from Ipswich to my home near Cambridge, then came with me to pick up Frank Rivett at Sandy and we drove to Painswick for a 10am start, Mellor Surprise Maximus scored, George on the tenor. From here we drove the 50 miles to Midsomer Norton, and scored the afternoon peal, 4 Spliced Surprise Maximus. Then home, a round trip of some 400 miles from Ipswich!

Edward P Duffield

In December 1988 a peal of 5,090 Stedman Cinques was rung at St Mary-le-Tower to mark the 90th birthday of Edward P Duffield, a highly respected ringer and past master of the ASCY. Ted rang a number of peals with the Pye band including the long peal of 15,312 Cambridge Surprise Maximus at Ashton under Lyne in 1929 which took 11 hours and 33 minutes. Ted came from an East Anglian milling family and was a friend of the Pipe family for well over 50 years. He devoted much of his life outside of the business to public service, for example serving as Mayor of Colchester. I am very proud that the name of Ted Duffield appears in my peal book.

Sampling very advanced twelve-bell methods

Much learning was done by George for a peal of 106 Spliced Surprise Maximus at St Mary-le-Tower in April 1989. Such peals demonstrate how dependent ringing is on teamwork because if someone drops out the day before you can't just replace them as you would in a 'normal' peal, as there would be no time for the replacement to do the necessary learning. Some wonderful method names too – Manitoba, Orion, Quex, Utah, Verulam, Xique-Xigue, Yahoo and Zanussi. Another big first was in April at Ipswich: Orion Surprise Maximus, a method composed and named by Rod and acknowledged by him as the most difficult blue line he had yet seen. Later, in July 1995, George rang inside to a peal of Rigel Surprise Maximus, his first in the method – Rigel, also composed by and named by Rod, is a sister method to Orion and also very difficult. It's quite possible that no other ringer has rung their first in this method at the age of 60 or above!

Letter and telephone

It sounds a little quaint these days, but in the 1950s and early 1960s most communication was conducted by letter – fax and mobile phones were a generation away for most people, and not everyone had a phone at home. George had always been keen on anything involving writing and drawing and had been a keen letter writer for years (as many ringers will know!) and with Cliff and one or two others formed a small bellringers letter-writing circle. With Cliff, George and Stephen Ivin as some of the participants the subject areas must have been wide and diverse.

George remained a committed communicator by letter to the end and made excellent use of the telephone as well. An example was his regular contact over a number of years with Joseph

Thornley, from Farnworth with Kearsley, Greater Manchester, who died in 2019, well into his nineties. Joe was a devout Christian, as was George, and they also shared an interest in Freemasonry. Joe, a bachelor, was a lift engineer throughout his career. It was no surprise that Joe was affectionately known as Joe Treble, since he rang the treble to 821 of his 1,130 peals, and rang just one peal of Surprise Major inside, which must have been a collector's piece! It's fair to say that Joe seldom knew much about the method being rung but he worked as a kind of informal conductor's assistant, regularly calling out 'half lead now', which still causes a smile years later on the odd occasion it is announced by others these days. Joe rang his last peal nearly twenty years before he died and sadly was forced to retire from ringing in 2005. However, he maintained his interest in ringing, The National Trust and English Heritage, beer and Church history. I expect these two met only a handful of times but that the telephone conversations and letters were long!

The peal of 106-spliced S Maximus, as recorded by George in his peal book

Collecting Royal Peculiars

Occasionally, a huge honour can arrive in a totally unexpected way. I guess that was the case when George received an invitation to ring a peal of Cambridge Surprise Royal at a Royal Peculiar, Westminster Abbey, on 13th October 2009. George was always keen on collecting anything, from postcards through to very large rings of bells all over the world, and 1986 had seen a major addition to the latter, with a peal of Grandsire Triples at the Curfew Tower, Windsor Castle, another of the Royal Peculiars, to mark the sixtieth birthday of her Majesty the Queen Elizabeth II. These days visitors are occasionally invited into peals at Westminster Abbey. These peals are requested by the Abbey authorities and are to mark significant events. Members of the Westminster Abbey Company of Ringers then join the visitors to complete the band. It is a great privilege to be invited.

Hitherto, peals at the Abbey had been rung almost exclusively by members of the Westminster Abbey Company of Ringers, but a decision was taken to invite visiting ringers on an occasional basis, typically centred around the Edward-tide celebrations, commemorating the founder of the Abbey church in the eleventh century. Invitations went to those who had made a major contribution to ringing in one way or another and perhaps in George's case it was fitting that ringers he knew well, like Michael Chilcott, Ian Oram and Howard Egglestone, were invited to ring. It is good that a number of other ringers have also been similarly invited in subsequent years.

*The Westminster Abbey peal band, October 2009. Left to right, back: Anthony
Bloomfield, Christopher Rogers, David Hilling, the Sub-Dean, Alan Frost,
John Hughes-D'Aeth; front: Michael Chilcott, Ian Oram, Howard Egglestone,
George Pipe and Adrian Moreton*

The collecting happened closer to home as well – in 1986, George rang in the first
peal at Great Glemham (installed 1553) and at Edwardstone, followed by Stedman Triples
at Merton College, Oxford (the oldest complete octave, cast by Christopher Hodson in
1680), and the centenary of the first ever silent and non-conducted peal of Stedman
Triples (Burton on Trent in 1886) was marked by a peal at Lavenham in November. The
same month also saw a St Mary-le-Tower 'awayday' peal of Lincolnshire Surprise Maximus
at Lincoln Cathedral. It is very pleasing to be able to take your band some distance and
get a good result.

Chapter 16

The 1990s – a decade of decades

Exeter Cathedral – again

In July 1991, George, Rod and David rang in a peal of Cambridge Maximus at Exeter Cathedral, where George and his father had rung the tenor to a peal of Bob Major in 1954. This was the first peal at Exeter since the fitting of a new headstock on the tenor. The original massive headstock on the tenor had made the bell very challenging to ring and this led to a number of 'glorious losses' in previous years. Peter Border had been the first person to turn it in to Maximus, in 1965, and Tim Collins had rung it to both Cinques in 1975 and Maximus in 1982. Prior to 1991 any single-handed peal, particularly of Maximus, on the huge old headstock, was a truly remarkable achievement. Now with the new headstock it is possible for 'normal' ringers to ring it to Maximus single-handed as a number of people have done in the past thirty years or so.

Alison Surry rings St Mary-le-Bow tenor to Maximus

One of the joys of ringing is its variety, and George's peal books are a treasure trove of contemporary ringing and non-ringing footnotes. A couple of peals George rang with Alison Surry illustrate the point. In December 1987, Alison came to St Mary-le-Tower and rang the tenor to Pudsey Maximus. She rang it superbly. George said '5 ft tall and 7¾ stone, nobody has rung the tenor better and I'm proud to have been in the peal'. Then in October 1991, George rang in a peal at St Mary-le-Bow where the 41cwt tenor was rung by Alison: 'a remarkable performance by Alison Surry, at 7 stone' is recorded in George's peal book.

Such assessments are usually a little subjective, but in this case George knew exactly what he was witnessing – Alison Surry was probably the best female ringer in history. She was a stylish performer who rang anywhere in the circle, an excellent striker who made it look easy, topped up with an unparalled ability to ring big bells. She rang several 40cwt+ tenors to peals, at Inveraray, St Mary-le-Bow, Southwark Cathedral and Worcester Cathedral. One of the peals at St Mary-le-Bow was Cambridge Royal (very tough) and two were Bristol Maximus. But it wasn't just about big bells. She was also highly talented on handbells and 492 of her 1866 peals were in hand, many of these on ten and twelve.

Alison learnt to ring as a teenager at Winchester Cathedral. She had already rung 400 peals and was an accomplished tower and handbell ringer when she moved to London to commence university studies in 1980. One of the people she met on arriving in London was Linda Garton. They became firm friends and both rang with the University of London Society at a time when the UL was achieving many firsts. Alison was also a member of the local band at Willesden for most of her time in London. What was really special about Alison was her tremendous loyalty and complete unselfishness. She was as happy teaching learners or ringing call changes at Willesden as she was ringing high level Maximus on handbells or ringing big bells. Her attitude was that it was never her that mattered, just what the band was looking to achieve and how she could assist to that end.

Very sadly, Alison Regan (as she became) died after a short illness in 2012, at the age of 53. Linda Garton spoke at her funeral and said:

Alison Regan (née Surry). Happy times, pictured at Linda Garton's 50th birthday party in January 2011. Alison died in July 2012, aged 53

> 'Alison was, in my view, the greatest lady ringer and one of the most accomplished and inspirational ringers of our generation, and I'm sure that very few who had the pleasure of ringing with Alison would argue with that. But she was also so much more than a wonderful ringer. She was a loving mother to her three children and a much loved daughter and sister. She was a dear colleague and friend. She was special to all who knew her and had time for us all. We will miss her dearly.'

First of 23 Spliced Surprise Major

In December 1990, at Hollesley, George recorded a rather surprising first, 23-spliced Surprise Major, but not composed by Norman Smith as one might expect, instead being an every-lead-different version arranged from Norman Smith's by James R Taylor. A couple of days later, the 500th peal at St Mary-le-Tower on the 255th anniversary of the first peal. Another very notable first was achieved in December 1990 with the first peal at Horham following the restoration of the bells. This was only the fourth peal on the bells, which are the oldest octave in existence (cast by different founders; Merton College in Oxford was mentioned earlier, which is the oldest eight cast by a single founder). In March 1991 George made a visit to Deeping St James in Lincolnshire and commented that 'this was specially arranged to score a peal on one of the finest sixes in England'.

George Pipe's 1,000th peal

George rang his 1,000th peal, 5,100 Stedman Cinques, at St Mary-le-Tower, composed and conducted by Rod, in February 1992, the 177th person to ring 1,000 peals, and in the band were members of the family and close friends over the years. As is usual with major milestones, lots of analysis followed, which summarised: 310 peals on twelve bells, 167

George's 1,000th peal, rung at St Mary-le-Tower in February 1992. Left to right:
Howard Egglestone, Frank Price, Rod Pipe, John Mayne, David Pipe, George Pipe,
Diana Pipe, Clifford Barron, Stephen Pettman, Simon Rudd, Stephen Ivin, Ken Hesketh

on ten, 381 on eight and 142 on six and five, conducted 203, peals rung in 291 towers, for 47 guilds and associations and with 1201 ringers. He commented on the difficulty of choosing a band when there were fifty people he would like to have asked. He recorded his indebtedness to Diana and the family in particular since over 750 of the peals had been rung since they were married and tempers the whole thing by commenting that 'this is a fraction of what the Exercise is all about. I hope to carry on teaching and supporting restoration work,' confirmed by a comment about possibly scaling down his peal ringing in the future!

John Mayne, a ringing friend of George's from childhood – they learnt to ring together at Grundisburgh in 1944, so a very longstanding friend – wrote an excellent and moving account of George's ringing career prior to becoming a new 1,000-pealer, from learning to ring at Grundisburgh through to the numerous achievements that have followed, in Australia, the formation of ANZAB, the St Mary-le-Tower restoration and new twelve, Central Council, Suffolk ringing and the Suffolk Guild.

As a result of this peal, George and Rod now belonged to the seventh family in which brothers have rung 1,000 peals, the others being the Pyes (three of them), Fellows, Randalls, Pauls, Prices and Moretons. What was totally unique was that Rod, Jim and George are the only instance of a father and his two sons all ringing 1,000 peals – the stuff of dynasties, I guess! John also wrote about the breadth of George's interests, his churchmanship and his leadership of others, particularly at St Mary-le-Tower. His one thousand peals were a well-worked thousand over nearly fifty years and he received many letters of congratulation which are on display in the trusted peal book, from John Chilcott, Kingsley Mason, the Suffolk Guild, Tom and Margaret Chapman, Ringing Towers (ANZAB), David Bleby (Adelaide) and Jack Cummins (Sydney).

Sheer eloquence

Following the 1,000th peal, in the peal book there is another one of those wonderfully eloquent retrospectives, which could only come from George, covering 1981 to 1992.

1981 was a kind of 'year of years', with the purchase of a permanent residential home near Mildenhall for East Anglian young autistic people, the culmination of five years very hard work. 1981 was George and Diana's silver wedding anniversary year, celebrated in the garden at 8 Lansdowne Road. There was the privilege of complimentary tickets for Björn Borg's last match at Wimbledon against McEnroe (which Borg lost), a business trip to Paris, the Royal Show, and the Halle orchestra at Ely playing mostly Elgar. Then there was a special service and tea at St Paul's Cathedral for all those who have rung a 'Royal' peal there. They took Ted Duffield along to this function. A thrilling NatWest cricket final at Lord's, a fete at Thornbury (Alison's last term there) and an Elizabethan feast at King's College Cambridge, at which George spoke. The year ended with a jolly good peal of London S Royal at Grundisburgh, which was the 5,000th peal for the Suffolk Guild.

Acknowledging the clergy

George was always keen to acknowledge and celebrate the clergy, sometimes with a peal to greet them in their new post. A good example was in 1995, when the Reverend James Atwell moved from St Lawrence, Towcester to become Provost of the Diocese of St Edmundsbury and Ipswich based at Bury St Edmunds. During James' time at Towcester the excellent 23cwt eight from Christ Church, Todmorden, were transferred to Towcester and augmented to twelve, an initiative pioneered by Andrew Wilby and his team at Towcester in 1989/90. James' arrival at Bury St Edmunds was marked by a peal rung by a mixed Towcester/Suffolk band.

Lay Chaplain and PA to the Bishop

In 1991, George was invited by Bishop John Dennis to become his Lay Chaplain. When Leslie G Brett (the last of the pre-war Helmingham band and a much loved ringer) died George delivered the eulogy at his funeral. Alison was to move to Ipswich in 1991. When the first peal was rung on the twelve at Grundisburgh, George's notes suggest 'much work to do to get them acceptable'! In March, Frank Price's 1,000th peal was rung at St Mary-le-Tower. At the Suffolk Guild's AGM in April, George retired after 27 years continuous office. He suggested in a note the previous year that this might happen as there was a little 'difficulty' and he fancied a break.

As noted earlier, Ipswich hosted the 1991 National 12-Bell Contest and came fourth, a great achievement. The St Mary-le-Tower band also received an invitation to ring at St Paul's Cathedral during the year, at a time when such invitations were uncommon. At the end of 1991, he rang a peal at Evesham, 'a lovely peal of Stedman Cinques on the marvellous twelve there, my word they are fine! So often one returns after twenty years and one is disappointed. Not so here – glorious ringing, glorious bells, belfry and composition to match' – and a thanksgiving for the life of Gilbert Thurlow. He rejoiced in the ringers' Songs of Praise from St Martin-in-the-Fields attended by over 1,000 ringers, for which he was asked to choose a hymn.

The Bell Tower, Evesham

Evesham – "a wonderful ringing experience ... my word they are fine ... glorious ringing, glorious bells, belfry and composition to match!"

'Scaling down' his peal ringing

In 2001, George indicated that he might scale down his peal ringing, and do some other things, which he initially did in some style by not ringing a peal for five years! This was due mainly to increasing back pain, but he made his comeback in September 2006 with a peal of 5,100 Stedman Cinques at Grundisburgh to mark the 100th anniversary of Jim Pipe's birth in which Rod, David and Diana all rang and which featured on the front page of *The Ringing World*. Otherwise, the scaling down wasn't a glorious success, down to around 25 peals per year for much of the rest of his peal ringing career! Finally, after Christmas, they started to teach a band at St Matthew's, Ipswich, a tower that has always been a little overshadowed by some of its more illustrious neighbours in the town. As usual, the Pipes got going – they were only 70, after all!

View of a nephew, David Pipe

David Pipe talked in 2019 about George and Diana's influence on him, good times at 8 Lansdowne Road and the importance of developing the family into the next generation:

> *"'I became the luckiest man on earth, David, the day I met your Auntie Diana.' This was a recurring theme from as far back as I can remember – usually said as we were sitting around the table at 8 Lansdowne Road, enjoying another spectacular meal prepared by Di. Indeed, it has been a privilege to be part of George and Di's extended family – and what a large family that is, one that includes ringers from all around the world. As a young ringer, it was very clear to me the exacting standards that George had in the belfry. Ringing at St Mary-le-Tower on a Sunday morning was no*

time for slacking. George's expectations were high, but he was also very proud of the achievements of what was entirely a provincial band. Twenty years ago, Cecilia and I were married and soon after started our own family. Our boys Henry and Alfie have benefited from George's advice and enjoyed his story telling as they have grown up – not forgetting the numerous hand-written letters we have received over the years! George's most recent peal was of Stedman Cinques on the relatively new ring of twelve at Great St Mary's in Cambridge in 2012. This was Cecilia's first with George and she is very proud to have rung with him. Afterwards, George admitted to having been in some pain. His performance, of course, had been faultless!"

George E Symonds's record equalled

1992 and 1993 were quieter, with less travelling, but peals were rung at Taunton, Leeds Minster, Llandaff Cathedral, Truro Cathedral, Our Lady and the English Martyrs, Cambridge and Salle, Norfolk, one of George's favourite churches. The 130-foot tower faced with Barnack stone and flint has been described as "the most perfectly composed of all late medieval Norfolk towers", and as "one of the first of the great East Anglian towers". The peal, conducted by John Pladdys, was rung at breakneck speed! Another interesting statistic from 1993 was George's 103rd peal on the 11th at St Mary-le-Tower, equalling the record of the great George E Symonds. A month later, also at St Mary-le-Tower, the first 1,000-pealers' peal of Bristol Maximus was rung.

'Revenge of the lawnmower' or 'Should have gone to the 12-Bell'

The National 12-Bell Contest Final took place at Newcastle Cathedral on Saturday 27th June 1992. Ipswich had hosted the 1991 final but unfortunately had failed to qualify for the 1992 final, therefore George was at home on the day. Mowing the lawn was on his list of things to do but sadly he tripped and fell and the mower passed over his left foot, severing the big toe and causing severe lacerations. He spent a couple of weeks in hospital during which time another toe in danger of being amputated was saved.

The surgeon who performed the three operations required was a local ringer from near Ipswich. George was out of peal ringing for four months. James Smith, from Ipswich, then in Australia, commented in *Ringing Towers* on the daunting nature of the surgeon's job, faced with the task of repairing one of the foremost feet in English ringing, but the repair job was a masterpiece of needlework. Of course James also made the link to George's six years in Australia when he worked for Ransomes, Sims and Jefferies, whose most famous product was … lawnmowers!

Some trips to the west

1994 saw peals at Bristol St Mary Redcliffe, St Luke's Chelsea (very rarely pealed) and the wonderful rings of six at St Buryan (now, by a whisker, the heaviest ring of six), and Paul, Cornwall. Further peals on the classic Taylor rings of ten at Loughborough Parish Church and Beverley Minster were rung in early 1995, and later in 1995 at Queen Camel (only ten peals on the bells) and Abergavenny. Finally, the 50th anniversary of

George's first peal was celebrated with a peal of London Surprise Major, once again at Ufford, conducted by Rod. In December, a peal of Cambridge Maximus by a local practice night band was rung to mark the departure of The Revd Canon Keith Jones, leaving St Mary-le-Tower after thirteen years to become Dean of Exeter, and later Dean of York.

'Siblings' 1,000-pealers ring an eight-bell peal ...

On Saturday 18th March 1995 a totally unique peal was rung, a first but not a record, but still an achievement that will find its way into the record books. This was a peal of four-spliced Surprise Major rung at Wicken, Northamptonshire, by four pairs of brothers all of whom had rung 1,000 peals: Graham & Alan Paul, Rod & George Pipe, Peter & Geoff Randall, and Frank & Richard Price. All pretty uneventful, good bells, good band, good ringing. They remembered other brothers who were also thousand-pealers, the three Pye brothers, Michael & Martin Fellows and Wilfred & Michael Moreton, together with a *Ringing World* article by George.

... and then a 'siblings' 1,000-pealers twelve-bell peal

On Sunday 30th September 2007 this concept was extended a little, with an interesting first at All Saints, Worcester. Arranged by Geoff Randall, this was a peal of Cambridge Surprise Maximus rung by a band of siblings all of whom had rung 1,000 peals. Frank Price died in 2005 so Graham and Alan Paul, Rod and George Pipe, and Peter and Geoff Randall were joined by Linda and David Garton, David and Phil Rothera and Robert and Adrian Beck. This was a great initiative to be involved in, with an article in *The Ringing World* by George remembering once again the three Pye brothers, (William, Ernest and George R), Wilfrid & Michael Moreton, Michael & Martin Fellows and Frank Price.

And of course, he posed the inevitable question 'what next?'

George and Diana's 40th, 50th and 60th wedding anniversaries

12th May 1996 saw George and Diana's 40th Wedding Anniversary celebrations, with a nice article in *The Ringing World* written by John Girt, who had known George and Diana for all their married life. For the 50th anniversary on 12th May 2006, I was pleased to ring in a peal at Monewden, which was followed by a special service at Bedfield church where they had been married. An excellent celebratory tea then took place in Worlingworth Village Hall and I remember George speaking at the event – clergymen excepted, I've never heard anyone speak without notes or repetition for fifteen or twenty minutes with everything so relevant and wonderfully structured. Adrian Knights, a man of few words but great wit, leaned over to me: 'See, he oopens his mowth and parls fall out', very apt. It was a lovely occasion and great to see the Beresford family there as well, making the long trip from North Devon. The anniversaries kept coming! George and Diana celebrated their 60th wedding anniversary in 2016 with a wedding lunch at Aldeburgh and a party at St Lawrence's, Ipswich.

George and Diana's 60th wedding anniversary at St Lawrence's, Ipswich

A gifted public speaker

Although I had heard him speak in public a few times, mostly many years ago as a youngster, it was when George spoke at their Golden Wedding celebrations that I realised what a gifted public speaker he was. In fact he has delivered a very significant number of eulogies (at least twenty), not just for ringers, but for family, friends and colleagues. This is highly skilled, but I suspect those who can do it have most of the skill as an innate component, with little to be learnt. It is selfless too, in that everyone is watching you, no one would really want to be where you are and you have to succeed. It's very unlikely George Pipe needed to learn how to speak, how to write and what to say to make it good. That's why he gave so very many significant eulogies, addresses and presentations over the years – for example Norman and Joan Summerhayes and Dennis Beresford from one family, Cliff Barron and Ken Hesketh, to name a few.

When Olive Rogers, a very well-known London ringer, died some years ago, George gave her eulogy. It was a great experience for Trish Hitchins (née Rogers):

> *"When Mum died in 2004, there was no question about who should give the address at her funeral, it had to be George. They had rung their first peal together in the late 1940s at Wakefield Cathedral and had been friends for over 60 years. In his gracious address he referred to the hundreds of people she knew and whose lives she had touched, These words describe you perfectly George, you touched so many lives and it was always a joy to meet with you and Diana."*

Chapter 17

The Pye brothers
and their legacy

A fusty old archive?

It's easy to underplay the importance of the securing of the Pye brothers' legacy. They were the greatest ringers of their generation but some ringers these days might see them just as chaps with moustaches, stiff collars and watch chains who rang a lot of peals over a hundred years ago. But they were ahead of most of the rest as far as advanced change ringing was concerned. Irrespective of the scale of their wonderful achievements at that time what they did would in its own way become normal in years to come but it would take some time, probably a generation, to happen. In its time though, from 1890 to 1935, what they did was a unique part of our ringing and social history.

To George Pipe, securing the archive was very significant and very high priority, given his family connections with the Pye family. These went back to when Jim lodged and rang with Bill Pye in the 1920s.

Early thousand-pealers

When John Coles, the grandson of Charles T (Tom) Coles, one of William Pye's band, generously gave Alan Regin access to his grandfather's collection of ringing books in 2014, George was delighted as it meant the archive was developing. The peal books contain a copy of the *Ringing World* record together with the towers where they rang. Tom rang 1,014 peals from 1905 to 1945. Another book contains single-line entries of both successful and lost peals. These books went to the London Metropolitan Archive with the Pye papers. Always interested in historical aspects of ringing, George wrote to *The Ringing World* at the time indicating how pleased he was that Tom's papers had been secured, and he also touched on his own childhood connection with the Pyes:

> *"When I started ringing in 1943/44 only 15 people had rung a thousand peals. My father suggested I learn all about these men, their background, job, dates and totals. He would then give me a little test! Now I believe 460 have reached the magic total. [543 as at July 2020.] How I wish I had met Revd Robinson, Ike Shade and the brothes Pye – Bill, Ernest, Bob, Jack Cheesman, Frank Bennett, Jim Davis, Keith Hart and Bill Fussell. Luckily I did meet the others, some albeit briefly – James George, Tom Coles,*

George Williams, Alf Pulling and Jim Bennett. Perhaps the thing we should remember most were the conditions in which they amassed such a total; transport, long working hours and minimal holidays, many rings of bells that were a tough proposition."

Charles T Coles

George said that Tom Coles 'was not only a top drawer ringer but, as the articles portray, a fine administrator, a servant of the exercise. He was, for his day, a notable photographer too, and several of his postcards adorn the Pye brothers' archive. Happily I have some in mine. And Tom's handwriting was exemplary. I remember Father saying to me (he had kept some letters from Tom, Charlie Roberts, Jim Davis, Ron Bullen and others from his Bishopsgate days in the twenties and thirties), "If you can write like Mr Coles, son, you can call yourself a scholar!" I tried. (With some success!)'

George saw this as a simple exercise, securing some of ringing's valuable history, and it was he who saw the opportunity and took it. So for readers of this book, what might have been a shortish chapter with a few highlights has burgeoned into something much greater, with some highlights from the Pyes' distinguished ringing careers, and I hope readers will enjoy it. Just because we have an archive doesn't mean that everything has been done, and the full 'Pye story' in a definitive sense is still unwritten – at the moment at least!

How it was in the 1890s

For generations, ringing had been organised and run by the landed gentry, village farmers, clergymen, aristocrats and, increasingly in the nineteenth century, by industrialists. These men often ran the churches and in some cases were the church benefactors. Such diversity leads us to think of Sir A P Heywood, an estate owner, who founded the Central Council; several of the founders of the Cambridge University Guild who were or would become leading ringing clergymen; and Squire Leonard Proctor from Benington, Hertfordshire, where the first peal of Cambridge Surprise Major was rung by estate workers in 1873. Ringing was a gentlemanly pursuit, definitely amateur in ethos rather than professional, and with the possible exception of J W Washbrook and Revd F E Robinson's activities, for the most part peal ringing had been practised locally or regionally.

Peal ringing goes national

The Pyes changed the established order. They were very different. Their bands were mostly working class men, railwaymen, carpenters, agricultural workers from the Essex or London areas. With their entry into the world of peal ringing in the 1890s, the long established order started to change. This happened quite slowly initially because few others at the time could approach the standards they set, but they started to travel further afield and often included local ringers in their peals. Their achievements were significant but what set them apart was the quality and volume of peals they rang over 45 years, through to the mid-1930s when Bill Pye died. 'Surprise' methods became an established part of their repertoire while others were still ringing simpler methods. As opportunities to travel grew easier, the Pye band developed ringing's early national possibilities, with regular peal

Photos of the Pye brothers on their own are quite rare. This one (from left Ernest, William and George (Bob)), taken after a peal at St Andrew, Enfield on 8th April 1912, shows the traditional dress for peals. (Photo courtesy John Coles)

tours all over the country. Few of the ringers had cars, luggage often went by sidecar, those without transport went by train or walked. It must have helped that Bill and Ernest Pye worked on the railways! In retrospect it was the Pyes that changed peal ringing.

What the Pye brothers achieved

Whilst many ringers will have heard of the Pye family, originally from Chadwell Heath, Essex, less well-known is the fact that they were a family of seven children, six boys and one girl. Sarah did not learn to ring, and John and Albert learnt to ring but did not ring peals. However, the four younger brothers – William (1870–1935), Ernest (1876–1915), Bob (George R, 1872–1945) and Alfred – were prolific peal ringers from 1889 through to the mid-1930s. Alfred rang around 200 peals, considerably fewer than the other three, due to extensive army service. Ernest Pye rang 1,007 peals, but died (in a railway accident caused by mental illness) in December 1915, aged 39. Bob rang 1,878 peals and died in March 1945 aged 72. Three brothers, three prolific peal ringers.

William Pye

Bill Pye (1870–1935) was the eldest of the four peal ringing Pye brothers and the undoubted leader of this band. He rang 1,969 peals and his achievements were remarkable: peals on heavy bells, handbells, first peals, long peals; for example, ringing All Saints, Loughborough tenor to 18,027 Stedman Caters in 12hrs and 18mins, Ashton under Lyne tenor to 15,312

The band for a peal of Stedman Cinques at Great St Mary's, Cambridge on Monday 5th August 1912. (Left to right) William Pye, Keith Hart, Ernest Pye, Isaac G Shade, Charles T Coles, Rev H S T Richardson, George R Pye, Reuben Sanders, Bertram Prewett, John S Goldsmith, John H Cheesman & Rev A H F Boughey. Some of them rang another peal of Stedman Cinques in the same tower that day! (Photo courtesy John Coles)

Cambridge Surprise Maximus in 11hrs and 33mins, St Mary-le-Bow, London, tenor (53cwt) to 7,392 Cambridge Surprise Maximus, Exeter Cathedral tenor to Stedman Caters, (the first time it was rung single-handed to a peal), and many more, including many records or firsts. He died in March 1935 at the age of 64 and the ring of six at Leytonstone was augmented to eight in his memory in 1936. One tribute was: 'There passes the greatest ringer the Exercise has ever known. Judged from every angle of performance the late master of the Middlesex Association (1912–1935) surpassed anything which ringers of this or any other generation have ever accomplished.'

Two peals of Stedman Cinques in a day and a clerical 'first'

By 1912 the Pye band was clearly getting to be a popular group and had received an invitation to visit Cambridge for a long weekend from Rev A H F Boughey, a Trinity man who was Vicar of Great St Mary's with its 27cwt ring of twelve bells. Most of the band travelled to Cambridge by train on the Saturday, when there was a peal of Bristol Major at Sawston, with London Major at St Andrew's unfortunately lost on the Sunday.

Monday 5th August was the big day, with two peals of Stedman Cinques at Great St Mary's. In the morning peal Revd A H F Boughey, vicar of Great St Mary's, and Revd H S T Richardson, his curate, rang their first peals of Stedman Cinques, with this footnote, 'This is the first occasion upon which a vicar and curate have rung a peal of Stedman Cinques

CAMBRIDGE.
THE MIDDLESEX COUNTY ASSOCIATION AND LONDON DIOCESAN GUILD.

On Monday, August 5, 1912, in Three Hours and Forty-eight Minutes,
AT THE CHURCH OF ST. MARY THE GREAT,
A PEAL OF STEDMAN CINQUES, 5007 CHANGES ;
Tenor 28 cwt., in D flat.

*REV. A. H. F. BOUGHEY	*Treble*	CHARLES T. COLES...	...	7
WILLIAM PYE	... 2	REUBEN SANDERS ...	...	8
GEORGE R. PYE ...	... 3	KEITH HART	...	9
JOHN H. CHEESMAN...	... 4	*REV. H. S. T. RICHARDSON		10
ISAAC G. SHADE... ...	... 5	ERNEST PYE	...	11
JOHN S. GOLDSMITH...	... 6	BERTRAM PREWETT...	...	*Tenor*

Composed by C. H. HATTERSLEY, and
Conducted by WILLIAM PYE.

* First peal of Stedman Cinques. This is the first occasion upon which a vicar and curate have rung a peal of Stedman Cinques on the bells of their own church.

CAMBRIDGE.
THE MIDDLESEX COUNTY ASSOCIATION AND LONDON DIOCESAN GUILD.

On Monday, August 5, 1912, in Three Hours and Thirty-eight Minutes,
AT THE CHURCH OF ST. MARY THE GREAT,
A PEAL OF STEDMAN CINQUES, 5007 CHANGES ;
Tenor 28 cwt.

ISAAC G. SHADE ...	... *Treble*	JOHN H. CHEESMAN	...	7
GEORGE R. PYE ...	... 2	*FREDERICK J. PITSTOW	...	8
BERTRAM PREWETT ...	... 3	FREDERICK PITSTOW	...	9
JOHN S. GOLDSMITH ...	... 4	KEITH HART	...	10
REUBEN SANDERS ...	... 5	WILLIAM PYE	...	11
EDWIN BARNETT, Junr. ...	... 6	ERNEST PYE	...	*Tenor*

Composed by GABRIEL LINDOFF, and
Conducted by JOHN H. CHEESMAN.

* First peal of Stedman Cinques.

The Ringing World records the two peals of Stedman Cinques rung in the same tower on the same day at Great St Mary's, Cambridge in 1912 on the bells of their own church'. There were some band changes for the afternoon peal, including two of the Pitstow family from Saffron Walden and Charles T Coles. These days the 'going off' course in a peal of Stedman Cinques is viewed as similar to most others. Not on this occasion, since there were four attempts to ring it in each peal!

These days, two twelve-bell peals in a day in one tower would require excellent sound control, a firm view on handling the complaints that such an exercise might generate and also very firm clergy commitment. I expect the Revd Boughey's invitation to the Pye band bore little concern about these matters. Society was very different then and I expect few questioned clergy authority. Interestingly, a similar band repeated the two in a day at Great St Mary's in 1913!

Record peals of 15,264 and 15,312 changes

On Monday 27th May 1912, at Hornchurch, a band led by William Pye rang a peal of 15,264 changes of Bristol Surprise Major in 9 hours and 49 minutes. This equates to effectively ringing three successive peals. To ring a peal of this length on a 19cwt eight was a significant undertaking, but at that time there was far less choice of towers for a long peal such as this. It meant they rang at a sedate pace for bells of that weight, but one which respected the task in hand. This was the longest length rung in any Surprise method. With 'Surprise' came connotations of complexity, since most peals rung at the time were of 'Plain' methods. Bristol, first rung in 1901, was seen as the most difficult method at that time and though the Pye band had rung peals of it on a regular basis there's no doubt that to ring 15,264 was a significant challenge, and the record they created would stand until 1950.

The band for this peal was the best that Bill Pye could muster, his 'A' band, and very much in their prime. As well as the three Pye brothers, he included Bertram Prewett from Bushey, John H Cheesman from Kent, Reuben Sanders, who would rang a peal on the eve of his 90th birthday in 1965, and Alfred W Grimes (both London ringers), and Isaac G Shade, from Greenwich, the oldest member of the band at 61, who rang 1,450 peals, including 875 with Bill Pye.

The photograph shown opposite is interesting, probably not taken on the day of the peal. We don't know why, but there are actually two photos, one of the band very smartly dressed up for a band photograph for something very special, whereas in the other they were in normal everyday suits and ties, dress more suited to a normal peal. They were proud men, proud of their achievement, looking good too.

Perhaps Bill Pye's greatest achievement, certainly as borne out by the *Ringing World* coverage at the time, was ringing the 26cwt tenor to the long peal of 15,312 Cambridge Surprise Maximus at Ashton under Lyne on 5th August 1929, in 11hrs 33min, at the time the longest peal on twelve bells. The coverage (more than five pages of it over several issues) started with a detailed setting of the scene via the notice of the attempt, (much more impressive than the brief adverts used today!) quoting details of the band, current records to be beaten if successful: a serious building-up of the occasion. The band was mixed, with several unknown to each other, a result of some ringers being secured from the North by Ted Jenkins. Worsley and Riding would have been unknown to Pye. Reeves and Dyke were from the South-West; the rest were from the London area. There was a limited number of ringers who could ring to this standard, only twenty

The band for the record peal of 15,264 Bristol Surprise Major at Hornchurch, Essex. The peal was rung on Monday 27th May 1912, but this photo is believed to have been taken on another day. (Left to right) Standing: Ernest Pye, Bertram Prewett, John H Cheesman, George R Pye. Seated: Reuben Saunders, William Pye, Alfred W Grimes, Isaac G Shade (Photo courtesy John Coles)

THE SURPRISE MAJOR RECORD.

HORNCHURCH, ESSEX.

THE MIDDLESEX COUNTY ASSOCIATION AND THE LONDON DIOCESAN GUILD.

On *Monday, May* 27, *1912, in Nine Hours and Forty-nine Minutes,*

AT THE CHURCH OF ST. ANDREW,

A PEAL OF BRISTOL SURPRISE MAJOR, 15,264 CHANGES;

Tenor 19½ cwt.

REUBEN SANDERS	...*Treble*	BERTRAM PREWETT	... ...	5
GEORGE R. PYE ...	 2	ALFRED W. GRIMES ...	...	6
ISAAC G. SHADE ...	 3	ERNEST PYE	... ...	7
JOHN H. CHEESMAN ...	... 4	WILLIAM PYE ...	... ...*Tenor*	

Composed by GABRIEL LINDOFF, and
Conducted by WILLIAM PYE.

The above is the longest length ever rung in any Surprise method and is the longest peal by the Middlesex Association. The band wish to thank the Vicar, the Rev. Herbert Dale, for the use of the bells, and Mr. J. Dale, the steeple keeper, for having everything in readiness.

The Ringing World's official report of the new record length of surprise

may still actively engage in it, not only as a mild occupation, but in the greater performances which are from time to time undertaken. To that wonderful ringer and conductor, Mr. William Pye, who was the mainspring in this gigantic undertaking, and to his equally wonderful companions in triumph, the Exercise will extend the heartiest congratulations upon a marvellous achievement.

TWELVE BELL RECORD PEAL.

ASHTON-UNDER-LYNE, LANCASHIRE.
THE LANCASHIRE ASSOCIATION
AND THE ASHTON-UNDER-LYNE SOCIETY.

On Monday, August 5, 1929, in Eleven Hours and Thirty-Three Minutes,
AT THE CHURCH OF ST. MICHAEL AND ALL ANGELS,

A PEAL OF CAMBRIDGE SURPRISE MAXIMUS, 15,312 CHANGES;

Tenor 25¾ cwt.

EDWARD JENKINS... ...	...*Treble*	JAMES BENNETT	7
THOMAS B. WORSLEY... ...	2	GABRIEL LINDOFF	8
GEORGE R. PYE	3	JOSEPH T. DYKE	9
CHARLES T. COLES	4	JAMES H. RIDING	10
ALFRED E. REEVES	5	EDWARD P. DUFFIELD ...	11
CHARLES W. ROBERTS ...	6	WILLIAM PYE ... ...*Tenor*	

Composed by REV. H. LAW JAMES,   Conducted by WILLIAM PYE

Longest peal on twelve bells and longest Surprise peal yet rung. First peal in the method on the bells.

The Ringing World records one of Bill Pye's greatest achievements: ringing the tenor to the record length of Maximus in 1929

years after the first peal in the method. However, the band assembled was very strong, although to nearly all today's long pealers the notion of not knowing some of the band as you assemble to ring for nearly twelve hours would be bizarre! There were no ringers from Ipswich or Birmingham, a little odd because the former band was very strong and known to the Pyes.

Two very full reports followed the peal, one a *Ringing World* account, good to read although a somewhat fawning account by today's standards since the writer seemed to be preoccupied with the age of the band ('anything but youthful' and 'one hardly looks for record-making among men who have passed the meridian of life'), and the other by Charles T Coles, scribe for Bill Pye's band, who was in the peal and told the story as one of the band, reading like an authoritative umpires' report, recounting how during the last two hours three previous records fell like ninepins in not much more than half an hour. There seem to have been no umpires – I guess trust and common sense prevailed in those days and in any case people like Sam Wood and Ben Thorpe, who had rung in the

The band that rang the record peal of 15,312 Cambridge S Maximus in 11 hours and 33 Minutes at Ashton-under-Lyne on 5th August 1929. Left to right: Edward P Duffield (11), Charles W Roberts (6), Alfred E Reeves (5), Edward Jenkins (1), James Bennett (7), William Pye (12), Charles T Coles (4), Gabriel Lindoff (8), Thomas B Worsley (2), James H Riding (10), Joseph T Dyke (9), George R Pye (3). This was the longest peal on twelve bells and of Surprise at that time.

12,240 Kent Maximus in 1911, were present on the day. Hundreds of people gathered to hear the finish and a press photo initially failed because two of the band were carried off by the crowd! The peal was the third longest peal ever in time. The local press seemed to eulogise about it. A cynic was 'sternly reminded that the passion for records is not confined to bellringers, but dirt track enthusiasts, cricketers and footballers also attach great importance to records'. As if the long peal wasn't enough, half of the band stayed at Ashton that night before going to Liverpool St Nicholas for a peal the following day.

Clearly the spirit of competition was alive and well, as a few weeks later notice was given of an attempt for 16,565 Grandsire Cinques at Painswick on 14th December, which if successful would eclipse the existing record of 13,001 set in 1920 and the 1929 Ashton record too. However, this was lost after two hours. The Painswick/Cirencester ringers were a strong group, one of several who had practised Cambridge Maximus in the early 1900s in a bid to ring the first peal of it.

Edward Jenkins

Ted Jenkins was a very interesting character. Born in Paddington in 1894, Ted Jenkins was adopted and moved to Baylham, Suffolk, where he taught himself to ring, his first peal coming in 1913 at the age of eighteen. After returning to Suffolk from World War One, Ted advertised his services as a gardener or carpenter, 'change ringer on all numbers, conductor 6 and 8' which resulted in a Mr Fairclough hiring Ted for building work, and also to instruct the local ringers at Stretton, Cheshire. Ted was also a member of the Frodsham band for some years and soon secured opportunities to ring on higher numbers across the North West. He then gave up ringing in 1935, returning in 1947 when he attended the dedication of Wakefield Cathedral bells and was persuaded to start ringing again. His later years from 1953 were in Oldham.

He was a small man of about 5'2" who rang heavy bells wonderfully well. For example, he turned in many of the tenors over 40cwt, including Wells Cathedral tenor when he was 62. Ted rang peals with most of the best ringers of that time. He may have been one of the first truly professional bell ringers, brought to the Cheshire peal band by Fred Dunkerley (a wealthy mill owner) as a tenor ringer, but given a job in Fred's mill as a carpenter! Sadly, Ted died intestate in 1971 and was buried in a paupers' grave.

Brian Harris (Cheshire) wrote a comprehensive and very well-researched article, 'The Suffolk Connection', which was serialised in the *Ringing World* in August and September 2013. It covered Ted Jenkins, Peter Laflin and Allen F Bailey (the second youngest of the famous Bailey brothers of Leiston, Suffolk.), all of whom came from Suffolk and all of whom moved to the North-West in the 1920s. George Pipe was one of several who contributed to the project, focusing on their early years in Suffolk.

Bertram Prewett

Many ringers were killed in World War One. The loss of Bertram Prewett, of Bushey, who died on the Somme on 31st August 1918, was very keenly felt, particularly by the Pye band, of which he had been an integral part since the 1890s. Born in 1878, Prewett rang 953 peals and at the time he died was reckoned to be one of the finest exponents of the art of ringing ever seen. He was a professional: Watford Grammar School, King's College, followed by joining the Civil Service. He rang in most of Bill Pye's record peals up to World War One, for example the long peals of 18,027 Stedman Caters at Loughborough in 1909 and 15,264 Bristol S Major at Hornchurch in 1912. The former was the first time a band rang round the clock (*see band picture on p.167*), and the latter was a remarkable performance which stood for 38 years until 1950 when it was eclipsed by the Cheshire band who rang 21,600 at Over. With Bill and Bob Pye, Bert Prewett rang in the first peal of Cambridge Maximus at Ipswich in 1908. He was also a very talented handbell ringer. For example, his first peal on handbells was Stedman Triples which he conducted from an inside pair.

Soon after he died, Bertram Prewett was featured in a *Ringing World* editorial which stated: 'But of all the ringers who have made the great sacrifice none, we think, will be more widely mourned or more greatly missed than Bertram Prewett who fell in action on the last day of August. Without any exaggeration one can say that Bertram Prewett was among the greatest of all ringers and had he lived there was no saying to what degree he might have extended his already remarkable record'. Also highlighted was his service to the church, willingness to help others and service to the Hertford County Association and to the Central Council, of which he was a member for twelve years.

During the run up to the centenary of the end of the First World War, Alan Regin drove an innovative project to install a ring of eight, tenor 6cwt, at St George's Memorial Church, Ypres, Belgium, the first installation of English-style church bells on mainland Europe. The ringing room at St George's Memorial Church, Ypres, Belgium, dedicated along with the new bells on Sunday 22nd October 2017, is named 'The Bertram Prewett Ringing Room' to preserve the memory of a great ringer. The bells were at the Menin Gate on Wednesday 30th August 2017 for the Last Post ceremony. Part of the delivery of the bells to St George's Church the following day was by Thorneycroft and Dennis lorries typical of those used one hundred years ago. The bells were blessed, in the church, that same day at 5pm. The handbells, formerly owned by Charles T Coles, who rang with Bertram Prewett, and given to Ypres by John Coles, his grandson, are housed in the Ringing Room and were rung during the service. Unforgettable experiences for those who attended!

Serious controversy

In those days, disbelief about high levels of achievement sometimes generated controversy. For example, on 26th January 1904, Bill, Ernest and Bob Pye together with William Keeble rang the first peal of London Surprise Major on handbells, conducted by William Pye. Nine months

"Without any exaggeration one can say that Bertram Prewett was among the greatest of all ringers"

of practice preceded this. Nevertheless, there were some in London who reckoned the ringing of two bells to such a difficult method to be impossible and stated so in *The Bell News*. The controversy that ensued was only partially resolved by the band repeating the feat in front of further witnesses a few days later! Some of the doubt emanated from members of the Ancient Society of College Youths, resulting in Pye falling out with that Society, but his resignation was not accepted. Another example was when William Pye called into question aspects of James W Washbrook's peal of 17,024 Double Norwich on the 23cwt eight at Kidlington, Oxfordshire in 1899. Washbrook was another brilliant ringer of that era and his band had beaten the Pye band's previous record of 15,072, which had been on the much lighter 15cwt eight at Erith only three weeks earlier! Bill Pye was used to being a winner in ringing, but Washbrook was an immense talent too. Unfortunately this matter was never satisfactorily resolved. Winners can sometimes be very proud!

Alfred Pye

Alfred was the eldest of the four peal-ringing Pye brothers. He rang at Romford and rang just over 200 peals, fewer than his brothers because of his 29 years service as a Staff Sergeant in the Army in India and South Africa, for which he received a number of awards. As well as peals for the Middlesex and Essex Associations he was a member of the Society of Royal Cumberland Youths, ringing peals for them on ten and twelve at Shoreditch, St Martin in the Fields and Chelmsford Cathedral. The four brothers – Bill, Ernest, Bob and Alfred – rang a number of handbell peals including Stedman Triples and Kent Major in 1897, Double Norwich in 1903 and Superlative in 1905, all claimed as firsts by a band of brothers. He was born in 1861 and died in 1939, aged 78.

Ernest W Pye

Ernest W Pye, son of the great William Pye, was born in January 1918 and died in March 1996. George Pipe wrote a very touching tribute in *The Ringing World* about a kind man rather overshadowed by his family's history. Much personal communication at this time was by pen and paper, which generated a considerable amount of historical documentation that would be of interest. Ernest and Bob Pye had no family of their own, so the only family was Ernie. He would become a pivotal figure in the retention and preservation of the brothers' papers, which included their peal books.

A reasonably good ringer, Ernie rang nearly 350 peals, including about fifty on handbells. His first peal was Stedman Triples at the age of thirteen, but he lived in his father's shadow, always relating decades-old stories about his father's achievements and talking about 'Owd Bill' with considerable regularity! At one time he lived in Woodbridge and rang at St Mary-le-Tower. His 'Uncle Bob' (George R), who had never married, had run a successful agricultural machinery business in Essex, and when he died in 1945 Ernie received a very significant inheritance. Ernie was a generous chap by nature, for example making a significant contribution to the Suffolk Guild Restoration Fund when it started in 1949, but he was given to be expansive. Thus he proceeded to spend it at some speed – 'keep the change mate' – this may explain his later employment in a paper mill!

I rang with Ernie as a youngster – he was an interesting character who at that time worked in the paper mill at Sawston, near Cambridge. My first peal with Ernie was in 1970, an evening peal at Grundisburgh on Tuesday 11th August, to mark the centenary of William Pye's birth, coincidentally my first peal on ten bells. At fifteen and with only a rudimentary knowledge of ringing history I already knew something of Ernie's impressive family credentials. The post card from Jim Pipe inviting me to ring said 'I have booked you for Grundisburgh, Cambridge Royal, 6pm, Tuesday 11th August.' Whilst it read well to me, it failed to impress my mentor, Leslie Mills, at Bures, where we practised on Tuesday evenings. Leslie prided himself on his outspokenness and his dislike of Jim was already clear. To his credit though, he was able to reconcile my opportunity to progress my ringing with this dislike.

A memorable peal and an even more memorable journey home

For the peal, Ernie conducted a well-known composition by his father, but what I remember most about the evening is the large amount of 'Owd Bill' Ernie drove through the conversation. We had it before the peal, after the peal and in the Dog afterwards, and as it turned out there would be more on the way home. I reckon I was a reasonably well-organised teenager: organising peals, planning journeys, scrounging lifts, (soon I would come across others who were incredibly adept at this), but that evening I hadn't organised how to get home and it was Ernie to the rescue! 'I'll take you back to Bures mate, jump in!'

Grundisburgh to Bures is about thirty miles, just under an hour, but it was a very different type of journey with Ernie at the helm. A map would definitely have helped since the route meandered somewhat, to Debenham, Stowmarket, Bury St Edmunds ('I think we'll go past the Norman Tower now old mate, 'Owd Bill' rang peals there'). The verbal input was still loud and clear, with another one-liner, 'If the ringing wasn't up to it mate, Owd Bill would put 'em on the sticks (stays), the lot of 'em, mate, he'd do it personally, no messin',' coinciding with our arrival in Hadleigh – still no semblance of any attempt at a direct route – followed by Sudbury and finally Bures at about 1.30am, over 70 miles distance and well over two hours journey time. If readers want to plot it, we'd followed a strange, vaguely horseshoe-shaped route with kinks in it, with what predictability there was provided by regular 'Owd Bill.' A memorable and very different experience for a fifteen-year-old!

George Pipe's links with the Pye family

George Pipe's links with the Pye family went back to the 1920s when his father Jim joined the Life Guards and for a time lodged with Bill Pye in Leytonstone. Jim also rang quite a few peals in London with the Pye band. As early as 1948, after George's first peal on twelve, Stedman Cinques at St Mary-le-Tower at the age of thirteen, to which Ernie rang the eleventh, Ernie made a very generous gesture, giving his father's and uncle's postcard collection to George.

The conversation might have gone something like this:

" 'Ere Jawge, Owd Bill would have been pleased to see your first peal on twelve at le-Tower and I'm sure he'd have liked you to have these cards, mate."

On another occasion, talking about band placing to the conductor, Ernie would say:

"Jawge, mate, Owd Bill, he would say, 'Put your good ringers round the front and the back, and your rubbish in the middle.' Where would you like me to ring, Jawge?"
    "Ring the 6th please, Ernie."

The value of the Pye family historical records

The album Ernie handed over to George in 1948 contained nearly 400 cards, Edwardian stamps and postmarks relating to correspondence from ringers such as John Austin, William Keeble, Gabriel Lindoff and many others, sent to Bill Pye at the three Leytonstone addresses he lived at over this time, at Sansom, Cecil and Canhall Roads. Some rarities were included, such as Star Street, Paddington, St Sidwell's, Exeter, St Stephen, Coleman Street, and All Hallows, Lombard Street on its original site – a priceless connection and a collector's delight.

Much later, in 1981, Ernie gave George a handsome album of 91 sepia photographs taken by Charles T Coles, a member of the Pye peal band and a noted scribe and photographer. This had been presented to Bill Pye on behalf of the Middlesex Association, with which he had a very long connection, in 1910. With it came more rare, probably unique, photographs of London towers; Christchurch, Blackfriars; St Andrew, Wells Street; St Mary Matfelon, Whitechapel and others as well.

Death of Ernie Pye and securing the archive

Ernest W Pye

When in 1996 Ernie died, his family – 'young' Bill' (William Edward Ernest Pye, an accomplished ringer as a young man who stopped ringing later), Anne, Robert and Caroline – generously gave George the entire collection of peal books, textbooks and ephemera, a wonderful gift. Although by then 'Young Bill' had become a Jehovah's Witness, he was nevertheless very enthusiastic that George should have the complete archive. In later years, Young Bill reverted to the Anglican faith.

This all shows that for George it was never 'just about the ringing'; many other aspects were important as well. Chris Pickford comments on the value George placed on the preservation and accessibility of historical records, and the Pye archive in particular:

> *"George did much to ensure that important historical records are preserved for the future. He was instrumental in preserving the archives of the Pye family and that all-time great, the legendary Bill Pye. No less important, he secured the records of the Ipswich bellfoundry – the Bowell family – which were literally rescued from a bonfire when a well-meaning neighbour was helping to clear Fred Bowell's house after his death. This was so much more than collecting for personal pleasure. Above all, George wanted to ensure that the material would be available – as it is, in collections accessible for public use – for others to enjoy."*

A visible archive

As far as the Pye family archive was concerned, George, as a keen collector, was ideally placed to deal with it. Indeed, it is unlikely that given the dynamics of the situation anyone else would have been able to do this. George felt that, with the collection of papers now complete, it was important that they should remain accessible for all to see. There were a number of possibilities for where it might be sited. The brothers had strong connections with Middlesex (Bill was Master for 24 years) and Essex (Bob was a Central Council representative for 27 years) so those ringing libraries were possibilities for storage of the archive. George felt that getting optimal exposure would be achieved by siting it at The London Metropolitan Archives (LMA), the principal local government archive repository for Greater London, and the largest county record office in the United Kingdom, based at 40 Northampton Road, Clerkenwell, London EC1. Fortunately the LMA could oblige and was keen to do so, and this is where the whole collection is now, beautifully stored and catalogued. It is important to be aware that this wonderful legacy could so easily have been lost.

Chapter 18

Momentum maintained in the late 1990s

St Paul's Cathedral once again

In 1996 George rang another peal at St Paul's Cathedral, this time Stedman Cinques with the Ancient Society of College Youths (again very highly rated indeed on the Ainsworth scale), so the Cinques and Maximus combination was achieved here, and peals on new twelves were scored at Broughton in Furness, Accrington and Bolton. Earlier, George rang his first peal on sixteen bells, Stedman Septuples, at St Martin's Birmingham. Two peals at Southwark Cathedral were rung in late 1996, the second of which was for Harold Rogers' 80th birthday.

A youngster's 2,000th peal

1996 saw my 2,000th peal, Bristol Maximus, rung at Great St Mary's Cambridge and followed by an excellent curry at Bottisham White Swan (a very early 'curry pub'). It earned a 'green diamond' award from George – a special sticker he placed in his handwritten peal books to mark some peals he felt were of unusually good quality. It was good that George and Howard Egglestone, such important mentors to me over so many years, were able to ring.

1997 saw the passing of Frank B Lufkin, marked with a peal at St Mary-le-Tower. Frank was the ultimate enthusiast. He gave great service to Essex ringing, was a creator of opportunity, a regular visitor to Suffolk and one of the nicest men you could meet.

1998 'Anniversaries' series at St Mary-le-Tower

1998 saw George fixing a series of monthly peals of Maximus to mark anniversaries of first peals in the various methods on the bells going back before the Second World War. Those who have visited St Mary-le-Tower will know that the walls are festooned with wonderful peal boards recording this history. The project involved mostly local band and practice night ringers and offered the opportunity to make personal progress.

I was privileged to ring in several of these peals and it was an initiative that definitely worked, even though there were odd losses along the way. After we lost Double Norwich Maximus early in the year, I went to see George at home at Lansdowne

Historic peal boards at St Mary-le-Tower:
"These six peals and [the first peal of] Cambridge [Surprise Maximus]
Aug 15 1908 are the first to be rung on twelve bells"

Road. He wasn't well and had missed the peal attempt due to a severe chest complaint. It didn't affect his ability to talk, however, and I spent much of the day there while he talked about the history of St Mary-le-Tower and its ringers over the last century. Apart from the first of Cambridge Maximus in 1908, most of this was new to me. Had I had a cassette recorder with me, I could have captured much of that history quite easily that day.

(I remember being told by George that I needed something to eat. I hadn't thought much about it in truth. I'd been focusing on a welter of information I knew I should have been recording (and still haven't; there are gaps in the very early stages). Anyway, 'Darling, can you get the boy some Welsh Rarebit, he's hungry,' was the call to Diana; it arrived in double-quick time, and I *was* hungry and thank you!)

Historic peal boards at St-Mary- le-Tower

The 1936 Suffolk Guild Report noted that a new peal board was erected across the whole length of one wall of the ringing chamber at St Mary-le-Tower. This board is stunning, due to its size and the range of first performances featured, with all the peals rung by the local band. This was unveiled by Mr. E. H. Lewis, the President of the Central Council of Church Bell Ringers (CCCBR), on 28th November. He spoke of the reputation which these two bands (he specified both St Mary-le-Tower and Helmingham) had gained throughout England for their pioneer work in exploiting new methods. Incidentally, eight peals are featured on the board, but one assumes that the original intention was to feature six peals, as stated at the bottom of the board, and they decided to add two more peals later!

E. H. Lewis was a real servant to the Exercise – he represented the Cambridge University Guild on the Central Council for 57 years and was President of the CCCBR for 27 years. A talented engineer, he made a significant contribution to our understanding of matters relating to towers and belfries.

Honorary Lay Canon at St Edmundsbury Cathedral

Another noteworthy event took place in May 1998, namely the installation of George Pipe as an Honorary Lay Canon in St Edmundsbury Cathedral, Bury St Edmunds. Installation took place as part of the Cathedral evensong where three lay canons and three honorary canons were appointed and all took their oaths of Allegiance and Obedience. George had a ring binder full of letters of commendation and congratulation. I guess when you have served in a diocese for many decades, as George did, you get to know many, many people and the letters of commendation and congratulation are very sincere. James Atwell, Provost, wrote 'Alleluia, it couldn't happen to a better person!' Bishop John Dennis, for whom George had worked

A joyous family occasion: George's installation as an Honorary Lay Canon, St Edmundsbury Cathedral 1998

earlier, said, 'Wonderful, wonderful, wonderful, we are so glad at your news, no one deserves it better'.

St Mary-le-Tower's March 1998 parish magazine said 'how good it is to hear that Bishop Richard has honoured our church warden with his appointment as a Lay Canon of our Cathedral. How richly deserved for one who has served the church throughout the whole diocese for many years and in many ways. For his work as Stewardship Advisor, Bishop's Chaplain and one of the country's foremost Bellringers. In so many ways George has served our Lord well.'

It was a great and much deserved honour, a joyful time, a shared celebration involving many people.

Suffolk Guild past Masters' peal

Something a little different was a Suffolk Guild Past Masters peal rung at Ashbocking in April to mark the 75th anniversary of the Suffolk Guild, with the band being, as photo (*overleaf*), Revd Lawrence R Pizzey, Howard W Egglestone, George W Pipe, Stephen D Pettman, David G Salter (current Master) and J Martin Thorley, a very worthwhile exercise on an excellent six.

This peal involved some travelling for Howard Egglestone, from Crediton, Devon and Martin Thorley from Keighley, West Yorkshire. Stephen Pettman and David Salter are active peal ringers in Suffolk. Lawrence Pizzey lives in Bury St Edmunds and rings at the Norman Tower.

A typically valuable snippet

There is so much in George's books to enjoy, particularly relatively small things of local interest. Just a small example – tucked away at the end of Peal Book number 3 is a 1948

Suffolk Guild
Ashbocking, Suffolk, All Saints
Sun Apr 19 1998 2h46 (10)

5040 Cambridge S Minor
Comp. R Bailey No.1

J Martin Thorley (1981–1983)	1
George W Pipe (1964–1969)	2
Howard W Egglestone (1969–1974)	3
Rev Lawrence R Pizzey (1974–1981)	4
Stephen D Pettman (1983–1990)	5
David G Salter (C) (1994–)	6

Especially arranged to mark the 75th anniversary of the Suffolk Guild.
Since 1923 there have been nine Masters, the above six plus Charles J Sedgley (1923–1957), Leslie G Brett (1957–1964) and Amanda M Whiting (1990–1994).

Past Masters of the Suffolk Guild, Ashbocking 1998: Lawrence Pizzey, Howard Egglestone, George Pipe, Stephen Pettman, David Salter and Martin Thorley

sketch of Bowell's Bell Foundry in Ipswich, with a note that it was taken over soon after by Ransomes, Sims and Jefferies Limited (George's employer, he joined RSJ in 1950 as an apprentice), and it was Ransomes who gave him the opportunity to go to Australia. Then they decided to use it as their fire station! Absolutely priceless!

90th and 100th anniversaries

A busy start to 1999 with peals. The first peal of Snow Tiger Delight Maximus was rung at St Mary-le-Tower, 5,100 Stedman Cinques at Southwark Cathedral for the 100th birthday of Lord Denning (a former Master of the Rolls), Canterbury and St Martin-in-the-Fields. Ever the 'anniversary spotter', George asked David House to compose and conduct a peal of 5,090 Stedman Caters at Beccles in April to celebrate the 90th anniversary of the long peal of 18,027 Stedman Caters at Loughborough Parish Church on 12th April 1909.

Sir Alf Ramsey

In May 1999, a peal of Stedman Cinques at St Mary-le-Tower was rung in memory of Sir Alf Ramsey, a long time resident of Ipswich, who managed Ipswich Town FC to win the Division One championship in 1961–2 and the England team that won the World Cup in 1966. Peals at Waltham Abbey and Wakefield Cathedral by Ipswich bands during May demonstrated how twelve-bell ringing in Suffolk was developing strength in depth. The 1990s also saw regular 'post-retirement' peals, typically on some of the fine rings in the Eastern Counties, usually with John Mayne, for example East Dereham, Diss, Long Sutton and Hollesley, to name just a few.

Kenneth J Hesketh and his early death

I mentioned earlier George's strong relationship with Ken Hesketh, which developed from about the mid-1970s onwards. Ken, from a Liverpool ringing family, was well-taught by his father at Halewood. He was always immaculately turned out and this transmitted to his ringing, which was accurate and neat and tidy, a fine ringer. He was one of George's best ringing friends. He was very loyal to those who rang in the peals he organised. His career was in the food industry, working for Chivers Hartley at Liverpool and later Cambridge, Cadbury Schweppes in Birmingham, TKM Foods in Essex and Lockwood's at Long Sutton, and thus shared an interest with George, who had worked in agricultural engineering and later high-value materials handling equipment. When in Lincolnshire, Ken had access to the excellent beer from Bateman's of Wainfleet and also black pudding from Cheshire!

Kenneth J Hesketh, outside St Mary-le-Tower on the occasion of George's 1,000th peal, February 1992

Ken built a regular twelve-bell band that rang peals all over the country, often ringing two peals in a weekend at twelve-bell towers in close proximity, before, for many of them, a drive home of a couple of hundred miles. The peals were every four to six weeks and the recipe was decent bells, high quality ringers and a well-developed social side! Ken was an excellent organiser, with everything confirmed in writing to each individual member of the band during the week before the peal. This generated opportunity for many of the band to achieve twelve-bell peals all over the country. George rang 156 peals with Ken, 104 on twelve, many of which he recalled as memorable. The method was usually Stedman Cinques or Cambridge Maximus, with the focus on quality of ringing rather than the method difficulty, and the band was selected from a pool of about 16–18 people. Good company, good fellowship, good ringing.

So, for example, in 1976 George rang the tenor to a peal of Cambridge Surprise Maximus at Southwark Cathedral. Other towers visited were new twelves such as Bedford, Guildford Cathedral, and Gloucester Cathedral as well as more regular venues such as St Mary-le-Tower. Manchester Town Hall and St Nicholas, Liverpool were towers not readily available for peals at the time and therefore much valued by those able to take part – peals of Stedman Cinques were rung at both. There are far too many to list, but some of the highlights were peals of Stedman Cinques at St Mary-le-Bow and St Michael Cornhill, City of London, and Great St Mary's Cambridge. Stedman Cinques at St Mary Redcliffe, Bristol in 1977 received the ultimate accolade from George: 'this really was a magnificent peal in every respect'. Howard Egglestone's peal of Stedman Cinques at Redcliffe in May 1978 was a memorable peal – Jim Towler talked only the other day about the amazingly good middle hour of that peal – and both peals at Redcliffe received a 'green diamond' award!

Sadly in late 1998, shortly after his band's usual peal in London on ASCY Dinner Day and another at Tewkesbury the following week, Ken became unwell and was unable to ring in a peal at Leeds Parish Church he had organised in December. The diagnosis was CJD (Creutzfeldt-Jakob Disease), a incurable degenerative brain disorder that leads to dementia and ultimately death, and Ken died about six months later in May 1999 at the early age of 55. This was a great shock to the ringing fraternity all over the country. Ken was a very close friend of George's and they rang over 150 peals together. Ken's funeral was at Pinchbeck, Lincolnshire in late May, at which George gave a memorable eulogy. John Fielden, a very longstanding friend and contemporary of Ken's, wrote an excellent obituary in *The Ringing World*. Ken contributed to ringing in South Lincolnshire in the '80s and '90s, but he was best known as a prolific organiser, particularly of ten- and twelve-bell peals, all over the country. Tudor Edwards and John Gipson also wrote personal accounts of Ken in *The Ringing World*. A peal in Ken's memory was rung at St Mary-le-Bow, London, Stedman Cinques by an 'Around' tour band. This is recorded in the tower with a peal board.

Chapter 19

The early 2000s

Anniversaries and losses, 2000 and 2001

On 1st January 2000, the first day of the new Millennium, the first peal on the restored bells at Boxford was rung, the first peal on them since 1896 and only the third peal ever rung at Boxford. In May at St Mary-le-Bow, London, George rang a peal of Bristol Maximus to mark the 50th anniversary of the first ever peal in the method, at Leicester Cathedral in 1950, followed in August by a peal of 5,100 Stedman Cinques at St Mary-le-Tower in honour of the 100th birthday of HM Queen Elizabeth the Queen Mother.

Peter Border, a much admired and popular ringer, died suddenly in October 2000 and a peal of Barford Surprise Maximus, a method composed by Peter and named after the Warwickshire village where he lived, was rung to his memory at St Mary-le-Bow. Peter, the original gentle giant, was a regular ringer in the Birmingham Cathedral Thursday night peals and rang 500 peals on the tenor. He was also a noted composer, particularly of Royal and Maximus, but also composed the long peal of Glasgow Surprise Major rung in 1966. He rang almost 3,500 peals and was the first person to reach 3,000 peals. He was also a keen knitter.

In January 2001 John Chilcott's 70th birthday was celebrated with peals at St Stephen's, Bristol, Birmingham Cathedral and St Mary-le-Bow. George and John were close friends over a number of years and were among the few remaining members of the 1964 Washington band. John also composed the then record peal of 15,699 Stedman Cinques rung at Birmingham Cathedral in 1966, so it was a special day, with all three peals of Stedman Cinques successfully rung. Later that month a peal at Selby Abbey, North Yorkshire, with its three towers and one of England's biggest parish churches, was an architectural treat for George. Norman Harding of Kings Lynn died in January 2001 and he was remembered in peals at Ipswich and Kings Lynn.

First retirement from peal ringing, 2001–2006

Having rung a peal of Yorkshire Surprise Sixteen, at Swan Tower, Perth, in April 2001, George was keen to ring Bristol, accomplished in August, at St Martin's Birmingham. The 9/11 terrorist outrage in New York happened in September and a College Youths peal of Stedman Cinques was rung at St Mary-le-Tower, remembering the victims, friends and families of the terrorist attack, with a minute's silence before the peal.

Peal band at Grundisburgh, 5th September 2006, on the 100th anniversary of
Cecil W Pipe's birth, with his grave in front.
Left to right: David Pipe, Rod Pipe, George Pipe, Diana Pipe, Stephen Pettman,
Mike Whitby, Andrew Wilby, Barry Pickup, Jim Towler,
Richard Munnings, John Loveless, Adrian Knights

After that peal, number 1275, George made a conscious decision not to ring any more peals. In his own words:

"I wasn't feeling well, mainly from breathlessness and fibrillation, resulting in a visit to Papworth Hospital and a week in Ipswich Hospital. Added to this I was finding peals very hard going and was in considerable pain too in the lower back (again), right arm and leg, nor did I want to perform at what I considered would be less than 100%, whatever that can mean.

"So I quite expected to ring no more quarters or peals and thus started to fill the remainder of peal book number 4 [about 80% of it!] with ephemera and items that interested me."

(The ephemera is varied, an author's delight, and of the highest quality!)

Return for special centenary peal

"However on September 5 2006, the centenary of my father's birth, the family persuaded me (pressurised me!) into standing in a special peal to mark the event, Stedman Cinques, at Grundisburgh."

Jim died in October 1980. Many of us who rang in this peal had rung with him in earlier years, and ringing high-quality Stedman Cinques at Grundisburgh that evening was a privilege, with David conducting and Rod, George and Diana all in the band.

"Thereafter I rang a few, mostly if bands were short. How long that continues time will tell. I confess I'm finding them pretty tiring and painful in arms and right leg. Happily the palpitations/breathlessness is under control it seems."

For 'a few' peals, above, read nearly 150! There were still lots of things to do, ambitions to be achieved in peal ringing, new twelve-bell towers, not to mention a very significant restoration right in the heart of Ipswich.

To Australia once more in 2007

In February 2007, George and Diana were off to Australia once more, this time a short trip with just one peal, Stedman Cinques on the augmented twelve at Goulburn. This was specially arranged in memory of John J F (Jack) Roper, George's great friend in Melbourne from when he arrived in Australia, a founder member of ANZAB and his wife Gwen. In June 2007, George received an invitation to ring a peal of Stedman Cinques at Worcester Cathedral to mark the centenary of the birth of Sir Edward Elgar, a great son of Worcester, and in September a peal at Southwark Cathedral, also Stedman Cinques.

Heavy metal

On 1st November 2007 George achieved a long-held ambition to ring a peal at East Pennard, Somerset, Grandsire Doubles, thus having rung peals on the heaviest rings of five, six, eight, ten and twelve. The conductor of the peal, Stephen Pettman, obviously not concerned with minimising risk, called 21 different 240s! Later in November, George and Diana were kindly invited by Stephen Coaker on a trip to New York where the new ring of twelve had been installed in the autumn of 2006. Peals of Cambridge Maximus and Stedman Cinques were rung, with Diana taking part in the Cambridge and the Stedman being George's 1,300th peal. George achieved another long-held ambition with a peal of Bristol Surprise Major on the fine 35cwt eight at Westbury, Wiltshire in April 2008. He commented this was a really superb peal, not a word spoken, except bobs and singles, and of course attaining 'green diamond' status!

Harold Rogers anniversary peal

Later in April 2008, a peal was organised to mark the 70th anniversary of 91 year old Harold Rogers' first peal, rung on the little five at Huntingfield, Suffolk. Harold, now 91, was going to ring in this peal, again at Huntingfield – of course he was, since he rang 85 peals after he was 90! Age was no barrier to him. His son, Chris Rogers, enjoyed the day:

"After Dad, my sister Trish and myself, there were just two places to fill – George and Diana of course, whom Dad had known for much of his ringing life and who were

delighted to ring and had much more experience of five-bell peals than the rest of us. We had decided to ring Stedman Doubles, but just before the peal George gave me an excellent piece of advice: 'If Dad appears to be tiring, change to Plain Bob.' That is precisely what we did – 31 extents of Stedman, followed by 11 of Plain Bob. Thank you, George, it was a memorable occasion."

Rod Pipe's 2,000th peal

This took place on Sunday 11th May 2008 at St Martin's Birmingham. George was in this peal. Always keen to push the boat out, Rod composed a fearsome looking composition of Spliced Bristol, Bristol Little, Littleport Little Surprise Sixteen and Stedman Septuples, duly rung in 3hr 42min.

100th anniversary of the first peal of Cambridge Maximus

On 16th August 2008 at St Mary-le-Tower, one of the Exercise's greatest 'firsts' was commemorated with a peal of Cambridge Surprise Maximus specially arranged and rung to mark the 100th anniversary of the first peal of Surprise Maximus (Cambridge) ever rung. This was at Ipswich on 15th August 1908. Then, in September, back at Ipswich, a peal of Stedman Cinques was rung to mark the 60th anniversary of George's first peal on twelve, also Diana's 100th on twelve.

Also noteworthy at this time was a peal of Yorkshire Surprise Fourteen rung at Winchester Cathedral. This included ten regular ringers at St Mary-le-Tower.

A sad loss at Bury St Edmunds

A peal rung at Bury St Edmunds on 8th November 2008 bears the footnote 'A get well compliment to the Dean, the Very Reverend Neil Collings, presently in Addenbrooke's Hospital, Cambridge.' Neil Collings was suffering from an incurable brain tumour and died in 2009 at 63. He had come to Bury St Edmunds from Exeter Cathedral in 2006, where he was Canon Treasurer. Soon after arriving at Bury, he provided the impetus behind the initiative to augment the existing Dobson ring of ten to a ring of twelve.

Crediton

January 2009 saw George in a peal of Bristol Maximus at Crediton, Devon, the fine new twelve which replaced the original Pennington eight. This initiative was the result of many years of hard work by a strong local team of people headed by Howard Egglestone. Howard lived in Suffolk in the 1960s and 70s and at that time he and George were close ringing colleagues, initiating many changes and improvements to the ringing scene in Suffolk. Initially Crediton only wanted ten bells (since they had had eight for about 200 years) and the ten were dedicated in November 2004. However, a twelve-bell frame had been fitted, and the two trebles were added in 2007.

The Band of Ringers who, on Easter Monday, April 12th, 1909, rang at the Church of All Saints, Loughborough, Leicestershire,

The Great Peal of 18,027 Stedman Caters,

In Twelve Hours and Eighteen Minutes.

The band for 18,027 Stedman Caters at Loughborough Parish Church on 12th April 1909, the first time a band of ringers rang round the clock.
Top row: Geo. R. Pye, Treble (Chadwell Heath); Isaac G. Shade, 2nd (Greenwich); W. H. Inglesant, 3rd (Loughborough); John H. Cheesman, 4th (Kent); Bertram Prewett, 5th (Oxhey); B. A. Knights, 6th (Chesterfield) Bottom row: William J. Nudds, 8th (Hampstead); Gabriel Lindoff, Composer, 9th (Dublin); William Pye, Conductor, Tenor (Leytonstone); William Willson, 7th (Leicester)

Centenary of Loughborough long peal

Easter Sunday in 2009 (12th April) marked the 100th anniversary of the 18,027 Stedman Caters rung at Loughborough Parish Church, conducted by William Pye. This anniversary was duly marked by a peal of 5,100 Stedman Caters, again at Loughborough. The composition, arranged by Rod Pipe from the original 18,027 by Gabriel Lindoff, was fitting for the occasion and an excellent peal was rung. We were commemorating a remarkable achievement (which was also the first time one band had rung round the clock) and every member of the band felt privileged to be ringing that day.

Ixworth bells were restored and augmented, with the first peal coming in March 2009. George's footnote says 'splendid tea afterwards'! He had given a talk during the project to assist the cause. Later, in September, the first peal was rung on the excellent new light Taylor eight at St John's, Felixstowe.

Maximum age difference

We were particularly pleased to host a peal of Double Norwich at Campton, Bedfordshire, on Saturday 16th May 2009. It was to mark the 100th birthday of Frederick N Smeaton of Adelaide, the oldest College Youth in the Society's history, still ringing and driving his own car. George and some Australians were in the band. The day before the peal there had been international conference calls to wish Fred well on his birthday. The treble ringer in this peal was Thomas Keech, who was eleven years old. He had rung with Fred Smeaton at Prospect, Adelaide, four years earlier when on holiday in Australia. A good day!

Mountaineers and football managers

A peal at Chelmsford Cathedral on 31st May 2009 was accompanied by a very unusual footnote, to congratulate Amanda Richmond on her achievement of climbing Mount Everest. Another footnote highly valued by many Suffolk people was that for a peal of Ipswich Delight Royal at Grundisburgh on 6th August, which was specially arranged and in thanksgiving for the life of Bobby Robson MBE, a wonderful manager of people and a former manager of Ipswich Town FC and England, who died the previous weekend aged 76. Sir Bobby, as with Sir Alf Ramsey before him, was revered in Ipswich and all over the country.

St Lawrence, Ipswich – restoration of the fifteenth-century ring, the oldest complete ring of five, in 2009

The St Lawrence's Bell Restoration Project

George Pipe always thrived on projects and another one was duly completed in late 2009 at St Lawrence, Ipswich. The church has a wonderful tower, by far the most prominent tower in central Ipswich. In 2006, as George discussed with Alan Hughes the possibility of restoring the bells, it became increasingly apparent that what was under discussion was not simply the restoration of an unringable peal of five bells. It was also about the retention of as much of the fifteenth-century infrastructure as possible, the key message to the outside world being about the re-creation of the sound that Cardinal Wolsey would have heard in his childhood years as he grew up in Ipswich.

That is what happened. The completion of the project in 2009 was marked by a peal of Grandsire Doubles on Wednesday 11th November, half-muffled for the Fallen, the first peal on the restored ring. The bells are a fifteenth century ring of five with a tenor

George with Dr John Blatchly MBE, pictured here with Helmingham tenor during another bell restoration project

of 14cwt, which had been sensitively tuned, the oldest complete ring of five. The peal was rung using the original fifteenth-century clappers! A couple of years later George invited the Ancient Society of College Youths to St Lawrence's for their country meeting in Ipswich, affording some members not just the rare privilege of ringing on five bells, but on a highly noteworthy and historic ring of five at that!

The St Lawrence's story demonstrates the strength of effective co-operation at work. St Lawrence's had a chequered history back to the 1880s and was made redundant in the 1970s, moving from the diocese to the County Council and then entrusted to the care of the Ipswich Historic Churches Trust. By 1996 the Church and the installation were falling into severe neglect. What remained was the church floor littered with rubbish and rubble, also being used to store parts of the bell frame and bell wheels. The bell frame, wheels and associated infrastructure, which had once supported a complete pre-reformation ring of five bells, was by now standing against the college-style pews along the walls.

By 2006, and largely due to the endeavours of John Blatchly, chair of Ipswich Historic Churches Trust and a former Headmaster of Ipswich School, it was announced that the Borough Council and Suffolk County Council would in future work to help develop St Lawrence's as a community resource. Involved parties included Age Concern, who had previously run a cafe in the Town Hall, and the project was to be coordinated by a local progressive 'social enterprise', Whitehouse Enterprises, which enables adults with disabilities to find work and focuses on catering and furniture products, both of which contributed to the reinvention of this church as the St Lawrence Centre, now a highly successful community restaurant and gallery in central Ipswich. Ultimately the centre was opened to the public in July 2008, with the cost of the whole project at £1.2m, much of this from the public purse.

In December 2009 a peal of Wolsey Surprise Maximus at St Mary-le-Tower, conducted by Rod and the first peal in the method, further cemented the Wolsey connection. Thomas Wolsey was the town's most famous son. This was a tribute also to John Blatchly MBE, Chairman of the Ipswich Historic Churches Trust, who died in 2009.

Parham – A typical Suffolk bell restoration

Ten days after the St Lawrence, Ipswich peal came the first peal ever at Parham, Suffolk, a tiny village of 263 people (reduced from 300 at the previous census) with all the classic attributes of rural Suffolk, which as far as a bells scheme is concerned means a very small number of people working incredibly hard over several years. Since the project is largely restorative, someone is required to research and apply for grants, a critical component in the mix. Then this is topped up with specific skills from a small number of individuals with, for example, wood working, metal working, general engineering skills and the ability to provide transport/haulage facilities and a willingness to put up bellhangers. All this will be donated free, which helps reduce the cost. Parham's fourteenth-century church will probably have an active congregation of maybe around twenty, so the project will succeed largely due to a huge amount of goodwill that will come from various people in the village, not necessarily people connected with the church, and often gently targeted. Or, though probably a long shot, a couple of major benefactors will come forward and cover much

St Mary's Church, Parham, Suffolk, in George's hand, 'early spring 2004'

of the cost. Some who give will wait for the project to gather momentum before they do so, meaning public relations and communication are important. Special 'bells' events may generate relatively little income, but masses of goodwill.

The talk to parishioners

People love bells, their bells, and that's where the talk in the church/village hall comes in. In fifty years George gave over two hundred talks about bells, ringing and restoration to parishes and other groups and there's no doubt some of these led to immediate results or confirmation of a parish plan to restore its bells and commence fundraising. Others are more about a slower moving situation where a restoration in a tiny village with little infrastructure is simply a dream with a plan yet to be finalised – it's all a dream until the end is in sight. A talk can help establish the potential and build the will to commence a restoration project. Either way, the knowledge and motivation provided by an excellent speaker who is an expert on bells and ringing really helps.

Ruth Suggett comments on the help George gave her at Ixworth few years ago:

"When you are raising thousands of pounds for a bell restoration project, the person you want to call you up and offer to help is George Pipe. When I was in the middle of running our project in 2008, George did exactly that – generously and completely unsolicited, he offered to give a talk about bells and bellringing. Apart from anything else, it was such a morale-booster. George and Diana arrived with several large boxes containing items from his wonderful collection of cards, photographs, models and

other memorabilia all to do with bells and churches. Charismatic and knowledgeable as ever, he held the audience, almost 100 people from local U3A groups, spellbound with his very personable and amusing style. The feedback from the event was glowing – he had clearly caught the imagination of everyone there, most of whom had no idea about the subject. We were very fortunate to have George as our ambassador that day, not only for his passion for ringing but he communicated it with such ease and confidence, and he helped us raise several hundred pounds more towards our total."

Chapter 20

More losses, more restorations, more new twelves, more cricket

Stephen Ivin

Stephen Ivin died on 7th January 2010, aged 72, after a long illness, another major loss to the Exercise. Steve was a very close friend of George's and was without doubt one of the greatest ringers of his generation as well as one of the brightest. As Steve Stanford put it (in an account featured across two issues of *The Ringing World*):

> *"Not only did he possess very considerable abilities in performance – as a composer, conductor and heavy-bell ringer – but he was equally a master of his instrument, with very extensive theoretical, technical, and practical knowledge of the tuning, dynamics, and hanging of bells; subjects in which he was widely recognised as an authority, and on which he was often consulted.*
>
> > *"His achievements during the '60s and '70s at St Paul's Bedford in developing and leading one of the finest Sunday Service bands of the day, followed by equally impressive developments of the bells and ringing in Oxford, from the mid-'80s until the time of his death, serve as lasting and fitting tributes to him."*

Cliff Barron

Cliff Barron died in January 2010 and this was marked by peals at St Mary-le-Tower and Kings Norton, Birmingham. A wonderful ringer, in some ways Cliff was a very complex man and George's well-written obituary reflected that.

More new twelves

When Ken Hesketh died in 1999 his band lost a great organiser and their supply of new twelves, formerly provided by Ken's arrangements, dried up as well. George, ever the collector, had new twelves to collect and the ground to cover to do so! I am also a twelve-bell collector, and George and I had many towers in common, typically some of the newer augmentations to twelve, so it was a pleasure to include George in several of these arrangements.

The first day out was in January 2010, to Hampshire, peals at Hursley and Bitterne Park. Then in February 2010 a peal of Bristol Maximus at St Magnus the Martyr, London, following the restoration and installation of the new Whitechapel twelve, with an East Meets West band. I remember this being a particularly good effort. To Northallerton, wonderful as always, and Ripon Cathedral in late October and an excellent peal of Bristol Maximus at Ripon, receiving a 'green diamond' rating. George described it as 'a super peal in every respect' preceded by a very convivial evening the night before as most of the band stayed in the Ripon Spa Hotel, just by the Cathedral.

Adrian Knights, a true man of Suffolk, who has lived in the county all his life, rang his 1,000th peal at St Mary-le-Tower on Tuesday 1st June 2010, marking his 63rd birthday. George had rung in 238 of Adrian's peals, with them third in each other's lists of collaborators.

More Suffolk augmentations

I mentioned earlier that augmentations from six to eight had taken place in many Suffolk towers over the years. This allowed George to ring peals at Rendham in 2008, Felixstowe (a new eight) and Ixworth in 2009, and Hopton-by-Thetford and Bardwell in 2010. This reflects the fundraising and restoration ethos in Suffolk, where the projects sometimes come thick and fast – as Ruth Suggett discovered when she was involved simultaneously in the projects at Ixworth and Bardwell in 2009/10 – assisted by talks from George to assist with the PR and stimulate the fundraising.

St Michael, Cornhill

In January 2011, George rang in the final peal to be rung on the old bells at St Michael, Cornhill, City of London, by the College Youths, a 'green diamond' performance by a very experienced band ringing Cambridge Maximus, one of five peals he had rung at Cornhill. The peal marked the centenary of the first peal of Surprise Maximus in London in 1911, which was only the third peal of Surprise Maximus ever rung, the first two being at Ipswich in 1908 and 1910.

Sadly, replacing the old, mixed and poor 42cwt twelve at Cornhill with a new 32cwt Taylor twelve, thus reducing tower movement by half and making the bells easier to ring, generated much controversy over some time. Projects in the City can move really quickly, but this one took about six years – the project had been agreed in 2005. Much of the controversy centred around a very strong character, Philip A F Chalk, who was a distinguished, retired medical consultant, a member of the St Paul's Cathedral Guild of Ringers for 25 years, a past master of both the Ancient Society of College Youths and the Drapers Company, and a former churchwarden at Cornhill. Post-retirement, he had developed his interests in the countryside, cake making and fly fishing!

George was a good friend of Philip's over many years and he wrote a long, well-argued article in *The Ringing World*, touching on a number of different themes and not forgetting Philip Chalk's contribution to ringing, a significant one, over many years. The tower of St Michael, Cornhill had a wonderful history, but George stressed the need for change, advocating a lighter twelve in future. There had been many instances over the years of towers in Central London where rings of bells were just too heavy for the tower. George posed the question, 'Why the obsession almost, for a two-ton tenor high up in such a tower?', given the constraints at Cornhill of an unbuttressed Hawksmoor-Wren tower. The Cornhill arguments became highly entrenched and came to involve legal input well above the normal level of faculty, etc., and it took over three years to resolve these issues.

George with brother Rod at the Ringing World Centenary event on 26th March 2011. Sadly Rod died a few days later, on 1st April.

The loss of George's brother, Roderick W Pipe

Rod Pipe's death, at the age of seventy, was a huge loss to the Exercise. A measure of how ringers valued Rod's life and achievements is that 57 peals in his memory were featured in the *Ringing World* that featured Richard Jones' brilliant account of Rod's life. In Suffolk there were peals of Stedman Cinques at Grundisburgh, where he learnt to ring in 1949, and Cambridge Maximus at St Mary-le-Tower, largely by resident bands.

Richard Jones's tribute started:

"With the death of Rod Pipe, unexpectedly on 1st April 2011, one of the most brilliant stars in the ringing firmament has sadly passed into history."

The Pipe family at the commemoration event in 2013. Left to right: Gill, Alfie, David, Diana, George, Henry, Helen (Rod and Gill's daughter), Cecilia and Stephen (Helen's husband)

The brothers had always been very close and George found losing his younger brother, five years his junior, very difficult to bear. He talked to me about how Rod was an innovator, composer, conductor and leader in ringing, who took others with him, particularly in the pursuit of raising standards and achieving the very best – 'levelling up' as professionals do, and actively pursuing ways of doing that. Outside the tower he was interested in astronomy, gardening, and sport. He was very competitive, banterish and fun.

Sometimes other ringers would get upset, since Rod could on occasions be coruscatingly direct (it happened to me!), but he saw ringing as a team activity which required collective responsibility. In 2010, some *Ringing World* correspondence about 'scary' ringers elicited an interesting response from Rod, stating:

> *"… errors in ringing frequently demand urgent action … I try to modulate the response to the person and the situation and of course I get it wrong at times, sometimes overreact, sometimes get angry … The point is that we are all collectively responsible to the band we are ringing with, first and foremost to do our best but also to accept that things can get heated, even scary. The time to sort out bruised feelings is afterwards."*

Rod was committed to the broad interests of ringing as an art and science. But he could be down to earth and had often talked about the importance of the ringing environment where we spend so much time. It had always been obvious when entering the ringing room that St Martin's, Birmingham was a historic tower going back over two centuries. In the modern era, it was the site of the first ring of sixteen bells, a concept pioneered by Rod, for which he led fundraising efforts and which was completed in 1991, yet in other respects it had changed little over a century. Thus, in 2013, the Birmingham ringers decided to mark Rod's contribution to ringing with a project to update and improve St Martin's ringing room, together with a commemoration weekend, fully involving the family, on completion of the project in late 2013.

Portsmouth Cathedral and two heroes

Another new twelve for many at the time was Portsmouth Cathedral, where we rang a peal on Saturday 12th February 2012, Bristol Maximus by an East Meets West band including George and Howard Egglestone. These two men were my great mentors from my early, formative years in Suffolk through to 1977 when Howard (and I, coincidentally) left for Berkshire. As it turned out, this was the last time they would meet and ring together and appropriately it was their 100th peal together. Howard suffered pancreatic cancer in 2010, for which he underwent major surgery. He recovered well, to the extent of walking the 87 miles of the Kennett and Avon Canal as a fundraiser for Pancreatic Cancer UK, but it recurred and he died in January 2013.

This was also the writer's last peal with George. Ringing allows high standards of performance to be maintained at a relatively late age, for example Harold Rogers rang 85 peals when in his 90s. At Portsmouth, George and Howard, both in their mid-70s, gave a high level of performance that most of us would love to emulate, and we rang a very good peal. All in all, this was an excellent day and I hope that in 2030, when I'm 75, that my performance level will be as high as theirs was in 2012. Footnotes for performances in ringing vary in importance. Trevor E Bailey, the former Essex and England cricketer and BBC commentator, had died in a house fire a couple of days before the Portsmouth peal. He had been George's cricket coach at Woodbridge School in 1948–9 so the peal was dedicated to him, a highly appropriate footnote to an excellent peal.

A love of cricket

George developed a love of cricket at a very early age, well before he came under the influence of Trevor Bailey, an Essex and later England all-rounder, at Woodbridge School. Someone once said to him, 'if you hadn't chosen ringing as your main hobby what would you like to have done?' He replied without hesitation 'play cricket for England or have been a pianist'. George continued, 'I suppose my sporting love is cricket in all its forms especially Test cricket and well-contested 50 overs a side matches'. He feels he has been very lucky to see some top quality cricket, which has given him much enjoyment along the way.

But there is just one 'beef' – that George went to Lords as a teenager three times to see the incomparable Denis Compton bat, but in all three visits the great man only just managed to get into double figures and never went on to make a big score! During the 1947 England *v* South Africa series in England, Compton was among the best batsman in the world and one of the greatest cricketers of his era, a swashbuckling figure who became the twelfth cricketer to score 100 first-class centuries in a cricket career lasting from 1936 to 1957. In 1947, Compton scored eighteen centuries, another world record, and his aggregate in all matches that season was 3,816 runs, which remains the most ever made in a season in first-class matches. Against the South African touring team, Compton scored five centuries, four of these for England. Operating simultaneously at a high level in two sports sometimes used to happen at that time, so for good measure he also played football for Arsenal FC between 1936 and 1950.

Compton's Australian rivals included the all-rounder Keith Miller, a fast bowler and an attacking batsman who could score very quickly. Keith Miller was a highly important part of the 1948 Australian team who beat England in England, along with another fast bowler Ray Lindwall, a devastating pair. Ray Lindwall was a natural athlete with a bowling action reckoned to be close to perfection.

Back to T E Bailey and his coaching spell at Woodbridge School; George commented that he was lucky to come under Bailey's eagle eye which stood him in good stead in another way. In the 1970s, there was a Gillette Cup match at Lord's that George particularly wanted to see, but he couldn't get a ticket for it. So he had the nerve to write to Trevor Bailey, by then retired, reminded him of his coaching time at Woodbridge, and asked, could he help George secure a ticket? By return of post two complimentary tickets arrived and an absolute refusal to accept more than George's thanks, a kind gesture indeed.

Living in Melbourne for seven years, 1956 to 1963, gave George and Diana the opportunity to see some wonderful cricket, not only at the Melbourne Cricket Ground but also Victorian country matches, and eventually all the test venues except the WACA in Perth. The most memorable was the great series between Australia, captained by Richie Benaud, and the West Indies under Frank Worrell's leadership (he was later knighted). Richie Benaud would later become one of the best ever TV commentators: highly intelligent, perceptive, quietly spoken, he let the match do the talking. Diana and George saw all five days of the 1960–61 Australia and West Indies Second Test at the Melbourne

Cricket Ground (what an experience!). This Test at the MCG followed the First Test of that series at Brisbane – this was the famous 'Tied Test', the first time this had happened in Test Cricket.

Australia – no better place to be for a cricket fan!

Chapter 21

Some retrospection

By 2011, George was having considerable physical difficulty ringing, but was still keen to ring peals on new twelves. True to form, he continued to show tremendous courage and determination in all his activities. He didn't ring peals after 2012, a matter of profound regret and frustration, even more so when ringing is something that one is particularly good at. However, these difficulties notwithstanding, 2011 and 2012 saw a good representation of fine East Anglian twelves featuring in his peal book: St Mary-le-Tower for the Queen's Diamond Jubilee, Bury St Edmunds, St Peter Mancroft, Norwich and Great St Mary's, Cambridge.

George's 1,400th peal was at St Mary-le-Tower in March 2011 and he then procured another peal book from his book binder. This book, Peal Book No 5 (that should be a method name!), is the best peal book of all even though it only contains eighteen peals, which is obviously disappointing. However George decided to fill the blank pages with photos and other images of 'favourite things,' and other memorabilia which readers in years to come might find interesting. Manna from heaven for someone writing a book about him! A peal at St Mary-le-Tower in June 2012 marked the Queen's Diamond Jubilee, the 50th anniversary of ANZAB, of which George and Diana were founder members, and George's 250th peal at St Mary-le-Tower. By 2012, when he stopped ringing peals, he had rung 251 peals on the bells, considerably more than anybody else, his first peal on the new bells coming in January 1977 and his total on these bells was 234.

The ring of ten at the Norman Tower, Bury St Edmunds, had been augmented to twelve in 2011. Given George's very long association with the Diocese of St Edmundsbury and Ipswich and ringing at the Norman Tower, he was very keen to ring a peal on the twelve, which he did, Yorkshire Maximus in August 2012. A peal of Stedman Cinques at St Peter Mancroft, Norwich, in November 2012, a 60th birthday compliment to David Brown, was George's 25th peal in the tower, achieving an ambition he had held for a few years. George's last peal was on the new twelve at Great St Mary's, Cambridge, in December 2012, Stedman Cinques with a Mark Eccleston 'special' composition and nephew David also in the band. If you needed to choose a venue at which to bow out, Great St Mary's would be a good choice.

The problem with peal ringing was 'all sorts of health problems necessitating major surgery at Papworth Hospital, Cambridgeshire, ulcerated legs, kidney failure, varicose eczema, all rather tedious for other people' – these worked against it. He noted shortly before his death that for him ringing was probably over, but Diana is still an active ringer and at the age of 80 rang a peal of Cambridge Surprise Maximus.

This, from George, is one of the most profound observations I've ever read about ringing:

> *"Ringing is so much more than peal, quarter or tower totals – it's about people, events, human anecdote and reminiscing, history, fine churches, some in glorious settings. I feel I have been very lucky, not least in Australia and North America."*

A little analysis

What emerges if one puts his first 1,400 peals under the microscope? Firstly, apart from six years in Australia, he lived nearly all his life in the Ipswich area, far from London or Birmingham, which are peal ringers' paradises. He always rang peals but was never an accumulator or 'numbers man.' It's fair to say he was a good record keeper who kept a watchful eye on his numbers, as normal bellringers do!

However, his is an impressive list. Over a third of his peals, just under 500, were on twelve bells. One or two organisers helped his efforts to achieve 500, but sadly it didn't happen. But trips to new twelve-bell towers such as Portsmouth and Ripon proved very worthwhile and received the 'green diamond', George's quality marque!

There is a standard mix of peals on six, eight and ten, with a third being Major and 12.5% Minor, the latter reflective of the earlier days, and often peals for others. It's a good 1,400, reflecting his commitment to ringing in Suffolk and travelling, often with Ken Hesketh's band, to new twelves all over the country, particularly in the 1980s and 1990s.

Then on to the summary of the 1,400 peals:

> *898 of the 1,400 were rung for the Suffolk Guild. The peals took just over 65 years at an average of around 22 per year, with the most in one year being 57 in 1988*

> *1,392 on tower bells, 8 on handbells (none on minirings)*

> *Peals rung with nearly 1,500 different ringers and 202 different conductors*

> *Rung for 56 ringing societies in 50 counties in 384 towers (122 of these in Suffolk)*

Holiday opportunities

Enid Roberts, originally from Swindon, but based in Sydney for the last sixty or so years, comes to the UK most years and George reported excellent holidays in Scotland, the three of them visiting nearly all the cathedrals (ever the collector), Iona, Orkney, Tulloch and Carlisle, South West Wales, and the Isle of Wight. George and Diana were regular attenders for a number of years on Brian Whiting's annual quarter peal weeks, relaxing and enjoyable holidays with a dozen or so people staying in a big house with quarter peal towers close by. Brian related what happened on one tour:

> *"Back in the mid-90s, the tour was based at The Queens Head in Milton Ernest, Bedfordshire. The pub had non-standard background music which provided the opportunity for a rather strange form of mini quiz, at least strange for most of those from Suffolk. One particular track stumped everyone, though. Returning from the gents, George announced that he had remembered the name of this track. "It was*

Outside Beaminster, Dorset, in 2018 on one of Brian Whiting's annual quarter peal weeks. (Left to right) Back Row: Roger Lubbock, Ralph Earey, George Pipe, David Stanford, James Sparling; Middle Row: David Sparling, Gill Sparling, Claire Smith, James Smith, Brian Whiting, Diana Pipe, Adrienne Sharp Front Row: Pat Lubbock, Peta Whiting with Max, Tristan Shaw, Claire O'Mahony with Ronnie, Tessa Earey, Ellie Earey with Friday. (Photo taken by Ralph Earey)

Harold Faltermeyer – Axel F", he said. The assembled company was amazed that he should know the artist, let alone the tune. It transpired that he had checked out the name with the barman on the way back from the gents."

Suffolk Guild summary obituaries

For many years George wrote obituaries for the annual Suffolk Guild report. He thought it was very important to remember members the Guild had lost and wrote hundreds of these. They are an object lesson in how to paint a picture with skilled use of language to describe what's really important when you have limited words to devote to your subject. Some of the subjects were well-known to George as writer, others he may well have met only once or twice, if at all. They are a great read.

Here are some examples from the 1973 Suffolk Guild report:

James Bennett – Grundisburgh

As a Royal Marine, he travelled the four corners of the earth and in his day, as a member of Bill Pye's famous band, he was a very well-known performer. Jim, a 1,000-pealer, member of the 15,312 Cambridge Maximus peal band in 1929, a Cumberland and a strong churchman was above all a disciplinarian, not least to himself, in all that he undertook.

Frederick Bowell – Ipswich

The talented, though somewhat eccentric, son of Alfred Bowell the Ipswich Bellfounder, Fred's lifelong interest was in teaching beginners. An able musician, and a member of the Guild since its formation, it was always regretted that he was unable to carry on his father's successful business.

Derek Lockwood – Thorndon

A farmer who in his day rang at Wetheringsett, Stradbroke and Fressingfield as well as Thorndon, Derek passed away at Eye in November.

Miss Grace Reeve – Hockwold

As Chaucer would have said, "A kind and gentle maid" who with her sister Dora supported the work of the Guild in the more remote areas of N.W. Suffolk. She will be sadly missed.

James Smy – Blaxhall

A countryman from the village and band of ringers immortalised by George Ewart Evans in 'Ask the Fellows who cut the Hay'. Jim Smy was a faithful servant, and occasional peal-ringer.

Charles J. Sedgley – Ipswich

One of the best-known figures in the Exercise, conductor, composer and in his prime, between the Wars, one of the foremost twelve-bell authorities. With George Symonds he built up a Surprise Maximus band without peer at St. Mary-le-Tower and helped give the Suffolk Guild its reputation in the Exercise. He served as Master from the Guild's foundation in 1923 until 1956, and rang 357 peals, 130 on twelve. A self-taught man in many fields, he was a splendid companion and we shall find his place hard to fill.

Henry Vince – Marlesford

P.C. Harry Vince, the village 'bobby', a man of humble ringing achievements, but nevertheless one who enjoyed his ringing and was a gentleman with it. He long declared the quality of Lt. Glemham bells!

May these past members and friends rest in peace, and the Suffolk Guild offers its sympathy to the bereaved.

The Suffolk Guild Veterans 1966

Suffolk veterans' events

The Suffolk Guild Veterans' afternoons, held on the second Wednesday in July, are one of those wonderful ringing institutions, a social event the aim of which is simply for the Guild to honour and respect senior members. I feel I should have attended one of these afternoons – both through desire and (just) qualification by age, although there is no prescribed age for entry – but as yet I have not done so. Maybe next year? One or two Suffolk ringers, notably Christine Knight, have given me a clear idea of the nature and significance of the event. It is a gem!

It is held at Debenham, a great venue, home to one of the finest eights in East Anglia: historic ringing chamber, stone seating in the porch, wooden benches outside the church room, a good supply of drinks and a pub just the other side of the churchyard wall in case of need. The event provides an opportunity for older members to meet with friends they might otherwise not see, have a ring on some fine bells and then enjoy a fine tea and a long yarn – tea at no cost to those attending, lavish, not paid for directly, but by donated draw prizes and the sale of tickets. Tea as it should be! A great afternoon out, and of course there are plenty of members who fall into this category. It sounds old-fashioned, but is the firmest of diary entries for those involved, and a wonderful atmosphere once people arrive.

Jim Pipe started the Veterans in the 1960s. What a wonderful photo from 1966, of George Symonds and Charles Sedgley and their contemporaries. When Jim died in 1980, the meetings were discontinued for a few years until they were revived in the early 1990s with a lot of hard work by Muriel Page, who ran the event for about 25 years – Muriel has boxes full of photographs which form a brilliant archive of the event over the years. She handed over to Jenny Scase, so the event continues into the future. The event is 'very Suffolk', seen as the important event that it is, but low-key, caring, friendly and an example of getting priorities right. In the past, noted ringers from afar would attend, with attendances sometimes over 100. These days about 50 attend – that's similar to a successful district meeting!

George, keen to socialise with old friends, always attended this event and was himself one of its focal points. With less travel away from Ipswich in recent years as he got older, the chance to make contact with old friends across the county was of increasing value to him – and to them, of course. There had been some doubt about him attending the 2019 Veterans meeting but he made it, no doubt after a considerable effort to do so, this at a time when most aspects of life were getting tougher for him. But the charismatic yet approachable George Pipe was still effective, with his trademark modesty and interest for others, renewing acquaintances, still a superstar at 84. If anyone could defy age and maintain a status of ringing stardom, he could. No need to 'work' the gathering; the queues of people surrounding him, all wanting to shake him by the hand, demonstrated the point. True class just gets older, that's all.

A key part of the proceedings for many attending had been George's vote of thanks to all involved, especially the helpers, lucid, no notes, no one forgotten and not time limited! His presence was synonymous with the event over so many years. Now it will need a new speaker.

Pure kindness

But it is the extremely kind 'unseen' gestures to a large number of ringers, particularly Suffolk ringers, which endeared George to so many. Here is an example, from Christine Knight, which demonstrates the point:

"The last two occasions Richard and I met George were at the 2019 Veterans and then about ten days later at Brian Whiting's annual fund-raising barbecue, another big event. Tim Forsey from Clare came with us to the Veterans meeting. Tim is nearly 70, a former call-change ringer who has now rung lots of quarters and a peal, an avid RW reader too. He had a very successful career in pharmaceuticals and got frustrated that the acquisition of change-ringing skills was difficult for mature learners, but he's now SW District Secretary and has been elected recently to the Guild Management Committee.

"Anyway, Tim's attendance led to an incredibly kind action from George, who must have felt exhausted from all the interaction with well-wishers. I had said to Tim that he couldn't learn to ring in Suffolk without being introduced to George Pipe, but when the moment came, many others were waiting so we shook hands, I introduced Tim very briefly, and we moved on. About an hour later, I was wandering over to the church room for a cuppa, when George caught my arm as I passed. He was mid-conversation with someone else, but said quietly, 'Don't worry, Chris, I'll speak to Tim.' He had read my mind completely! True to his word, he did just that, and Tim later told me what an encouraging chat it was.

"At Brian's barbecue, George pressed into my hand an envelope, containing a copy of the book he co-wrote with Ranald Clouston. A lovely letter for us was inside, confirming that he hadn't been feeling at all well at Debenham, and he even apologised for not having been 'brighter'! The book itself was a signed copy for Tim, with the inscription 'A long & happy ringing life – so nice to have met you at Debenham'. A very special man indeed!"

*Alan Regin with the Ypres bells at the Loughborough Bell Foundry Open Day,
29th July 2017 (Photo courtesy David Potter)*

An MBE proposal – What to do and how to do it

Ian Campbell writes about the proposal of Alan Regin for an honour, an MBE, in 2018.

"*When Alan Regin became Steward of the Rolls for the Central Council of Church Bell Ringers he found many names missing mainly from WW1. He continues to do so although the list is now very short. His stated wish was to have a Memorial peal of bells cast to their memory and installed in a church in mainland Europe, which was achieved at St George's Memorial Church, Ypres, Belgium in 2018. Allied to this, is his enormous input for helping other ringers and developing ringing, both in the USA and UK, over many years. Given these major positives, I felt that it would be worth investigating the possibility of getting a "gong" for Alan.*

"*I believed the process to be reasonably straightforward, with good supporting letters very important. I managed to get twelve initially, including one from George. What a letter it was, beautifully handwritten on his home letterhead and full of passion – he really does have magnificent skill for finding the right words for the occasion. Accompanying it was a note saying "if you want to type it out on your PC and send it back to me I will sign it and return". I rang him straight away and told him the letter was what I called a "work of art" and would be sent as is! George also helped me with a covering nomination letter but before sending the package off to the Cabinet Office he said "we need one further supporting letter – one from a high ranking clergyman". We were grateful to The Bishop of Salisbury – Nick Holtam (a former vicar of St Martin-in-the-Fields and a former ringer too) for his help. So it was that 3 years later Alan was awarded the MBE.*

"Of course, during this time the Ypres project was well underway and it was decided that it would be fitting to have a prayer prepared for the ringing room at Ypres which would be read out before ringing took place. Who could write the prayer? There was only one person who could find the words required – yes it would be George! He provided two and they are both so beautifully written that it's almost impossible to read them without stalling – they soften even the hardest hearts. Thank you George!"

George had visited Ypres with Andrew Wilby and Laith Reynolds some years before Alan Regin's 2017 project was mooted. Sadly, despite his keenness and enthusiasm demonstrated above, George never rang at Ypres due to the health reasons that restricted him in the last few years, but was pleased to participate and contribute by providing the prayers.

More ill health

In 2017, George was diagnosed with giant temporal arteritis, a potentially dangerous condition which frequently causes headaches, scalp tenderness, jaw pain and vision problems, being treated with steroids and other medication at home and at Ipswich Hospital. To bear all this, and the regular visits to Ipswich Hospital that came as a consequence, showed significant fortitude. It would have been easy for him to have become negative about life, but as a man with many interests he stayed optimistic. The only thing he complained about was that 'I can't really do anything.' Diana was his rock, staying in wonderful health, and they were sustained by their family and friends. They had both been thoroughly involved in assisting me to write this book, particularly regarding the earlier part of George's life and then the years in Australia 1956 to 1963, a very long time ago. His powers of memory remained quite remarkable until the end.

Chapter 22

George's death –
Tuesday 3rd March 2020

Laith Reynolds called me on 4th March to advise that George had died the previous day – we were in New Zealand on holiday and not back for another week. The news was a shock to us, but not completely unexpected since George's health had declined over the last few years, and while he had maintained contact with local Suffolk ringers, it had been increasingly on a social basis rather than in the tower. His last peal remained his first on the new bells at Great St Mary's, Cambridge, in December 2012.

Only a day or two after his death, Cecilia Pipe observed that

> *"… it's really heart-warming to read so many messages about Uncle George and how he touched the lives of everyone he came into contact with. I think he gave us all something to aspire to in his generosity, encouragement, the way he treated others and his lust for life. His last, recent letter to us (we have hundreds), told us how very proud he was of all of us and I wish we had taken the time to write back and tell him the same. He was one of a kind! We will miss him enormously."*

Richard Munnings's Suffolk Guild Blog

Social media was filled with moving tributes from all over the world (see later), from which the sense of loss and respect for George was palpable. Through Richard Munnings's daily blog on the Suffolk Guild website we were able to gain a feel from 11,000 miles away for how the news had been received. Richard had known George all his life. Here is some of what Richard said:

Wednesday 4th March 2020
> *"Expected but sad, sad news came out today as it was announced that the great George W Pipe died yesterday.*
>
> *It has been some years since we have had the privilege of ringing with him and indeed now some time since he was last able to join us in the ringing chamber at St Mary-le-Tower. He was particularly missed at the Twelve-Bell Striking Competition named after him in February 2020.*
>
> *There was much said today and much more will be said in the coming days about him from across the world and if I were to go into depth of all he has achieved there*

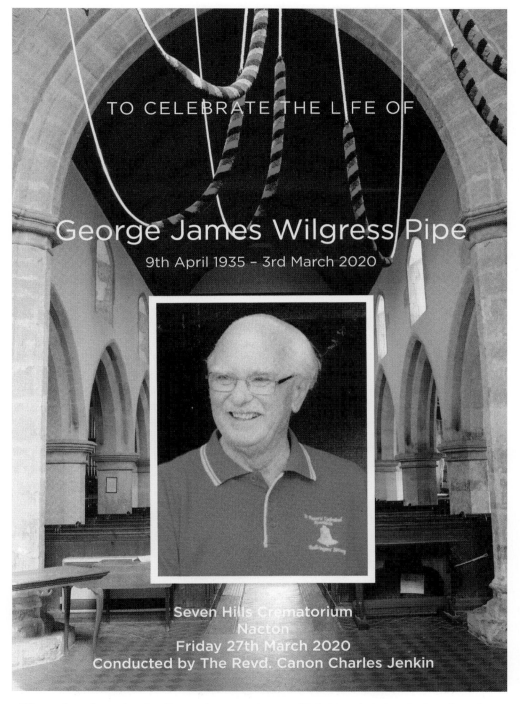

TO CELEBRATE THE LIFE OF

George James Wilgress Pipe

9th April 1935 – 3rd March 2020

Seven Hills Crematorium
Nacton
Friday 27th March 2020
Conducted by The Revd. Canon Charles Jenkin

The order of service for George's cremation on 27th March 2020. Only a few close family were able to attend, due to the 2020 spring coronavirus lockdown

would be about a year's worth of blog in this one entry! And yet on this Guild website it is important to stress just how much he did for ringing locally, nationwide and globally and what a gem we had in our midst.

At St Mary-le-Tower he took a band that was apparently just ringing Plain Bob Doubles, led the project to get the bells rehung and many of them recast in 1976 and turned them into a band ringing local peals of Bristol Surprise Maximus and reaching the National Twelve-Bell Final on multiple occasions.

For the Suffolk Guild he was the Ringing Master from 1964-69 (incredibly only the third Ringing Master in its history!), Chairman from 1974-77 and was a driving force behind its success over many years.

Nationally he was hugely respected. Peal boards across Suffolk bear witness to many of the biggest names in the exercise being willing to travel here to ring in peals with him. They saw him as a part of the country's ringing 'elite'.

Internationally he was best known and most fondly remembered for being instrumental in forming the Australian and New Zealand Association of Bellringers (ANZAB), but he also rang in the first peal at Washington Cathedral in the USA in 1964, which in those days was a huge deal and contributed to his status as a ringing superstar.

Quite simply, he was one of the most well-known and most loved ringers on the planet. There are countless stories of ringers from within our borders travelling the country and indeed the world, and once their hosts realised where they were from would be met with the questions "Do you know George Pipe? How is he?"

He was gently teased from time to time, particularly around the extremely rare occasions he went wrong, a memorable example of which was the St Mary-le-Tower piece in the 1990 Rose Trophy Eight-Bell Striking Competition at St Margaret's, Ipswich, when the touch of Stedman Triples was too short! He was always more than happy to laugh at himself though, once going wrong in something at SMLT and chuckling afterwards that it "will be around the county soon!" Yet he was a rock you could rely on in everything he rang, especially on higher numbers.

Personally, I have wonderful memories of him, especially from my youth. Even before I started ringing he was an imposing yet kind figure and when I began ringing I aspired to be just like him. I got nowhere near of course, but through observing him, ringing with him and listening to his advice I became a far better ringer than I otherwise would have. He struck fear into the hearts of ringers, lest they went wrong in a piece he was ringing in, yet he was a gentleman when the ringing finished, always happy to guide and advise.

Beyond ringing he was also a good friend to our family. He was one of the first to phone us when the boys were born, he was Godfather to my brother Chris and he and Diana always gave the children presents at Christmas.

His artwork adorns many a ringers' wall, including ours with a drawing of St Mary-le-Tower he very kindly did for our wedding nearly eight years ago. The huge archive of information and history on ringing and churches, both physical and from his mind, frequently recounted to captivated audiences, were invaluable to ringing and beyond. Witness his exhibition at the 2015 Suffolk Guild AGM in Felixstowe, highly absorbing. Although it is sad he won't be there with us at its launch on 30th

May, thank God for John Loveless' biography of him which immortalises a man who at times appeared immortal. Sadly it wasn't so and thoughts are with his family and especially Diana. They say that behind every great man is a great woman and rarely has this been more the case than here!

Ringing reacted in its droves to the news today. Social media was awash with heartfelt messages and footnotes began appearing on BellBoard to his memory. Four were here in Suffolk, with the QPs of Double Norwich Court Bob Major at Bardwell and Elveden dedicated to him, as were the 120s of Grandsire Doubles at St Lawrence – the rehanging, and subsequent regular ringing of the historic pre-reformation five, is another achievement of his – and Ipswich Surprise Minor at Pettistree, whilst beyond our borders he was remembered with the 1344 of eight Major methods spliced at Our Lady and the English Martyrs in Cambridge and the handbell peal of Lessness Surprise Major rung at Lower Broadheath in Worcestershire. I imagine much more will be rung for him in the coming days and arrangements are already underway for a peal attempt at St Mary-le-Tower.

However, it was George and Diana on our minds today with this expected but sad news.

RIP George W Pipe."

UK ringing tributes

The coronavirus pandemic of 2020 played a significant role in ringing at this time, with peal-ringing ceasing from mid-March 2020. Many bands must have been disappointed by the enforced cancellation of ringing to George's memory. Nevertheless, around 75 ringing performances – peals, quarters and shorter touches – took place to George's memory, across the UK and further afield. Approximately half of the tributes were in Suffolk and surrounding counties. Tributes from Australia (14) and the United States (Washington Cathedral) showed that ringers all over the world were remembering him.

The footnotes to these performances demonstrate how loved and respected he was. For example:

Bardwell, Suffolk, *4 March 2020. This was the first ringing in memory of George, and by a band that knew him very well, but most of whom on arrival hadn't known of his passing. Of course, this news was not totally unexpected and the footnote was brief, 'In memory of our dear friend, George W Pipe, who died yesterday, just over five weeks before his 85th birthday.' True to form, Brian Whiting composed at very short notice a quarter peal of 1,284 (in line with George's 84 years) of Double Norwich. Bardwell village Facebook pages noted that 'this was a sad occasion on which to ring a quarter peal – the loss of George Pipe, a friend of Bardwell and a giant of ringing worldwide.'*

Ipswich, Suffolk, St Lawrence, *4 March 2020, 120 Grandsire Doubles, 'Celebrating the life of George W Pipe. Rung during the weekly lunchtime ringing at St Lawrence. George was heavily involved with the restoration of St Lawrence's bells in 2009. He will be missed. Also present were Gillian Wakefield and Tracey Scase'*

Norwich, Norfolk, *The Mancroft Ringing Discovery Centre, 5 March 2020, 1,260 Double Grandsire Triples. 'Remembering a great man. Rest in peace George Pipe.'*

Ipswich, Suffolk, St Mary-le-Tower, *9 March 2020, 360 London No 3 Surprise Royal: 1 Richard J Munnings, 2 Jill D Birkby, 3 Diana M Pipe, 4 Stephen A Cheek, 5 Jonathan J E Williamson 6, Chris Birkby 7, Ian J Culham 8, David I Stanford 9, David A Potts (C), 10 Colin F Salter: 'Rung by an SMLT Sunday service band at the end of practice night in memory of George W Pipe'.*

Pettistree, Suffolk, *9 March: Ringers rang a quarter with this wonderful footnote: 'In fond memory of George W Pipe (1935–2020). George gave a talk about Bells & Bellringing in Pettistree WI Hut at the start of fundraising for the 1986 Bell Restoration. He was part of the team who taught the original band. George was known worldwide as a fine ringer and taught many to ring across the globe. He will be sadly missed by the Pettistree Ringers.'*

Merton, London, *14 March, 5,084 Stedman Caters by the SRCY, conducted by Lucinda Woodward. 'Affectionately dedicated to a Great Man. Rest in Peace George W Pipe 1935–2020.*

The footnote to the quarter at St Chad's Shrewsbury *was 'Remembering George W Pipe and rung on one of his favourite rings of twelve bells.'*

Amongst the UK peals were two notable peals of Stedman, both on handbells: **Stedman Cinques** including three Willingham (where they live) Pipes, and **Stedman Triples** rung again by the Willingham Pipe family. One wonders what George might have said!

And from abroad …

Ringers in Australia demonstrated the love and affection he generated, nearly sixty years after they returned to the UK. David Bleby from Adelaide Cathedral, who learnt to ring towards the end of the Pipes' time in Australia (and witnessed George's pursuit of the first peal on Adelaide Cathedral bells!) said, 'I am sad to report that George Pipe died today. His gift to Australian and New Zealand ringing, and indeed to the whole Exercise, is immeasurable. He was indeed the driving force for the formation of ANZAB. May he rest in peace.'

The **Adelaide** quarter noted 'Rung in celebration of the life of George W. Pipe, a friend and inspiration to many ringers around the world.' The photo of the band demonstrated social distancing! The **Armidale** quarter was 'Rung in memory of George Pipe, a firm and enduring friend of the Armidale bellringers.' The **Burwood** quarter noted 'Remembering George Pipe who did so much for Australian ringing'. At **Burnley**, Sue Pacey conducted a quarter 'In memory of George W Pipe. A grateful celebration of his ringing life and with thanks for teaching the conductor 58 years ago in Melbourne, Australia.' At **Melbourne Cathedral** a quarter of Plain Bob Major was rung on Sunday 8th March 'to celebrate the life of George W. Pipe. George joined the band in 1956 and was Tower Captain at St. Paul's, 1959–1960 and 1962. He took the band and Australian ringing to a new level. Ringers 1, 2 and 3 (David Heyes, Helen Pettet and Sue Pacey) learned under his tutelage.' At **Manuka** a touch of Grandsire Triples was rung by ANZAB officers and members, 'Rung in memory of George W Pipe (1935–2020). He made an immeasurable contribution to Australian ringing and the creation of ANZAB.' At **Lismore**, the ringing was 'In Memory of George W. Pipe (with 2007 photo!). George visited Lismore in February 2007.' Reading these quarters, it struck me that his last visit to Australia had indeed been in 2007, so a few participants might not have met him, but the sentiments were the same. At **Goulburn**, the ringing was 'in affectionate memory of George W Pipe, a great friend to ringing in Australia and New Zealand.' At **Perth**, the band rang 'In celebration of the life of George Pipe, a great inspiration to many in the Ringing fraternity.'

Finally a peal at **Yass**, famous as the venue of a GWP 'mishap' in 1959 and never forgotten by Australians! 'Rung in memory of George Pipe who rang a peal at this tower in 1959. He also famously, after reading the first edition of *Dove's Guide*, drove to this tower expecting to ring at a 27cwt five before seeing the tower and realising it was a misprint.'

The impact of coronavirus increases

By mid-March, the status of many of the summer's major sporting events was coming into question, and our own National 12-Bell Contest, with eliminators on 28th March and Final on 20th June, was cancelled on 15th March. Concerns over the virus started to affect aspects of what we would normally consider to be everyday life, with a rapid shutdown or reduction in normal services and restrictions in travel.

This also affected George's funeral, scheduled for 27th March, at Ipswich Crematorium; because of the restrictions it was only possibly for close family to attend.

'Zoom' meeting

In normal circumstances many people would have attended the funeral, but that was not possible, so a virtual meeting was set up concurrent with his funeral using Zoom videoconferencing technology. It was the best we could do and but it was a valuable and moving experience. The jury's out on how George might have viewed this technology versus a more normal type of funeral, but some thirty of us, representing the US, Australia and the UK, were on the call.

We started with prayers from Linda Garton, reflecting George's deep Christian faith. David Sparling, former Master of the Essex Association, then opened up proceedings by talking about George's influence on him, particularly when he was learning to ring twelve bells, and the importance of setting high standards.

Rick Dirksen mentioned May 1964 and 'the ten' who travelled to Washington, of whom George had been the sole survivor – they truly established change ringing in a country where there was none before. One evening during the week George Pipe and Frank Price were at a social event, failing to remember they had also been booked for a media appearance. They eventually arrived just in time. The host's name was Steve Allison, known as "The man who owns midnight". (The Dean termed him 'a jerk', to introduce a little perspective.) In 1964 Allison was the toast of the town where late-night radio was concerned, and appearing on his show was considered a very big deal. Steve had a reputation for rough questioning aimed at belittling and maintaining superiority. Anyway, George and Frank buried him in change ringing jargon and it never happened. They literally left him speechless for, as he said, the first time in his career!

David House talked about his fifty years of friendship with George, their St Peter Mancroft (David was at UEA) and ASCY links. David Brown talked about George's remarkable ability on handbells. He seldom rang handbells but two of his eight handbell peals were Stedman Cinques, in 1953 (his first peal in hand) and 1978, the latter conducted by David.

Tina Sanderson talked of being taught to ring by George at St-Mary-le-Tower in 1971 and drew attention to the dismissal of the thirty York Minster ringers, including her husband, Peter, and herself, in 2016. George felt particularly strongly about what he saw as an appalling injustice. But it would be wrong to assume that George was principally about pursuing topical ecclesiastical injustices. Far from it. George was a very well-read person and any church-related observation from him, irrespective of topic, came from a position of real knowledge.

One of his major drivers was his desire to help others, in particular his friends, and readers can find plenty of examples in this book. He would go to amazing lengths to help. This was partly about his faith, but in my view it was mostly innate. Being a prolific letter writer (many thousands) must have helped (particularly pre-phone), but he also gave freely and regularly of his time whether it be on the phone (the familiar 'John – George') or visiting or helping in whatever way was needed. Here are just three examples illustrating this caring side of his nature:

Peter Sanderson recounted how he was temporarily hospitalised in Ipswich many years ago. He hardly knew George at this stage. During Peter's short stay an unlikely visitor, George, looked after the little known visitor from Yorkshire who received five star treatment. David Stanford mentioned George's kindness and steadfast support to him when he faced difficulties in his personal life some years ago. I suffered mental illness back in the 1980s and remember George's pragmatism and good advice as to how this might be resolved at a time when the involved parties seemed to be treading water. None of these actions in themselves changed the world. Indeed, life would have progressed satisfactorily without them. But they demonstrated perfectly George's desire to go the extra mile when people needed help. From a ringing perspective, this was the case in Suffolk, where he knew most of the ringing fraternity and ringing influencers, from agricultural worker to senior clergy. There was the vast number of talks to parishes, demonstrating that for him a significant restoration for a tiny rural parish differed little to a prestigious, shiny new job.

In Australia, he achieved what can only be described as reverence, as all the ringing to his memory in Australia during March 2020 shows. His visits to Washington were relatively few, but his status as the last surviving member of 'the ten' who went to open the bells in 1964 meant he was highly respected – after all, these were the men who brought change ringing to Washington in 1964, with all that has followed since.

Philip Earis reflected on what turned out to be George's last peal in December 2012, Stedman Cinques at Great St Mary's, Cambridge, his first on the new twelve. He rang the treble to a Mark Eccleston composition, which he thoroughly enjoyed. Several of the band agreed it as a superlative performance and the best peal they had rung on the bells.

Alan Regin talked about George's support for the Ypres project in 2017. George composed two appropriate and very moving prayers for St George's Memorial Church. These are located in the ringing chamber, to be said before the bells are rung.

Among other compliments, the words 'great', 'remarkable', 'inspirational' and (inevitably these days) 'legend' were used. Other recurrent themes were his faith, his modesty, his welcome to visitors at St Mary-le-Tower, his politeness, consideration for others, team building and standard setting, with his mere presence making ringing better.

Simon Rudd, who succeeded George as Ringing Master at St-Mary-le-Tower thirty years before, described George as 'friend, mentor, a deeply Christian man and source of boundless enthusiasm for ringing.'

The author's view was that 'George was very widely respected and greatly loved, a positive influence on others in many walks of life who will be greatly missed.' Several of us had known George for fifty years or more and the thirty of us exchanged happy memories, anecdotes and prayers about George for an hour and a quarter on what would otherwise have been a rather empty Friday afternoon. Thanks to Simon for the Zoom inspiration.

Epilogue

Underlying all the words I've written are some very simple observations about ways of living a fulfilling life and also making a difference. Firstly, George and Diana's partnership was as strong a marriage as I've ever seen – they married on 12th May 1956 – a great team. Secondly, they always had a deep Christian faith and this sustained them through good and not so good times. This helped shape their journey. They were committed to their family as their absolute top priority and, as if to give added stability, they lived in the same house, a home of homes for so many, since they came back from Australia in 1963, a mere 57 years ago. They travelled widely and enjoyed many great times, and of course there have been some difficult times too. When autism came into their family in the late 1960s they might have buckled, but instead their faith came to bear and they responded by helping to effect improvement for all those affected in East Anglia, not just themselves.

They shared a commitment to St Mary-le-Tower church, community and, of course, tower, over those 57 years. They headed efforts over thirteen years to fund the restoration of the bells in 1976 (and what a result it was) and then over the next ten years developed twelve-bell ringing in Ipswich to a level few thought possible. They have been great servants to bellringing in Suffolk and further afield too, and inside or outside of ringing, think of all George's talks, watercolours and pen & ink, all of which came free, some on our walls at home.

That's a quick run through some of the history. What's so special then? Well, lots actually. Everyone was treated in the same way, with politeness and respect, irrespective of who they were: that's a gift, rather than a 'given.' Many of those who didn't know him probably saw George as a charismatic front man with excellent communication skills (which is true), but underneath was a sensitive, kind, considerate man. George and Diana shared some outstanding personal qualities, which mean that they attracted others and often took others with them – for example in Australia, Melbourne particularly, and also at St Mary-le-Tower. They have acted as great role models for people of any age, and for the young they have been great encouragers. Kind, tolerant and caring deeply about others; it's very simple really, 'good people'. 8 Lansdowne Road has been a 'go to' haven for many over the years, no better place to be when things get a bit difficult.

It has been my privilege to have been asked by George to write this book. The sheer breadth of the story of George and Diana is huge, and it has been a much bigger job than I was expecting. When people ask how this spot of authoring has been, I say 'long'. The breadth is because as a youngster George knew men born back in the mid-nineteenth century and his life went right through to the brilliant youngsters of today, born in the 21st century (some in his family, of course), many of whom he knew and even more of whom know who he was!

I guess this book is largely about bellringing. Whether or not readers will see it as such, there's little doubt in my mind that there can be no more compelling story about bellringers in the modern era than theirs. George and Diana's story covers a lot of ground. I hope you have enjoyed covering the ground as much as I enjoyed working on it!

John Loveless
August 2020

Thanks and acknowledgments

I'd like to thank a great many people who have assisted me in bringing this project to fruition.

One day a couple of years ago after one or two previous refusals (too busy, need to retire), I found myself embarking upon this project. I suppose, modesty aside, that I reckoned it was likely no one else would do it as well as me because of the good working knowledge I believe I have – of George, Suffolk ringing and the Exercise in general over the last seventy years or so. I am an avid *Ringing World* reader, a 'cover-to-cover' person, a campanological 'wonk' perhaps, all positives in this exercise. As time went on this view hardened a little, and I found myself wanting to do it because I couldn't face seeing someone else do it, and perhaps not as well as I would. Incentive enough then!

I'd particularly like to thank George, a particularly helpful subject even when he sometimes wasn't feeling great, who I'm sure had forgotten more about this topic than I will ever know. He kept me fully abreast with anything I might be missing without being in anyway interfering. George had a welter of information spread across about seven peal books or scrapbooks dating back to the nineteenth century and covering the whole of his ringing career right up to the early 2000s. All his peals are handwritten, which is unusual these days, and a treat to witness. The presentation of the information is vibrant, anything but hundreds of pages of peals with little or no comment. There are photographs, lots of them. George had a policy of trying to collect a photograph of every tower he pealed. Then there were comments about all sorts of things, a real treasure trove.

The researching of the history of bells, ringing and ringers is such a valuable part of our social history. It can be particularly rich, as in George's case, and yet ringers tend to pay relatively little attention to it. The Suffolk Guild's policy of scanning all its annual reports back to 1923 is a masterstroke. It means that history can be brought alive, so thank you to all of those who have been involved in this exercise. I'm sure other researchers will find it worthwhile in the future. Certainly this book would have been a poorer effort without it.

The Ringing World, as one might expect, is a very useful and comprehensive source of information for an exercise of this nature, and the same applies to *Ringing Towers*, the Australian publication dating back to the time when George and Diana were still living there, and the formation of ANZAB in 1962.

This availability of detail has enabled me to move significantly 'off piste' at times, into areas I've found particularly interesting, though not always hugely relevant to George himself, such as Albert J Lancefield, the achievements of the Leiston and Helmingham bands, the opening of Washington Cathedral bells (of which I have not seen a comprehensive account apart from George's account of the week of the dedication, 'Ten Men Went to Sow'), and the Pye Brothers and their legacy, where the link goes back a century, the latter considerably beefed up quite recently. I hope readers enjoy these sections too.

I definitely didn't want everything to come from me so I approached about 25 people from diverse backgrounds for input, recollection and general comment. This came from people across George's ringing career. Their recollections confirm the view that he was a widely liked, respected and able man with his biggest strength being his common touch! This is backed up with scores of written commendations about all sorts of matters, career, church-related, ringing and more. To be fair, it's unsurprising that he would be good at securing business references (as many are), but his file contains letters that are usually congratulatory and expressing heartfelt thanks.

I'd also like to record my thanks to a number of individuals who have been very helpful. David Bleby, from Adelaide, who learnt to ring shortly before George left Australia, supplied me with very useful information about George's impact on ringing in Australia. David and Elizabeth Bleby are authorities on ringing in Australia and Elizabeth has published two books recording Australian bells, ringing and people on a location by location basis. The first was *We Sing in a Strange Land: A History of Change Ringing in Australia and New Zealand to 1988*. The pace of development by 2001 meant this required updating with *Their Sound Has Gone Forth: A History of Change Ringing in Australia and New Zealand to 2001*. These are valuable and lasting contributions that chart the tower-by-tower development of ringing in these places. Tom Goodyer and Laith Reynolds provided very useful information on the formation of ANZAB in 1962. Similarly, my thanks to Rick Dirksen. Rick was at Washington when the bells went in back in 1964, but moved away a few years ago. He clearly still knew the key people at the Cathedral to help resolve my queries!

I'd also like to thank Linda Garton, my wife, who has been very supportive throughout this project, but particularly when we needed to go through the process of selecting the photos. I'm reasonably good with the written word but not very practical. She is extremely adept with practical things requiring common sense – I'm not! Selecting and referencing 100 or so photographs from multiple books mentioned above and then positioning them in the text together with relevant comments brought with it some challenges.

Finally, let's see more biographies. We're good at short biographies, of which there are plenty due to the excellent work of people like John Eisel, Bill Butler and the Central Council. Very recently the excellent work of Richard Pullin has brought to life many of history's great composers, about whom we previously knew little. In recent years there have been comprehensive biographies of A J Pitman (my hero!) and now George Pipe (also my hero). Robert B Smith wrote an autobiography some years ago. Revd F E Robinson's *Among the Bells*, written over 100 years ago, was a weighty 637 pages! But I struggle to think of too many more. What about biographies of the fine ringers of today? If we do not write them today then interesting biographies will not be on our smartphones tomorrow and the Exercise will be the poorer.

I've thanked some people chapter-by-chapter. My grateful thanks go also to:

Keith Jones, Dean Emeritus of York, Vicar of St Mary-le-Tower, Ipswich 1982–95, for providing a thought-provoking foreword to this book.

Michael Wilby, for providing the review of this book. Michael is steeped in ringing, comes from a ringing family and is a top quality ringer with a wide perspective on all aspects of bells and ringing. He took up the role of MD at John Taylor and Co. in 2019.

Christine Knight, who learnt to ring at the same time as I did, for proof-reading several drafts and for some useful suggestions about additional Suffolk-related content that might be worth including!

Simon and Judith Reading from Sheffield are professional indexers. I'd like to thank them for doing a wonderful job in providing the indexing for George's biography which I'm sure will benefit readers.

Mike Whitby, for his help with providing some of the photos.

The Ringing World for backing this venture, particularly Will Bosworth, Editor, for his help and encouragement.

Index

References in bold are to illustrations. 'P' indicates the colour plates section in the centre.